Praise for Laura Waterman's *Calling Wild Places Home*

"A legendary mountain figure and revered voice on backcountry ethics, Laura Waterman is an American treasure. Her new memoir illuminates the challenges and rewards of homesteading and wilderness stewardship. It also dives deeper into her marriage to the prolific writer and climber Guy Waterman, whose shadow looms over the Northeast because of his tragic decision to intentionally freeze to death atop Mount Lafayette in New Hampshire. In sharp contrast, Laura chose life—and this book is an embrace of all its mystery, pain, and joy."

— Stephen Kurczy, author of *The Quiet Zone: Unraveling the Mystery of a Town Suspended in Silence*

"In this latest memoir, celebrated wilderness steward Laura Waterman reflects on her years of homesteading, and her relationships—with herself, her late husband Guy, and the world they dove headlong into together. Examining a world under our modern noses, should we slow down to see it, *Calling Wild Places Home* rings like a clarion bell: honest, unflinching, and true. Now more than ever, we need Waterman's voice."

— Michael Wejchert, author of *Hidden Mountains: Survival and Reckoning after a Climb Gone Wrong*

"*Calling Wild Places Home* is timely in its portrayal of a remarkable life centered on the essentials and, through it, the much deeper connection we can realize with ourselves and natural spaces. Through a series of vulnerable and poignant essays, Waterman demonstrates that the standard definitions we so often rely on to validate how we love, sacrifice, renew, and persevere most likely require some focused introspection."

— Ty Gagne, author of *The Last Traverse: Tragedy and Resilience in the Winter Whites*

"Laura Waterman's *Calling Wild Places Home* is an extraordinary story. She and her husband, Guy Waterman, authored the bestselling book *Forest and Crag*, a history of hiking and trail blazing in the Northeast Mountains. Her new book, part memoir and part anthology of Laura Waterman's previously published essays, focuses on two interrelated stories: their lives together and their experiences as mountain climbers, homesteaders, and stewards of nature. Part of the power of the memoir lies in her depiction of her husband's demons, which culminated in his suicide in 2000. She writes sensitively and honestly about this event, offering us insights gleaned from a twenty-year perspective. As she observes, 'There is nothing like the passage of time to help us gain clarity with which to see long-ago events.' Yet *Calling Wild Places Home* evokes the spirit of Thoreau's *Walden* in its affirmation of self-reliance and resilience, but Laura Waterman's voice is uniquely her own. Readers will remember her inspirational, revelatory, life-affirming book for a long time."

— Jeffrey Berman, author of *Dying to Teach: A Memoir of Love, Loss, and Learning*

Calling Wild Places Home

Also by Laura Waterman

Losing the Garden: The Story of a Marriage
Starvation Shore, a Novel

Also by Laura and Guy Waterman

The Green Guide to Low-Impact Hiking and Camping, previous editions
  published as *Backwoods Ethics*
Forest and Crag: A History of Hiking, Trail Blazing, and Adventure in the
  Northeast Mountains
Wilderness Ethics: Preserving the Spirit of Wildness
Yankee Rock & Ice: A History of Climbing in the Northeastern United States
A Fine Kind of Madness: Mountain Adventures Tall and True

Calling Wild Places Home
A Memoir in Essays

LAURA WATERMAN

Illustrations by
Nancy Kittridge

EXCELSIOR
EDITIONS

Cover: Franconia Ridge Trail on Mount Lafayette, White Mountain National Forest, New Hampshire. Photograph by Darin Horst. Shutterstock

Published by State University of New York Press, Albany

© 2024 Laura Waterman

Excelsior Editions is an imprint of State University of New York Press

For information, contact State University of New York Press, Albany, NY
www.sunypress.edu

Library of Congress Cataloging-in-Publication Data

Name: Waterman, Laura, author.
Title: Calling wild places home : a memoir in essays / Laura Waterman.
Description: Albany : State University of New York Press, [2024] | Series: Excelsior editions | Includes bibliographical references and index.
Identifiers: LCCN 2023032954 | ISBN 9781438496245 (pbk. : alk. paper) | ISBN 9781438496252 (ebook)
Subjects: LCSH: Waterman, Laura. | Waterman, Guy. | Outdoor life—White Mountains (N.H. and Me.) | Outdoor life—Vermont. | Suicide victims—White Mountains (N.H. and Me.)—Biography. | Widows—Vermont—Corinth—Biography. | White Mountains (N.H. and Me.)—Biography. | Corinth (Vt.)—Biography.
Classification: LCC CT275.W32225 A3 2024 | DDC 974.2/20092 [B]—dc23/eng/20230825
LC record available at https://lccn.loc.gov/2023032954

10 9 8 7 6 5 4 3 2 1

For my parents,
Catherine R. and Thomas H. Johnson, wellsprings and guides.

The enjoyment of solitude, complete independence, and the beauty of undefiled panoramas is absolutely essential to happiness.

—Robert Marshall, *Forest Service Bulletin*, August 27, 1928

Little feels better than knowing where you are, and having a reason to be there.

—Craig Childs, *Atlas of a Lost World: Travels in Ice Age America*

Contents

III. Lighting Out for the Territory

Preface and Acknowledgments

After Guy Waterman, my husband, took his life in 2000, my life, by necessity, changed. Yet much of the old remained, and a piece of that was writing.

In 2005 I published a memoir titled *Losing the Garden: The Story of a Marriage*. I wanted to write about our nearly thirty years together as homesteaders. This would also include our life as climbers and hikers, and, through our writing, as advocates for the mountains we loved. An important part of that memoir was an attempt to understand my role in my husband's suicide. In the sense that Guy's death necessitated my choice to move off our land, I was "losing the garden." (We both saw "Barra" as a metaphorical Eden.) But I was not "losing" gardening, that is, growing vegetables as I always had. With my relocation I saw myself only moving deeper into my own life with the creative acts of writing the memoir and growing a fully productive garden on a different piece of land. Both the gardening and the writing, as time passed, began to feel redemptive to me.

Guy and I had done a great deal of writing collaboratively over those thirty years. Now, I was on my own as a writer, and I found my subjects continued much the same: issues of stewardship that so deeply concerned us as climbers, hikers, and conservationists in the mountains of the Northeast was one subject. Another that complemented it was the history of our mountains. Who were the people who made the first ascents, began building our trails, establishing hotels in the notches as well as on the treeless summits? (The first hotel on the rocky top of Mount Washington opened in 1852.) Who formed the early hiking clubs? Who were the pioneer rock and ice climbers? All those books that resulted made up an important part of my life with Guy, and continuing that writing felt both productive and full of pleasure.

But I had always wanted to write a novel.

I had written short stories but wanted to take on a much longer, more sustained piece of fiction. I found my subject in the course of writing my memoir. From the beginning I had established a routine of listening to music before I began work. I'd brought my opera recordings with me from New York that had sat unplayed under Guy's piano for nearly thirty years. Particularly, I was playing a Maria Callas recording of Bellini's *Norma*, and after I'd finished my morning's work I would play those arias again. This bookending worked two ways. I had, without much conscious thought, constructed for myself an emotional exercise program. Callas was well along in her career, her voice—no longer beautiful—the steely edge grown steelier, harsher, a wavery, frayed torn sound like old cloth ripping. Her tenor, Franco Corelli, had maintained his youthful animalistic sound, vibrant, blazing, glowing. I found this contrast heartbreaking. But Callas made use of this. Awareness that her voice was coming apart seemed only to drive her deeper into the emotional depth of the song, to where she could pull up a kind of truth from her own rich emotional storehouse. I was, by listening to Callas, priming myself for my morning's work, readying myself to confront and tease apart my own emotions in an effort to commit them to the page. At the end of the morning I turned to Callas again. This time as release, a cooling down, from the intensity of my own thinking and feeling. I was moved by this great singer's fearlessness. She had become my guide.

This attempt to write a novel based on the life of Maria Callas went through a number of drafts but found no home with a publisher. It needed more work, which I felt, at the time, unable to give it. I set it aside. Nonetheless, my desire to write a novel was as strong as ever. When a young friend, a former steward at Barra who knew of my love of polar history, suggested I read Clint Willis's *Ice: Stories of Survival from Polar Exploration*, and drew my attention to the chapter containing David Brainard's diary entries, this cracked open a door. A small crack at first, but one worth exploring at the Dartmouth College Library, thirty minutes down the road, that was referenced in Willis's book as containing diaries of this particular expedition. I knew this library also housed the Stefansson Collection, a wealth of polar material.

So I found my subject in a little-known American Arctic expedition of the 1880s, historical fiction that allowed me to expand my scope, in this case, to include people abandoned in an indifferent landscape that tested and rewarded them in ways that elicited emotions through their own human interactions. *Starvation Shore*, a ten-year project, was new territory for me as a writer, both exciting and hard. But it felt good! I could draw on the memory of the many days Guy and I had spent in arctic conditions in the alpine zones of our home mountains. I could call on the books we had read together set among the world's largest mountains or at the poles. All this gave me a path into the daily existence of the twenty-five men on the Greely Arctic Expedition as they fought for their natural lives. *Starvation Shore* was published in 2019.

When my literary agent suggested I write a second memoir, I welcomed the chance. Already I had material with the essays I'd written since Guy's death that sprang from our homesteading life and the work we had done tending trails above treeline. Working in both these landscapes had taught me much. I had learned that the work each requires is similar, if you kept in mind that what you wanted to preserve and perpetuate was the health of the land itself.

As I began to focus on this project, I was taken back to my childhood in a search for the origins that led to my writing collaboratively with Guy that had come so naturally. I had long thought that my English teacher– writer father had served as a model for me. But how, and why? This led to another essay that would be about books, books I grew up on, books Guy and I had read aloud together, and what the edifices—small-town to large-city libraries—that housed books had meant to the life of my mind and my heart, as well.

While I had written *Losing the Garden* about our homesteading life, I had not looked closely at my relationship with the twenty-first century when I moved into it soon after Guy's death. I was still too close to the world we had lived in, a world without central heating, electricity, plumbing, telephones, and road access. Though we might have successfully grown a large organic vegetable garden, though we might have built a plentiful library and made room for a Steinway grand piano, for various reasons we had chosen to plant our feet in the nineteenth century. Now, with my life on the brink of change, I had some choices to make. How did I feel about living in an electrified house? I quickly discovered that a light bulb or two could cut me off from looking out the window and seeing the stars, as I could do when I was living with kerosene lamps and candles. Would I still heat my house as well as cook with wood? Would I work up the wood myself as Guy and I had done with crosscut saws and axes? How about refrigeration? We had depended on a root cellar. Also, now, I would be living on a road. We had had, in winter, a mile-and-a-half walk from the village where we kept our car to our cabin. We had become very comfortable with that walk that fit seamlessly into our life, a life spent largely outdoors. We had fostered a connection to nature that I knew was going to change. Yes, my adjustment to the twenty-first century merited a closer look!

For one thing, I would no longer be sugaring. Sugaring deserved its own remembering, its own essay. It was our favorite time of year. I wanted to capture that period when the sap from the sugar maples runs clear as a mountain stream from a small hole drilled in a tree into our waiting buckets. Just the act of boiling out the water over (in our case) an open fire, turned this sap into an elixir fit for the tables of kings and queens. Sugaring required our greatest devotion and our hardest work. I wanted, in memory, to call up that period when winter loosens its grip and spring returns to the earth.

I began writing these essays in my late seventies. By then much had changed in my relation to mountains. I wanted to capture that, too: how aging had increased my joy of being in the mountains at the same time that it limited what I could accomplish. And how this limiting of ambitious mountain days had focused me on explorations from my door, my own home territory, where I found unexpected beauty and experienced a sense of discovery.

I wanted not just to scrutinize my whole relationship with Guy, a daunting task in itself, but to be able to reply to those bold enough to ask me, "Laura, how could he do that to you?" In other words, didn't I feel anger? Those mostly unspoken words did not occupy me. I had always felt Guy's sense of fairness. He was a principled man. He understood obligation. Now, though, I had come to see that he was a desperate man as well. We were good at working as a team, though in this case, Guy's overriding need to get out of his own life upset the balance and put me in the position of responding. Yet, I never felt that Guy was not respectful of what was important to me, what I needed, particularly in a practical manner, to continue on without him. His suicide, as I see it, was not so much a selfish act as a desperate one. I loved him. I would, I knew on some level, be able to live without him. More than that, I could support even his ultimate overwhelming need to take his own life, which meant leaving me.

When we were in the middle of this, in the heat of our own lives together, I was acting the way I always had, intuitively. I knew he loved me. It was his own angst that he was refusing to face that was causing him problems. And I also saw, or felt, that our loves were different. Different because I could love myself, whereas, I believe, Guy could not.

I have come to understand that Guy was a driven man who carried a crushing burden of charisma. He was a man in pain and his pain caused me pain too. Though I was unsuccessful in helping him break through his unarticulated pain, I could write about my own journey. I could write through the pain. I found liberation in this. Liberation through the pain. I have come to understand much about myself that turned this book into an exciting excavation. This is why I can say that *Calling Wild Places Home* is a joyous book.

All this is the stuff of memoir. Often we don't fully understand, or even start to see, what leads us in one direction or another until later in life. Hindsight can focus memoir writing. Or such has been my case. That's why writing memoir—a reflecting back—is so compelling, even exciting to me. It can be scary and unsettling as well. Do we want to risk unearthing material that we fear has the power to disturb and shock? On the other hand, we might unexpectedly delight ourselves, giving us the courage to continue.

Do we ever completely understand what shapes our lives? How can we? Something happens today that changes the way we've thought of a particular past event, past encounter, past conversation, that throws a new light, a new eye-opening meaning on the large and small turning points of a life. But why am I writing about myself? That's the question the lurking stumbling-block false modesty demands. You set the work aside. It does no good. You are driven by something that cries out for resolution. It floods your dreams, your daytime thoughts. You are overtaken, driven a little crazy until you pick up the pen again.

I have introduced each chapter with a headnote, intended to support the memoiristic nature of the collection. I have given new titles to some previously published essays, have trimmed some of them to eliminate redundancies, and have added material to draw connections between the essays. These headnotes also give me the opportunity to acknowledge and thank publishers and the publications where some of these chapters have previously appeared.

I'd like to thank Rebecca Oreskes, Doug Mayer, Annie Bellerose, and Louis Cornell who gave helpful and encouraging comment on the material about Guy. Thanks to Dave Govatski and Ryan Harvey for our day on Mount Washington, and for their comments on chapter 16. Hannah and John Narowski supplied me with updates on sugaring that appear in chapter 8. I give deep gratitude to Robert Rubin who skillfully gave shape and story to a hodgepodge of essays. Thanks to Stephen Kurczy whose comments, late in the game, served to focus these chapters and tie up loose ends. Christine Woodside's insightful comments benefited chapter 14. Steve Jervis took a helpful look at chapter 18 under a tight deadline. Thank you, Steve! Chip Brown made a crucial appearance near the end of this journey that I recount in the epilogue. Hearty thanks to Jonathan Strong, Susan and John Morris, Sue Foster, Tania Aebi, Carl Demrow, Eleanor Kohlsaat, Brad Snyder, and Jon Waterman for standing by me. Your readings, conversations, letters, and emails helped to make this a better book. Thanks to the librarians and volunteers at the Blake Memorial Library who support me in countless ways. To Sue Foster, my amanuensis, I send everlasting gratitude. My thanks to Nancy Kittridge for her illustrations that capture both a sense of wildness and a home place. Here's a special shout-out to my agent, Craig Kayser, who got me started and steered my thinking in exciting and unexpected directions. James Peltz, my publisher who shares my zest for mountains, knew how, along with his able staff, to reach the summit. To echo the scholar Willard Thorpe's words (see chapter 4), "Such fun we have had!"

Prologue

Wild Places

Above all let me be thankful for something rarer than gold—
Viz.: that at 11:07 A.M. I'll be 27¾ years old.
Oh let my future be as lucky as my past!
Oh let every day for a long time not be my last!

—Ogden Nash, "Hymn to the Sun and Myself," in *Hard Lines*

Back in 2005 I was doing a reading for my latest book when, during the question period, a large, solidly middle-aged woman in the audience said, in a voice too loud for the small group, "You should have stopped him!"

1

That stunned me. I was caught off guard and left speechless. She was referring to the suicide of my husband, Guy Waterman, the subject of the memoir I was reading from. Several friends in the audience, who knew Guy well, covered for me: "If you read Laura's book," they said, "you'll see that Guy couldn't have been stopped." It took me a long, long time to see that this begs the question: *Why not?* Why couldn't I have stopped my husband from taking his own life? Despite the generosity of my friends, I had not fully answered that question. This second memoir is an attempt.

The questions that afternoon in that bookstore in Peterborough, New Hampshire, proceeded on to our homesteading—an off-the-grid life of nearly thirty years—our climbing, and the books we'd written on environmental stewardship of the mountains here in the Northeast. But that woman's statement—or was it an accusation?—stuck with me.

Other people in other audiences had broached it, if in softer tones. I had learned from these readings that people's questions could come from deep within, some place that my words had touched, perhaps a little too immediately—like metal producing an electric spark from a wall socket. In my case, this was *the* question, and one you only needed to have read the jacket copy to be prompted to ask. To come to some understanding of it—*How could I have supported my husband's plan to commit suicide?*—was largely why I'd written *Losing the Garden.*

Doing those readings was good for me. Hazardous, yes. I often felt like a PhD candidate defending her dissertation. I might know my material better than anyone in the room, I might be the authority, but there is nothing stopping your examiners from tossing out questions that hit a raw spot. Unlike a dissertation, what I'd written was highly personal, and at first, some of those questions from my audience were hard to confront. But quickly I came to see that with each hit I was given a chance to think again, think deeper. The bookstore woman's question has given me that opportunity.

What I've discovered from writing memoir is that it's the emotions that need going after. As for memory, Stephen Dobyns wrote in his contributor's note for *Best American Short Stories, 1999*, "Memory distorts. Psychology, emotions, good health or bad—all drag their feet across events. The details that I might remember one day are not those that I might remember on another day."

Memory cannot be trusted. Memory is a shape-shifter. Others' memories of the same event often conflict, and they do so because of the emotions we bring to the event itself. Emotions don't change. Their impact can be sudden, like a punch. The psychic mark is indelible and cannot be influenced. Emotions can be complex and confusing, but they speak truth. There is an emotional truth to events that we disregard at our peril, and it is the grist in the memoirist's mill.

Guilt, remorse, fear, shame, anger, and pure hatred—emotions can also make us feel happiness, joy, and love, those are of interest too, but the writer of memoir is, more than likely, on a search for language that can simulate as well as articulate the hard-to-confront emotions in an effort to understand events that have deeply affected a life. Yes, there is a search going on here.

We gather our courage and start to dig, with a trowel perhaps, like an archeologist, tentative at first. If we keep at it with diligence, we end up behind the wheel of a bulldozer, going for the roots! When that happens, all those bad feelings loosen up, all that discomfort caused by strong, painful, chaotic, uncontrollable emotions dissipates. Exciting work, with a big payoff, like digging into a diamond mine. Also scary.

I was shocked to silence by that bookstore woman's statement. She was telling me I hadn't reached the roots when I was sure I had. Yet my shock at her words that I was doing my damnedest to ignore was now shouting at me that I hadn't finished the job. It took me nearly two decades to pick up the pen and start digging again. This would not have happened if my agent hadn't suggested that I write another memoir focused on the last twenty-plus years since my husband's death. I didn't see Guy—our relationship, his death—playing much of a role. I'd covered that ground in *Losing the Garden*.

How wrong I was! I was well into this second memoir when it became abundantly clear that Guy could not be left out. I protested this, to myself, at the same time the handwriting on the wall grew larger and larger. Had I backed myself into a corner by agreeing to write this second memoir? I had, and the only way out was confronting the beast. By this time I realized I was ready for it.

Why didn't I, couldn't I, prevent my husband from taking his own life? Now I had the opportunity not only to take ownership for the moral support I had given him, but to puzzle out *why*.

There is nothing like the passage of time to help us gain clarity with which to see long-ago events. My thoughts about Guy's suicide, and my part in it, have evolved—and, I imagine, will continue to evolve. When we pause to think deeply about what appear to be unsolvable questions or situations, we rarely, if ever, hit the bottom. We merely come to a resting point from which we can launch further explorations.

In my case, as I dug (quite literally) into this second memoir, I could sense that the process of writing was opening up a passage into deeper self-discovery. I learned as well through the writing that my life with Guy contained many of the ingredients I needed for moving into a life without him. Understanding our life together was key to my own personal liberation. It had been vital to articulate my life with Guy in *Losing the Garden*. Now, in the hard work of writing and thinking, this second memoir was turning into a celebration of my new life. I knew that was what Guy had hoped for. He had said as much in the final note he had left for me.

Memoir writing is immodest; it can be seen as selfish if not self-indulgent, but it can also be immensely validating. It can be healing. I felt it was important for me to write about Guy's suicide, for instance, in order to see what the experience itself wanted me to do with it. I hoped that through the writing—through this introspection—I would continue to grow and be changed in healthy ways. I wanted to be the agent of my own opening to a future rich with possibilities. These were my subliminal thoughts, not well articulated, certainly not deliberate. I could not see into my future, but I was driven to write, and I knew it was important to embrace that persistent grappling that had a headlock on my being.

I discovered, along the way, that this writing was an act of sharing: I was writing for an audience. Again, this realization emerged slowly, out of the muck encountered after my headfirst dive into the urgency of telling the story of my own life. The writing was for everyone who had cared for Guy and me, everyone who supported us—especially for everyone who supported me after Guy's death. I was also writing for everyone who had read our books, which extended to people I had never met and would never meet: people who had heard about Guy's death—the shocking manner of it—I was writing for them, too.

I knew from letters and conversations I had—and continue to have—with people after *Losing the Garden* was published in 2005, that the book had been helpful to those in a similar situation of trying to weave the path between "supportive" and "enabling," between fostering a "partnership" and "codependency." These were words Guy and I never used, had almost never heard, though they might have been helpful to describe what might have been transpiring in our marriage. Yet even if I had known how to use them I would have thought twice about introducing them into our conversation. Such clinical language—jargon in Guy's book, and because he saw it that way, so did I—would have met with his disapproval, his dismissal, his silence, and I'd be sorry to have upset him. What I was asking him for was an emotional response, and that territory my dear husband would not enter, though I had no insight of that at the time.

Most of all, though, I was writing for myself. And as I wrote, I discovered I had made the right choices. I knew this because I found comfort in what I was putting on the page, something that extended to all the writing I'd done since Guy's death.

"Listen to your life," wrote theologian and philosopher Frederick Buechner in *Now and Then: A Memoir of Vocation*, who had taught in my father's Lawrenceville School English Department when I was a child. "See it for the fathomless mystery it is. In the boredom and pain of it, no less than in the excitement and gladness: touch, taste, smell your way to the holy and hidden heart of it, because in the last analysis all moments are key moments, and life itself is grace."

Life itself is grace. As I worked daily on this memoir, Frederick Buechner's words resonated with me. I discovered them when I was well into this project and took delight in their power. In my imagination Guy and I are sitting at our table in our cabin, and I ask him, "What do you think of Freddie's words?" (I called him Freddie since I knew him from childhood.) I don't get back an answer, at least not verbally. I see my husband turning away. My question is making him uncomfortable. He stands up and walks across the pine board floor and looks out the window. I am facing his back. I debate pushing it, but experience with topics that turn Guy silent causes me to fall silent, too. It's an uncomfortable silence for both of us and I regret I brought it up.

But his reaction helps me to see that, for this well-past-sixty-year-old man who has told me he wants to take his own life, *life*—being alive—holds little interest for Guy. Whereas for me, it holds a great deal of interest. I can't fathom what must plague Guy's mind—a creeping darkness? a soul-numbing despair? a just plain gut-wrenching regret-filled sadness?—that has him shut out Buechner's joyous words. At least they strike me as joyous, and they fill me with anticipation of what life holds. I know that Guy once felt joy when he was climbing rock, when we were living through our first decade at Barra—when the demons had, for a period of time, gone underground.

I have called Guy's death a new beginning. At first it left me in an unusual position for a so-called survivor of a suicide, that of explaining and offering comfort. His death generated news, including an obituary in the *New York Times*. News spread fast. Friends snowshoed in to our homestead, and my post office box filled up. For them, his death was unexpected and shocking:

a suicide can provoke that reaction. Those left want answers, they need to understand. I was the only one who could "explain" why Guy had chosen that path. I couldn't, really, but I could fill them in on the backstory, and my role. We could all—family and friends—talk about it together. Talk about Guy. Many tears. Many stories of fond memories, seasoned with quiet laughter.

I had indeed known, I could tell them. I did not experience the shock, and I could already feel myself moving into my new life as I shared what happened after Guy had returned to tell me he had tried to jump off Cannon Cliff and failed. The conversations, the letters, went on for months, for years. They have never stopped, because the "why" behind suicides can never fully be understood.

Yet every conversation, every letter from friends and strangers answered, was a healing step for me. Because I'd known Guy's plan, I felt, then, neither anger nor betrayal. I knew where I stood with him; while I had been unable to lead him away from Franconia Ridge, I did not resent or blame him for climbing to the summit that day. He was clear about his choice—"I am getting out of a world which I find increasingly unbearable"—he had written me in his last note. That misery was what I wanted to help those who loved him and would forever miss him, as well as those who were angry with him, come to understand.

I met my friend Andy Tuthill at the Haverhill airport in New Hampshire. He had promised to take me for a spin over the White Mountains and I jumped at the chance. Who wouldn't? I was going to see the mountains that I'd climbed and hiked and written about for much of my life, *from the air!* Andy was motoring around the tarmac in his Cessna 172—"the most popular small airplane ever made," he'd assured me. He pulled up, and, boosting myself in, I told him that my only experience with small planes was when Guy and I had been flown into the Alaskan mountains, but not in a plane this small, I said, as I tucked my arms and legs into the requirements of the seat. Andy just smiled. He'd been flown by bush pilots many times into the mountains for climbing.

We had a three-pronged sightseeing mission for this June afternoon. The first leg had us crossing back over the Connecticut River and flying over my own house. I was just getting used to this bird's-eye view when there it was, a cozy log structure resting comfortably at ground level: 6.5 acres of field edged by woods, the 30 ft. by 40 ft. fenced-in vegetable garden, the sprawling, colorfully overcrowded perennial beds, and the pond housing aquatic life, all in place. Andy dipped down. Suddenly I could count the incipient blueberries on my six highbush blueberry bushes. My home since 2000, settled in a peaceful Vermont landscape.

Andy winged us upward and within an eye-blink we were over the village. There was little time to name the landmarks, or who lived where in the cluster of quiet houses on either side of the road. But there was the library, a snug brick building, warm and welcoming, a house for books, called by one local denizen "the intellectual hub of Corinth," which made us laugh. There was the post office where I pick up my mail daily, a twelve-minute walk from my house.

Our second viewing target was soon upon us as Andy made a left-hand turn and we crossed the Tabor Branch that runs behind the village houses, and in less time than it would take a darting hummingbird, we arrived by air over my old homestead, which my husband Guy and I called Barra, and where we had lived from 1973 till Guy's death in 2000. I see in the clearing our cabin we'd stained green to blend in, porch attached, then down two steps to the woodshed. A steep forested hillside rose behind like a protecting bulwark. There had never been road access or electricity or telephone, or even running water. Downslope from the house was the vegetable garden and the circle of sixteen blueberry bushes. It was a few hops to reach the stream and the path through the woods that leads to the sugar shed—I could see it all in my mind's eye—in the center of a productive acreage of sugar maples. Barra, surrounded by woodland, made for us its own contained world, and so it still appeared, though I noted the clearing was not quite as open as it used to be.

With the feature attraction our next flyby, Andy directed our course back toward New Hampshire and the White Mountains. As we skimmed past Mount Moosilauke we both excitedly pointed out the mountain's familiar features: the South Peak and the open sweep of alpine leading to the main summit, the great glacial cirque of Jobildunk Ravine, the drop into Kinsman Notch, all old friends.

Suddenly we were moving up alongside the Franconia Ridge. I was gazing at the bare, stony summit of Little Haystack that marked the start of the nearly two-mile ridge walk, almost all above five thousand feet, as homelike to me as Barra, and as dear. The skyline trail stretched up toward the summit of Mount Lincoln. From our discrete distance, the hikers on that summit looked about three inches tall. As we putted along a little above the ridge, our view slightly angled down, I was struck by its pronounced spine: picture looking at the tilt of a roof where it slants down from the ridgepole. This airy traverse is called a *knife edge*, but when you're hiking it you're not really aware of how narrow the ridge actually is. Andy and I were chatting about this when Mount Lafayette entirely filled my vision. The majestic rise of it soared into the sky, massive, yet only in comparison to Lincoln or the other minor peaks. Its shape from the air was one of great beauty: graceful, almost delicate, the largest jewel in the string of eminences threaded together by this narrow pathway. I was happy, yet my eyes were tearing. How Guy would have loved this! So much of our lives were spent caring for this sky-walk alpine trail. Andy kept looking at me and smiling.

We were past it too soon, and approaching Mount Garfield. "There's the cliff," I shouted above the engine. We both knew the Garfield cliff. No trail led to it. Andy had climbed it, as had Guy. The Pemigewasset Wilderness lay under the tiny plane. We pointed out the slides we'd climbed on the cirque that composed the Bonds, and also in the Twin Range. The Pemi itself was an ocean of green, staggeringly thick with trees. There were trails down in that foliage we couldn't see, yet we called out their names because we knew they were there.

We both knew the story of the small plane that had crashed in the Pemi in the 1950s. We told each other the tale: two doctors on their way to Portland, Maine, a hospital needing them, wintertime, caught in a snowstorm. They carried no snowshoes; unable to walk out, rescue failing to reach them, they perished. It was the tragic, sad accidents that turned into legend, and Andy said, with the joking black humor of climbers, "If we crash-land, Laura, we can always walk out." He sent me a grin, which I returned. But looking down at those densely packed trees, the steep-sided ravines, no paved roads for miles—I was pretty dubious of *my* walking out.

We had left the Pemi in our wake and, with what felt like the speed of light, were sweeping above the Crawford Path as it crossed over Mount Monroe. There was Lakes of the Clouds Hut a mile and a half below the summit of Mount Washington, which bristled with its cluttered cluster of buildings. Washington: huge and bare-sided and rocky. The landscape spread out below our wings—such a contrast to the delicate arrow-like ridge of the Franconias. Here the great shoulders of mountains—Clay, Jefferson, Adams, Madison—drop down into deep ravines. Andy and I began naming them: Jefferson's, King's, the Great Gulf. We had been in all of them, winter and summer. Even so I was stunned by their bowl-like depth, glacier-carved, cliffy and rocky. No easy ascents or descents here. And I felt a glowing pride for these rugged mountains I was seeing from the top down. What Guy and I had loved was their very difficulty. They were not of great height compared to the world's ranges, but to feel at home in them, as we had felt, can give more than enough challenge and joy for a lifetime.

I was lucky to have had these mountains, I thought, as Andy turned the little plane toward home, concluding the afternoon's scenic tour of my life. Up in the air, this three-pronged gift of a backward glance of my homes, past and present, had let me see it all, from the work and fun Guy and I had known in our homesteading life together, to the trail-tending on Franconia Ridge, to where I am now, still, like Huck Finn, about ready to light out for the territory.

I

Getting Started

1

A Camp in the Wild, 1945–1952

What writer can resist exploring with words the places they feel deepest in their bones? It might take them back to their childhoods, as it did in my case; along the way I saw how those early summers formed a foundation, a cornerstone, for my whole life.

I published the original version of this chapter in Northern Woodlands, *a magazine founded by Stephen Long and Virginia Barlow with the mission of drawing together loggers, foresters, and woodlot land owners who shared common ground but could otherwise be at cross purposes. My essay appeared in the Summer 2013 issue, in the back-of-the-book column called "A Place in Mind." Writing this was a special pleasure since* Northern Woodlands *was published in my small town, and Steve and Ginny are friends. I also acknowledge Elise Tillinghast, and this story is reprinted courtesy of* Northern Woodlands *magazine, northernwoodlands.org.*

This camp, the camp of my childhood, was in the woods. It was surrounded by greenery and smelled of spruce, balsam fir, and loamy soil. It was every child's dream camp, though being a child myself during those years I did not discover this until I began to write about it.

Here was where I and my brother encountered Nature head-on. There was nothing to distract us like playmates or neighbors. No one stopping by.

Our mother helped us create a terrarium in a shallow pottery bowl. She guided our hands around the trowel as we selected mosses—low and soft under our searching fingers, or ones that branched like miniature Christmas trees. We proudly placed our offering in the center of the dining table made of oak. It was hard to keep our hands from exploring this wild world we'd just made.

My mother was the grandniece of Frederick Law Olmsted, among the first great visionary landscape architects. Through his genes, I like to think, she possessed a subliminal connection to nature that had us—her children—looking, and soon naming the plants when we took our evening walks through the woods or along the infrequently traveled dirt road.

"We shall not cease to explore," T. S. Eliot, in "Little Gidding," wrote, "and the end of all our exploring will be to arrive where we started and know the place for the first time."

Loggers, foresters, and owners of woodlots were all children once, too. When each discovered the woods their world enlarged and became real. Real enough to sustain a life and a livelihood.

∼

We arrived by train, an overnight trip, and were met at the Brattleboro station by a family friend, my father's colleague. They were working on a book together—the reason we had come to spend the summer in Vermont. We had no car. It was 1945, the last year of the war. I was five, my brother two.

"Smell the air!" my father exclaimed, as we wound up from the Connecticut River into the forests near Wilmington. We all breathed in air that was so cool and sweet. My father knew Vermont air. He was born in Vermont. That was the other reason we were here. My father wanted his children to know Vermont, too.

The camp was on a lake. There was no telephone. "Your ice will be brought weekly," Mr. Barber, the real estate man who opened the camp said to my mother. "There's your icebox." We saw a shed through the window. A woodstove took up half the kitchen floor. "Could roast a moose," Mr. Barber said, patting the stove's cast iron flank. My mother blanched. "But you'll cook on this." He gestured to a two-burner oil stove sitting on spidery legs. "Here's your oven."

He picked up what looked like a bread box. "You set it on top." He demonstrated, to show my mother how easy it would be to prepare meals for her family of four. He turned a knob at the sink. Water gushed out in a silvery stream. "It comes from the lake. You'll heat your hot water on the stove. Don't drink it," he said, turning the water off. "The well's out back. Send the kids for the drinking water." He grinned at us. "Make sure you prime the pump, otherwise you'll wreck it."

My mother walked into the living area and sat on the couch in front of the fieldstone fireplace. The couch swung back and forth, and squeaked. It was a swinging couch on springs. My mother burst into tears. Our father saw Mr. Barber out.

We spent the next eight summers there.

The camp was in the woods. The air around us smelled of balsam, fresh and tangy. There were other camps on the road, but we couldn't see them. Across the lake the woods were undisturbed by people. Our camp had a porch across the front from which we could look deep into the surrounding woods—thick, dark, and green. My brother and I scanned for movement there.

We became fascinated by chipmunks. When our parents had drinks on the porch with guests, who came because of my father's work, my brother and I would strew cocktail peanuts up the porch steps to entice chipmunks. Chipmunks, shy of adult talk, remained aloof. But when we came out after dinner to inspect the steps, the peanuts were all gone.

When it was just us kids, a chipmunk might hop up the first step, grab a nut, and retreat to a nearby rock. We'd be extra still. The chipmunk would come back, hop up two steps, scarf a peanut, scamper to the same rock, and nibble rapidly, working the nut between his paws. Our goal was to entice a chipmunk up the six steps to the porch itself. One day this happened: the chipmunk took the nut from the porch floor, only a few feet away from where we crouched, motionless as any woodland creature who doesn't want to be seen.

One became our friend. Well, not a friend exactly, but he became identifiable because he lost his tail. In a battle with another chipmunk? For several weeks it dragged behind him until it fell off. Then he became

Chippy. We were relieved to see Chippy could climb, scamper, and scurry as well as if he still had his tail. Each summer, as we drove up from New Jersey, our whole family asked, would Chippy be there? Chippy always was, until suddenly he wasn't. My brother and I roamed those woods hoping to encounter him. We never did.

In the evenings we walked along the road with our mother. "That's Indian paintbrush," she said, pointing out the orange tuft on an upright stalk. "And that's black-eyed Susan. See the dark disk of her eye?"

My father found picnic spots for us: a field of ferns and steeplebush, an old woods road leading to a rushing stream. We'd bring our bathing suits.

Our parents transplanted by the porch a jack-in-the-pulpit and a pink lady's slipper from the loamy woods. "Be careful around them, children," they said. We were, because they were so undefended and beautiful. Would they be blooming when we arrived the next June? They always were.

We made balsam pillows under our mother's direction, clipping boughs, stripping the needles, and sewing little sacks to be filled. We took them back to our winter home and tucked them in our dresser drawers. On days when school bore down, and summer seemed far away, I would open up a drawer and release that tangy balsam smell. Vermont's summer would come again—the woods, the chipmunks, the lake where we learned to swim. It was sleeping for the time being. And waiting.

2

Books in My Life

I wrote this chapter because I wanted to articulate what books and reading have meant to me, their seminal importance in my life. What I have read has shaped who I am as much as living has. When I was a teenager, I made a silent vow to read all the great books, by which I meant books by famous authors. All too soon I saw the hopelessness of fulfilling this. While I might have been able to make a dent in the past, over the course of my lifetime keeping up with the future is impossible. This was frustrating until I realized how lucky we readers of the world are to be assured of a never-ending supply of books.

 Imagine that you're somewhere in the world in a library or a bookstore scanning the shelves. You can do this—run your eye along the spines of books—because you can read. I bet it's hard for you to pin down that exact point when words made of letters began to contain meaning and emotions that could make you laugh or cry, make you mad or just plain happy. That is, you were happy when you were reading. You had entered that magic world of books and there was no escape.

Sir Walter Scott wrote in his novel Waverley, *"Nothing perhaps increases by indulgence more than a desultory habit of reading, especially under opportunities of gratifying it." When you've reached that point of instant gratification when you pick up a book, whether you're aware of it or not, you'll very likely be a reader for a lifetime.*

But how about those of us who did not learn to read when our young brains were right at that pliable moment for this learning to take hold? Books are closed. Any printed word is shut down, carries no meaning, you are blind. An illiterate adult can learn to read but not with the ease of unconscious absorption of the six-year-old. For the illiterate it would be like adapting to an amputated limb. Or worse, because the whole world of printed words is lost to those who can't decipher letters.

In the childhood bedroom I shared with my brother our mother had tacked up the twenty-six letters of the alphabet along the wall, upper case and lower case. Our bedtime ritual was to sing the alphabet song as she pointed out the letters. In this way I learned that each letter has its own sound, its own word. She made it a game. She made it fun! She made sure we were letter perfect before we entered kindergarten.

In 1956 I read J. R. R. Tolkien's The Fellowship of the Ring. *Or rather my mother read it to me. I was sick in bed and she had gone over to the Lawrenceville School library asking the librarian advice about a book her daughter would like. This librarian, who knew me, handed my mother Tolkien's book, the first to be published in his great trilogy that had just arrived from England to America. Both my mother and I were completely swept away by this tale of hobbits, elves, and dwarves, their encounters with good and evil as they journeyed toward Rivendell.*

When I returned to school, I was so much in Tolkien's world that I began telling my classmates all about this great book I'd just read. Isn't that always our instinct after we have read something that takes over our imaginations, even our lives? But I got nowhere and I felt an overwhelming disappointment that no one was interested. How do you explain a hobbit? They hadn't heard of Tolkien, though that was about to change.

As I see it now, this sad story is about our obligation to spread the word, whether or not we are listened to, about books and reading. With The Fellowship of the Ring, *at fourteen, I had become a missionary for the reading life. My instinct was to share, to lavishly spread the news of the great pleasure of reading.*

David Crews, who published "Books in My Life" in his Platform Review *(platformreview.org) on March 21, 2021, did so because, as he told me, he wanted to open his readers' minds to what a reading life can give us.*

~

Reading is the sole means by which we slip, involuntarily often helplessly, into another's skin, another's voice, another's soul.

—Joyce Carol Oates, "7 Rules for Writing"

When I was small, my father showed me how to prepare a new book for reading. There was a process I must go through, he explained, so as not to break the book's spine. When my father used the words "break the book's spine," a sudden shudder went up my own. I certainly didn't want to harm my book! "First," he directed, "open the book in the center, and flatten the evenly divided halves. Yes, you've got it!" he said as I applied a gentle, steady pressure with my palms to the pages. "Now close the book, and open the first quarter." I did that, and flattened those pages. "Open the book again," my father said, "this time a quarter of the way from the end." At this point I'd caught on to the process and continued to divide the book into small portions, opening and flattening from side to side, until I was satisfied that the spine, on my brand new copy of *The Wind in the Willows*, would not be taxed when I began to read.

I can't say I have followed my father's instructions to the letter with every new book I have ever owned or read, but his tutorial, my silent and alcoholic father at his best, is a precious memory of my childhood.

My father loved books and imprinted that love on me.

As an English teacher at a preparatory school, he was sent books by publishers who hoped he would select them for his classes. I was the beneficiary of many of these books for my own library, which I was building on my bedroom shelves. I wasn't conscious of constructing a library, but that was what was happening. I loved to read! If my mother asked me to help her with a task—peeling potatoes for dinner, weeding a flower bed—my constant answer was "Wait until I've finished this chapter." But my mother was not inclined to wait, or to let me delay. Waiting until I'd finished an entire chapter was much too long for her! But I could get away with "Wait until I finish this paragraph."

My favorite place to read was—and it still is—in bed, before falling asleep. The comfort derived from the bedclothes, the pillow, and the book can only be expressed in a great wordless contented sigh.

One early book that I read over and over, and have continued to use as a reference, is *Classical Myths That Live Today*, by Frances E. Sabin of New York University, published in 1927. In 1940, Ralph V. D. Magoffin, also of New York University, a professor in the Department of Classics, came out with a revised and enlarged edition. That's the edition I have, one of those books a publisher had sent to my father because it contained questions to be answered and other teacherly aids. I didn't pay much attention to these; I was interested in the stories. My father had written, on the inside front cover, my full name: Laura Bradley Johnson, followed by "from her father, Christmas, 1948." I was nine.

Classical Myths That Live Today is the cornerstone of my library. It was far from the first book I placed on my shelves, or that I read to myself, but it was the first "adult" book, in the sense that it did not tell the stories of these myths in the way a book intended for young children would. Its text contained words I didn't know. Sometimes I looked them up, but probably more often I didn't—not wanting to interrupt my reading—and guessed at the meaning through the context. *Classical Myths* was illustrated with photographs and drawings of the classical sites where the myths were set, as well as the mythic figures themselves as they appear in sculptures and paintings. There are more than two hundred illustrations and one lovely fold-out map showing the Mediterranean lapping at the shores of Asia Minor, Greece, Italy, and North Africa where these myths originated. If I were an ancient Egyptian of noble birth, such that certain cherished items would be sealed in my tomb to accompany me into my afterlife, *Classical Myths That Live Today* would be among those objects.

It was our mother who read to us—my younger brother and me—before bedtime. *Mother Goose*, R. L. Stevenson's *A Child's Garden of Verses*, Babar the Elephant, Dr. Seuss, Peter Rabbit. We sat on my bed, on either side of our mother. *The Blue Fairy Book*, *Grimm's Fairy Tales*—so delightfully scary—and Hans Christian Andersen's tales, so sad and so beautiful. (My family spent 1951 to 1952 in Copenhagen where we felt the power of Andersen's stories firsthand, especially in the beguiling statue of the Little Mermaid in the harbor.) Our copy of *The Wizard of Oz* finally fell apart, but I still have it carefully shelved, some of its illustrations crayoned—no doubt!—by my brother. I would not have performed such a disgraceful desecration, though my little brother's vandalism could be seen as claiming ownership, even as an act of love.

My father read the *Alice* books to me when I was seven and a half exactly, Alice's age, as he made a point of telling me. This was the only book my father read aloud to me, I believe because he loved it so much himself. I heard years later from a colleague of my father's from when he was a graduate student at Harvard, that he had memorized many pages, and, after the lubrication of several stiff drinks, could be coaxed into reciting them.

My father put many books in my hand, and I read them all. *Oliver Twist*, *The Pickwick Papers*, Charles Kingsley's *Water Babies*, and John Ruskin's *The King of the Golden River*. So I was heavily indoctrinated by the Victorians from the beginning. Indeed, if *Classical Myths* is the cornerstone, the British writers of the nineteenth century form the rock-solid foundation of my reading life. I return to them as a palate cleanser when I've had a bit too much of late twentieth- and twenty-first-century fiction. Sinking into Dickens or Scott or the Brontës, or my beloved Jane Austin, or the amazing George Eliot's *Middlemarch*, is like easing myself into a warm, welcoming bath. The tub is long—I can stretch out—and on sturdy clawed feet. There is a window, and I look out on a view of mountains. I breathe in, and then slowly out. That's what reading those nineteenth-century Brits does for me. And the Americans too: Twain, Poe, Melville, Hawthorne.

My mother, a lifelong reader, always a book on her bedside table, was born in western New York State. She had grown up with Cooper's *The Leatherstocking Tales*; Scott's *Kenilworth* was also a favorite of hers, as it is for me. An English major at Mount Holyoke College, she'd been invited to participate in an honors English seminar, but finding out the time the group met, replied, "Oh, I can't possibly do it. I play golf then." She told me this story more than once, always accompanied with a wry, regretful look that said, How stupid we are when we are young!

When Guy's mother, a Vassar graduate, moved into her retirement home, she took with her only a few books, ones she had already read many times—reminding me of Joyce Carol Oates's words: "the voices of strangers are closer to us than the voices of friends, more intimate, in some instances than our own."

I began keeping a book list in a small notebook, leather-covered, measuring 4½ by 7¼, lined paper, six-hole punched, the summer I graduated from eighth grade, 1954. I wish I had started it sooner. Books that are not on my list, but are still on my bookshelf, include *The Yearling*, *Swallows and*

Amazons, *Oliver Twist*, most of *Dr. Doolittle*, *The Wind in the Willows*, the *Alice* books, Twain's *Life on the Mississippi*. And because I can't stop writing down these titles that continue to shape my life, I'll add, *Mutiny on the Bounty*, Thor Heyerdahl's *Kon Tiki*, Stevenson's *Treasure Island* with the N. H. Wyeth illustrations, *Uncle Tom's Cabin*, *Annapurna* by Maurice Herzog, and *The Conquest of Everest* by Sir John Hunt. I mention these last two only because they struck a chord in me that revealed itself later, when I was in my late twenties and discovered climbing. That is the beauty of books. We never know where they will lead us.

My book list now occupies three notebooks, the same size, the same six-hole punch, on lined paper. I include solely the author and title. I knew myself well enough to realize that if I attempted to write a book report or any kind of description, I would fail. My book list would stop before it had even gotten started.

I particularly love this quote from James Boswell that I pasted into the front cover of the third notebook, which I started in 2012: "If a man would keep an exact account of everything that he reads, it would much illustrate the history of his mind."

If a man . . . Yes, it's impossible to overlook that Boswell has only men in mind here, but what he says rings true. One of the great pleasures of looking through my book list is remembering what I was doing when I was reading, for instance, Carlyle's *History of the French Revolution*. Guy and I read it aloud. We had embarked on writing our large history of the Northeast's mountains and wanted to read a revered history written on a very different subject, but one from which we could learn the art of writing history.

From June 1972 to June 1973, I read only four books. (To explain: since I had started my list in June 1954, I continued to make my reading year go from June to June.) Those four books all had something to do with the mountains and climbing that had taken over my life. The sparsity of the list was because that year we were in the midst of the major life change that took us from working in New York City to homesteading in Vermont. The next year, June 1973 to June 1974, I read twelve books; most again reflecting my interest in climbing, except for five that featured the Brontës—their own works as well as biographies.

I can turn to any page in my book lists and tune in to what currently occupied me. I can often spot from a title a book suggested by a friend. Guy and I read books aloud. I noted those with an asterisk. We favored British and American nineteenth-century writers, but there is a smattering of children's books (such as *Charlotte's Web* by E. B. White and *The Secret Garden* by Frances Hodgson Burnett, that are so loved by adults), and Shakespeare.

I have kept a list of the number of books I read in a year. The high point was June 1961 to June 1962, my senior year in college, with 102 books—skewed by the books I read as an English major. The total of four books in 1972 to 1973 was the rock bottom. I'm not a fast reader. I'm a slow reader who prefers to savor. For many years I averaged about two books a month, or three; around twenty-four to forty-six books a year, that is. Over the last two decades, with more time for reading, the number has increased to a book a week, or even a book and a half a week.

At some point in the 1990s, Guy indexed my entire book list by author and by title, two separate lists. By that time, many years had gone by. It had become difficult to find whether I'd read a book or not. I'd experienced several embarrassing occasions of reading a book, recording it, then discovering that I had already read it. To add to this humiliation was that I hadn't the faintest memory of reading the book!

One of my missions in life has been to encourage anyone, but especially children, to keep a book list. Guy, a record keeper of all sorts of data having to do with our homestead, claimed my book list was *the* most important statistic kept at Barra. Perhaps. Perhaps not. But if you look at keeping a book list as a lifetime occupation, as Boswell seems to have, it's a list worth keeping. If you are a lover of reading and you decide to keep a book list, I can promise that ahead of you are hours of pleasure from reading over your lists, a pleasure that only accumulates as the years roll out.

Guy Waterman! I knew he was the man for me when, shortly after we got together—it would have been on our first commute into New York's Grand Central from the Beacon rail station—Guy pulled out Macaulay's *History of England*. My eyes opened wide. This was one of the great literary works of the nineteenth century! I gleefully added what I'd read, in terms of great histories, Herodotus; he had read Herodotus, too, *and* Thucydides. This made me very happy. In high school I had not had much luck with the young men I had an interest in when I disclosed what I read. In college, it got better, but when it came to conversations when titles were exchanged, I generally felt I held the aces and was not happy to sense myself holding back for fear of appearing excessively literary. With Guy, this was not going to be an issue. And, as it turned out, books and reading would be our lives.

You don't need to take a book off a shelf [in the library] to know there is a voice inside that is waiting to speak to you, and behind that was someone who truly believed that if he or she spoke, someone would listen.

—Susan Orlean, *The Library Book*

I spend many hours looking through my father's books, the books he had collected that were housed in our living room, on floor-to-ceiling shelves on either side of the picture window. There was very little fat. Indeed, none. It was a working reference library for a man who was a scholar. The little fiction that had wedged its way in came from me, contributions from my college English courses. I must admit that John Dos Passos's *USA* and Faulkner's *The Sound and the Fury* seemed light fare beside Edmond Gosse's *Life of William Congreve*, or Jay Leyda's *The Melville Log*, or Dumas Malone's *Jefferson*, in five volumes.

A number of these books were written by my dad's friends and colleagues, like Perry Miller and Kenneth Murdock, authorities on the Puritans. Or the aforementioned Jay Leyda, an Emily Dickinson contributor. Willard Thorp of Princeton and Robert Spiller of the University of Pennsylvania had their share of shelf space. They were all men I knew, and some were my friends, too—friendships that began when I was very young and helped form my life. I have my father's edition of Samuel Eliot Morison's *The European Discovery of America: The Northern Voyages*, with the frontispiece, a colored plate, tipped in upside down.

(Alas, these publishing goofs happen. A book of mine omitted the endpapers, a crucial map, though this was on a short batch of print-on-demand copies needed for a bookstore reading. No great harm done. A shock at the time, but nowhere near the shock for Professor Morison when he realized his whole first print run displayed this frontispiece, a colored plate entitled "Frobisher's fight with Eskimos at Frobisher Bay," turned on its head. Ah well, because of it, the book is among my most cherished.)

After my parents had moved into a nursing home, it fell to me to disperse my father's library. Guy aided me greatly in this task by listing all my father's books, sorting them into categories. I got in touch with the librarian at the Lawrenceville School, where my father had taught for thirty years, and invited him to come take what would be useful. Then Guy and I picked out books for friends and family, particularly my brother, and we made our own selection.

I contacted Richard Ludwig, the Princeton Librarian for Rare Books and Special Collections, who ended up taking sixty-nine books and pamphlets that had been collected by my father about Emily Dickinson, as an aid to his own work on the poet.

All this work on behalf of my father's library was wonderfully rewarding for me. I particularly valued Dick Ludwig's note to us expressing his gratitude that ended, "I shall be seeing Willard tomorrow for Thanksgiving dinner and sharing with him the good news that Tom's books and papers have found their proper storage place. And I know Bob Spiller will also be pleased. What those three men have done for the study of American literature in this country is tremendous."

Libraries have the power to reverberate down through our lives, as my father's library has for me. Susan Orlean writes, "It wasn't that time stopped in the library. It was as if it were captured here, collected here. . . . In the library, time is dammed up—not just stopped but saved. The library is a gathering pool of narratives and of the people who come to find them. It is where we can glimpse immortality; in the library, we can live forever."

It was in my father's library that I made tentative stabs at reading Shakespeare. The boys at Lawrenceville put on a Shakespeare play every year, and when I was old enough, I was taken, sequentially, to *The Taming of the Shrew* and to *Romeo and Juliet*. After each one I pulled the play off the bookshelf in our living room, in an effort to find the parts I remembered: Petruchio's many attempts to "tame" the beautiful and witty Katharina (Kate) by, for instance, getting her to say she sees the moon when, clearly, it is the sun that shines so bright. In *Romeo and Juliet* it was, inevitably, the "balcony scene." Seeing the plays was a good way to begin my acquaintance with Shakespeare, with his language, that was pushed a little further by spending the occasional half hour with his words on the page. Strange words, but they held a fascination that kept me coming back.

Orlean, in *The Library Book*, writes about the fire that laid waste to the Los Angeles library's Central Branch in 1986. Hundreds of thousands of books were lost to fire, smoke, water, and mold. The city pulled together and built a new library, a decade-long project. In my Vermont village, East Corinth, the Blake Memorial Library suffered a similar devastation. The library burned in November 1945; the only books that survived were those few hundred in circulation.

The idea for a library in our rural community originated with three young men from farm families, one of whom became a minister. In 1893, they went from house to house in the village collecting books in a wheelbarrow. The idea took hold, and neighbors began weeding their own collections, bringing books to a house in the village where they were given temporary shelf space. Library hours were established and the three young men who had the idea took turns as librarian. This was the beginning. It took several years to raise the money for a building, for which the town was helped by the generosity of the family for whom the library was named.

I love this story. It's the story of a community pulling together to build a house for books. And at the story's heart shines the beauty of libraries themselves: that anyone can borrow a book, take it home, read it, and return it. Libraries are free. They are built on trust. Everyone is welcome.

In Vermont there are more public libraries, per capita, than in any other state in the union. There are 237 towns and 9 cities and our state has 195 public libraries. All of them would have their own origin story to tell—a story that would speak to perpetual learning, to gaining knowledge, or, perhaps most important, the ability to enjoy a pleasurable read. Vermont towns, when our town library was founded, were separated, if not in miles, in the geography of steep-sided narrow river valleys. Travel between them was slow. A village needed a library of its own.

Guy and I, of course, had begun using the library as soon as we became residents in 1973. Then, when we began research for a book we were writing about the mountains of the Northeast, that was when we became acquainted with the amazing service of the interlibrary loan system. For those who live in a rural area, interlibrary loan is like a miracle, like a magic trick. You fill out the request form, wait a week, and the book appears. I always look to see the library it came from. Many come from libraries in Vermont or in New Hampshire, just across the Connecticut River. But one came from a library in Oregon once, and I like to imagine that librarian across the country pulling the book off the shelf, knowing that she (or he) was going to make a reader in a small New England town very happy.

Guy and I began volunteering at our library in the 1990s. The librarian at that time, Alice Thompson, suggested we go through the basement, where musty old books and long-out-of-circulation magazines were stored. It seemed that nearly everyone in the towns of Corinth and Topsham, who found their own library shelves cracking under the weight of old *National Geographic* magazines, had shuttled them over to the Blake Memorial Library. Alice wanted to do a house cleaning so that the basement space could be turned into a children's library. We spent most of a winter there, with our dog for company. It was a dusty, dirty job, but the end result was a lovely space for a children's collection.

My favorite library in all the world is the main branch of the New York Public Library at Fifth Avenue and Forty-Second Street. When I walk up the wide steps between the two guardian lions today, I'm happily awash in memories of when I lived in New York in the 1960s. One of my jobs as an editor at the publishing company where I worked was to fill out my authors' bibliographies. This work took me to the card catalog at the NYPL. The card retrieval system was housed in wooden drawers that could be easily slid out from the wall. The main sound under the vast ceiling of this room that included the circulation desk was the sound of these drawers—scaled to fit a three-by-five card, sliding open, and then shut, with a dull wooden *thunk*. Through this work I got to know the young people who worked behind the circulation desk, a few of whom became my friends.

I couldn't have foreseen, then, what this great public library would come to mean to me. After Guy and I had moved to Vermont, once a year or so I would find myself back in the city, walking up between the Library Lions, up the long flight of stairs to the catalog room, where, as the decades moved along, I witnessed the changeover when the card catalog drawers were replaced by computers. I felt the loss. I had enjoyed such an intimacy with those three-by-five cards, some with penciled notations from librarians of the distant past. I wondered what had happened to those lovely wooden drawers.

But change is constant, perpetual. The old is made obsolete by the new. There is a gain, but there is also a loss; the library itself remains. Books are housed there and anyone anywhere can walk into a nearby library and request a book. They can use the computers, search for articles, put in an interlibrary loan request, or seek out a reference librarian. There they will find a community based on books and learning, or a happy few hours spent browsing.

In the New York Public Library we sit with hundreds of other readers in the reading rooms—spaces with ceilings three or four stories high (or so it feels), sturdy wooden tables, chairs with arms, rooms that stretch for seeming miles, shaded lamps on the tables, chandeliers on the ceiling, and paned windows letting in natural light. A community of readers, researchers, and a few who have just come in from the cold, are gathered here.

The same scene goes on at my library in the village. A volunteer is at the circulation desk ("circ desk" for short). Readers sit at our one long table, some at work on their own computers, or on the library's computers, some with a book or magazine or the newspaper. The natural light filters in, though I would not say there is the sort of dusty hush I have experienced in the New York Public Library. Our library is a community gathering space where friends come to drop off a book, comb the shelves for another one, and have a chat, too. But the space is sacred in the same way the NYPL feels to me, a public house for books, for learning, for enlightenment, for sharing. It is perpetually open to anyone who steps across the threshold.

If we are lucky enough to begin to build our own libraries when we are very young, we find, as we grow older, that we have kept many of the books we started with. Some of these books have moved along with us. We feel protective of them, and it is likely that they have protected us, allowing us to recover our childhoods and recalling the many changes in our lives. Our libraries reveal our histories. I find it nearly impossible to weed my shelves for our twice-a-year book sale at the Blake library: I pull a book off the shelf, determined, this time, to put it in the box marked "For the Library Sale." But I can't resist opening it, and I begin to read its opening paragraph. I remember what stage of life I was in when I bought it, or who gave it to me, and I put it back on the shelf, where it immediately looks at home. Not yet. Because, really, I know I'll never be able to part with that book or any of its neighbors. The bond is too strong. It's permanent. Face it, I tell myself: only in death will we part.

3

Growing Up with Emily Dickinson

As a child, it never crossed my mind to reason out or to ponder the impact Emily Dickinson would have on my life. But that impact was profound and life-forming, giving me a slantwise view of not just the poet, but of my father too.

The writing life: as a writer, there are all kinds of ways to live this. In my case, I didn't begin to think about it until my agent suggested I write about it.

What does it mean to live the life of a writer? A friend of mine, a rock climber, who had set the standard for his generation, famously remarked, "Climbing is something I do, not something I talk about." He meant it was so much a part of himself, his nature, that talking or writing or thinking about it in an analytical way would trivialize what it meant to him. Climbing was too important to his life and well-being to break apart, to place on the examining table under the microscope.

Did Emily Dickinson articulate to herself that she was leading a writer's life? It makes me laugh to think this! Whether she did or not, she undeniably was, even though she was rarely published in her lifetime, and not for lack of trying.

Did my father ask himself this question? I can offer an unequivocal NO. He had probably never heard the phrase. Or if he had, would not thought much of it. Yet, he lived it every day by rising at 4:00 a.m. and getting to work. Both were geniuses and suffered the demands of what that meant.

Partially it meant a tremendous absorption into the work itself. This could result in a shutting out of everything that competed with the work. There is an astringency here that is frightening. Whether or not you articulate to yourself that you are a writer who is living a writer's life, and what that means only you can define, doesn't matter. It's the act itself that tells the story.

The writer's work is carried on in isolation no matter how many people fill the house. By its nature, intensely private, impossible to share in the heat of creation.

And the result? That's for the world to evaluate, and often, the verdict isn't given out until long after death.

I extend a generous thank-you to David Crews, who published "Growing Up with Emily Dickinson" in his Platform Review, *December 2022.*

~

When Thomas Johnson presented the *Complete Poems* to the public, he restored not only the capital letters used so liberally but the unorthodox punctuation for which she is now well known. . . . Since the publication of Johnson's text, Dickinson's "dashes" have been taken seriously.

—Judith Farr, *The Passion of Emily Dickinson*

Most of my life people have asked me about Emily Dickinson. They think I have a special knowledge of the great American poet, and, in a sense, they are right. I was ten or eleven when Emily Dickinson slid into my father's study and took over our family.

People want me to answer their questions. She is a poet who causes people to ask questions, because her life and work raise questions, many of which appear unanswerable. I give their questions my best shot because I'm helpful by nature. But I can hear in the way they politely thank me, and see in their eyes, that I have failed. As I knew I would.

My father was Emily Dickinson's editor. How this happened is a tale simply told. The *Literary History of the United States* had come out in 1948, and its four authors, my dad being one, made a splash with it. Then, his previous literary work alone, with the parson-poet Edward Taylor and the philosopher-preacher Jonathan Edwards qualified him, in the eyes of Harvard University Press, to be capable of tackling Dickinson. At this point, the early 1950s, her work was little known. Some poems were anthologized, but those in print had been forced into conventional poetic forms by her previous editors. Her main point of punctuation—the dash—was routed out for the traditional comma, or period.

Thomas H. Johnson's job was to restore what Emily Dickinson had originally written. He did this. He began the work in 1952, and the editions in three volumes were published in 1955. Next followed a three-volume set of Dickinson's letters in 1958, which he compiled with our dear friend Theodora Ward as his assistant editor. (My brother Tommy and I adored Theodora. She was humorous and sharp and as "wren-like" as Emily Dickinson described herself. The kind of scholarship Theodora was providing with Emily's letters was uncommon work for a woman of her generation.) My dad's *Emily Dickinson: An Interpretive Biography* followed on the heels of *The Poems*, also in 1955. At one point, Robert Hillyer wrote in a *New York Times* book review, "There is no greater achievement of editing and research in the field of American Literature."

The amount of work undertaken and brought to fruition—in less than a decade—still leaves me breathless, especially when I know that my dad continued to show up in his classroom at the Lawrenceville School where he taught seventeen- and eighteen-year-old-boys at 8:00 a.m. He never took on the athletic duties that usually went along with a preparatory school teacher's life. This is not, however, to say that he didn't appreciate the natural world. He was expert at discovering perfect picnic spots for our family. I remember an open hillside, where our mother taught us to recognize steeplebush, that looked out on the distant swells of the mountains of southern Vermont. There was a stream where my brother and I could slide down rocks into water only slightly above freezing. On the bank, my father would grill a steak over an open fire. If we had visitors—often his colleagues—the main course was preceded by martinis transported in a thermos to keep them cold.

He was an early riser: 4:00 a.m. He took no vacations, though we were spending summers in the mountains as a family, having by that time changed our destination to southern New Hampshire, under the shadow of Mount Monadnock. His discipline could only be described as steely. He seemed not to require downtime, in the ordinary sense, though we in the family were aware he did require, at certain times of day, a liberal amount of alcohol. Yet, why not?

His relationship with the poet must have been intense beyond words. I suppose it's no wonder that people assume I have a special pipeline to Dickinson. On one level I did—and do—but it is not that of the scholar or student; I understand little of what her poetry conveys. Yet, through my father, through her residence in his study—and, basically, she never left—I feel and understand much that is not easily put into words. My understanding of what Emily was like, of what she was trying to do as a poet, is largely intuited from an understanding of my father. Those few who knew my father well saw that Emily resonated with his own nature; during those early morning hours in communion with her words, he made her a part of his life. She seeped into his. I have heard them called soulmates.

My father had this to say about the weight and cost of Emily Dickinson's genius:

> All who have had access to material touching upon Emily Dickinson's life and writing agree—I think without exception—that she knew during her twenties that she was uncommonly gifted; that by the time she was thirty-one, when she sought advice from Thomas Wentworth Higginson in the now famous letters written in April 1862, she did indeed crave assurance regarding a talent which at times literally overwhelmed her. "Alone I cannot be," she wrote at this time in a remarkable poem:
>
> > Alone I cannot be—
> > For Hosts—do visit me—
> > Recordless Company—
> > Who baffle Key—
>
> How was this gift to be shared? She must have been somewhat prepared to accept Higginson's hesitation to advise publication, for it matched the opinion of other writers and critics whom she knew and respected, gentlemen who knew something of her writing, notably Samuel Bowles and Josiah Gilbert Holland. She should delay submitting any letters to the world, they all told her in effect, until she had learned "control." Since she could

no more "control" the quality of the hosts who visited her than she could alter her wren-like size, she must therefore, in her own lifetime at any rate, sublimate her desire for public recognition, however compelling the wish for it may have been.

My father delivered these words in an address read before the English Institute on September 7, 1951, when he had barely begun. What had to happen first was for all the scraps and bits of paper or letters to which Emily Dickinson had committed her poems to be rounded up. By the time we returned from a year in Copenhagen, where my father had been invited to set up a program in American studies at the university, Harvard University Press had collected most of what turned out to be nearly eighteen hundred poems. The bulk came as a gift of Gilbert H. Montague, a Harvard alum, class of 1901, who turned over his collection to his alma mater in 1950. This got the ball rolling in terms of the desires of scholars, publishers, and librarians to produce a variorum edition, meaning, "Including variant readings critically compared with all known manuscripts," as stated on the title page.

Before we left for Copenhagen, Mr. Montague had issued an invitation to my parents to be his guests at his home in New York City. (I pictured a Fifth Avenue mansion.) They took the train from Princeton, knowing that this overnight visit was a visit of inspection. Was a prep school teacher capable of such a plum assignment? They were amused by this, and appropriately nervous, or so it felt to me, by the tone of their banter—casual, but high pitched—when they left the house for the train. But it must have gone well. They were in excellent spirits upon the return, my mother launching into a description of an elaborate dinner, just the three of them, at a long dining table illuminated by candles highlighting the heavy family silver. Maids to serve and a butler to pour the wine that changed with every course. The downstairs bathroom, my mother reported, was painted black in memory of Mr. Montague's wife who had died not long before. This detail stuck to the story, and to our minds, something I pondered over that was sad—the *death* of his *wife!*—yet in the way of sad things to which we have no connection, especially as children, more than slightly risible.

Others of Emily's poems had ended up at various city libraries (New York Public, Boston Public) and institutions (the Jones Library in Amherst, as well as Amherst College's Converse Memorial, Yale's library, the Pierpont Morgan in New York, and more). No fewer than forty individuals possessed at least one Dickinson letter or poem. Seeing publication was barred to her, this was her way of sharing her output with, if not the world, at least with friends.

So, when we returned in 1952 from our magical year among the Danes, Harvard University Press sent my father what were called photostats—an early form of photocopying—that showed each poem in white letters against a black background. For the next several years when I walked into my father's study—if the door were open, I knew I would be welcome—that's what I saw thumbtacked into the pine paneling of his study wall. He was ascribing a date to her poems—*she* had dated none of them—by changes in her handwriting.

How did he do this? By close and exacting scholarship that he explains in the paper he read before the English Institute, later published as "Establishing a Text: The Emily Dickinson Papers," in *Studies in Bibliography: Papers of the Bibliographical Society of the University of Virginia*, volume 5, 1952–1953. He has this to say about it:

> The progressive unlinking of letters, in this case over an eighteen-year period, is enormously useful, and made possible by a physiological change that perhaps is comparatively rare. In her case I believe it theoretically possible, if enough manuscript existed, and if each manuscript used enough letters in sufficient combination, to track down dates of composition within the limits of a given week. But the quantity of manuscripts is wanting, and even if they existed it would take years to compute and equate the frequencies without the aid of an electric eye and a robot tabulator.

Yes, my father's painstaking work predated computers!

"He's in there with Emily," my mother would pronounce, waving her hand toward the study door when a visitor came, wanting to talk with my father. She also called Emily "the other woman" in her husband's life. Of course, this made everyone laugh. She said it to amuse, to joke, but everyone knew there was more than a little truth in it. How could it have been otherwise? My father, true to his nature, remained silent. He had long ago mastered the poker face—in fact was very good at the game. My dad played his cards right up against his chest. (Poker, and bridge, too, that they played in the evening with friends.) No one knew what was going on behind those watery blue eyes.

No scholar could cross swords with a poetic power of *her* caliber without some bloodshed. It was to be expected if you're fooling around with an off-the-scale genius, who happened to be a woman whose interior life was a mystery—my father's interior life was a mystery as well—that you end up paying a price. Singed fingers from incandescent verse was not the least of it.

When my parents' friends—fellow teachers (called masters at Lawrenceville) and their wives—who were my friends, too, came to our living room for cocktails, I might hear conversation like this: "How does she compare to Whitman, Tom? Is she pushing him off his podium?" My brother and I hung around, and I was fascinated by this adult conversation, shrill with women's voices, and deep, solid, and virile with men's, men who coached sports along with their teaching duties. The ashtrays filled and my father poured the drinks amid laughter on these evenings, and everyone heard from my father just what kind of new poetic genius was emerging from this wispy white script tacked to the pine paneling in his study. I found all this exciting. I felt a compelling energy, as when I rode my bike farther than I ever had before and started to fear getting lost and missing dinner. Would anyone come out looking for me? How would they know, even, where to look?

As for answering that question about Whitman, the current top American favorite, my father wouldn't say much except, in effect, stay tuned, adding, "her originality doomed her to obscurity," or some such opaquely perceptive comment. My father was famous for those, and to my mind, they made him sound like Emily. Both went for short, pithy, elliptical sentences or phrases that I either "got" instantly or broke my head against trying to make sense of.

My father would show me a poem from time to time. The one that made a permanent impression, "A narrow fellow in the grass," I could appreciate. The way it ended: "zero at the Bone," these words certainly described my own snake encounters.

They had in common that both were born in the Connecticut River valley, Emily in the college town of Amherst, my father a few hundred miles up the river in Bradford, Vermont. He grew up on a prosperous farm until, as he was just starting high school, his family moved to the state capital when his father became the adjutant general of the state. Emily and Tom were linked as well through the staunch connection of eighteenth- and nineteenth-century philosophical thought, with its religious underpinnings through the Puritan divines that had guided my father's earlier work. He and

Perry Miller of Harvard had written a book called *The Puritans*. And there was the manuscript of Edward Taylor's poetry that my father had found, most unexpectedly, in the dusty basement stacks of the library at Yale. He was well prepared to contend with Emily's poetic output.

It seemed important to scour the hedgerows. That is, Harvard University Press and my father wanted to make sure they had shown due diligence in searching out as many poems as could be found before launching into print. Since he had begun the work, bits and pieces from letters long saved in airless attics, damp basements, and the dusty backs of closet shelves had already turned up. My father was convinced there were more out there.

Ouija boards—a nineteenth-century occult game of making contact with the spirit world—had made an appearance in the homes of the Lawrenceville faculty. No one took seriously the idea that fingers lightly resting on a wand could be steered by a question to pick out the revealing letters on the board, but my mother, always alert to the ridiculous, had the idea. Let's contact Emily and see if she'll be forthcoming with the mailing addresses of friends to whom she had sent her poems!

It so happened that a young poet named James Merrill, a Lawrenceville School graduate, was back for alumni weekend. He had two books out, at that point, of which *First Poems*, the latest, had been published in 1951. He also, apparently, had a great affinity for Ouija boards. Jim came up to the house, and we all gathered around the board spread on the table in our living room. We were all—children and adults—in some kind of crazy high glee. Ouija boards did this to people. Yes, this *is* silly, we don't *really* believe, but let's see what happens! As the wand skittered from letter to letter under Jim's deft fingers, my mother transcribing as the words formed—well, by gosh, we *did* believe.

None of the names were recognizable, but my father wrote the letters anyway. The envelopes appeared in our post office box a week or so later marked "return to sender," news that was received, even by my brother and me, with merely a shrug.

In those early morning hours—daily, weekly, over the months and years—my father, I think, came to see the poet as a version of himself. Her love of words, her entirely original use of language, met with his own. In his *Interpretive Biography* my father wrote, "She seems generally to have conversed, as she wrote, in epigrams . . . in twists of phrase which haunt the memory and could often startle." This was true of my father as well. Bruce McClellan, Lawrenceville's headmaster, who had known my father long and well, described this in an unpublished article titled "Tom Johnson: The Emily Dickinson Scholar": "So, too, with Tom. His colleagues as well as students were often stopped cold in their tracks by something he said, and often would discover later, sometimes much later, that what he had said conveyed an important insight and was memorable." I was aware of this. Sometimes what my dad said seemed to make no sense. And indeed it didn't if it was following the cocktail hour. He was at his best at our family Sunday dinners, a meal I always looked forward to. Then I often reached the meaning behind the words in the epigrams he offered.

While this ability was what made him such a brilliant teacher, it also made him the right person to take on Dickinson. Similar minds. Both geniuses. Bruce McClellan, in that same article, called my father the only genius he ever knew, and went on to say he was "exactly the right person to resonate with the genius of Emily Dickinson."

I could add another shared characteristic—their reclusiveness. Both were obsessively shy. In my father, as in Emily, these traits became more obvious, more enigmatic, with age. When Julie Harris was portraying Emily in *The Belle of Amherst*, she made a point of inviting my parents to the production in New York around 1976. He turned down her cordial invitation. My mother was annoyed with him about that. *She* accepted with pleasure, and went to see it with the McClellans. Ms. Harris invited them to come backstage after the show and asked my mother to take her greeting home to her husband.

When the play was scheduled for performance at the McCarter Theatre in Princeton, Ms. Harris tried again. She telephoned. She invited my parents and then expressed the hope that she could come to our house and meet my dad. None of this happened. By now, my mother was thoroughly disgusted with my father. I thought he was carrying his repeated refusals pretty far myself. It would have been a lovely thing for them to talk about Emily together. But, no, I concluded, after looking at it from his point of view. Emily was too real to him. As great an actress as Julie Harris was, he did not want to confuse *her* interpretation of Emily Dickinson with the poet who maintained a life tenancy in his study. She was a part of him, more integral, I'm quite sure, than his own family. He had no interest in hearing (in fact was willing to appear rude to avoid hearing) Julie Harris's view of the poet. Sharing his own was unthinkable too. It would have been like baring his own soul! Emily resonated completely with his own nature; too much was at risk.

Years later, long after my father was dead, my mother was living in a retirement home, and when someone asked her if she liked Dickinson's poetry, I would watch as she gave a small, polite smile that did not encourage conversation. As she aged, and the censor dropped, she left out the smile and her "Not at all" was forceful, causing the questioner to take a step back. In this way she opened up for me just how challenging it was for her to live with her husband, who had turned his life and mind over to Emily Dickinson. She was proud of him, of course, but my mother would never have talked about what could have appeared to others as a triangular love affair, bounded by possible jealousy on her part with a hint of infidelity on his with this dead poet. She was true to her class and upbringing at a time when society compelled educated, intelligent, ambitious women to sublimate all that, remain in the home, and raise the family. My mother, after her brood was mostly grown, worked her way out of this by dealing in real estate in Princeton, New Jersey, for twenty years.

I would bet my life that she never articulated her deepest thoughts to anyone, whatever they were, about Tom and Emily. That would have been disloyal. It would have undercut her husband. It would have turned quickly into gossip. She was too smart to let this happen.

As for me, though I remain unable to answer the questions put to me about Emily Dickinson's life and poetry, I recognize how formative for me she has been. She remains elusive, yet I feel a familiarity with her because of my father's work, that intense period in our household when he brought her to life through her handwriting tacked to the pine paneling of his study. This familiarity works the other way: it leads me to a deeper understanding of my silent father.

I have many favorite Dickinson poems that I have read over and over in the course of my life, hoping, each time I pull out the book, that enlightenment will spring forth. But revelation is not essential. Sometimes there can come a glimmer, a spark—I'm so close!—then that narrow fellow in the grass slithers off into the underbrush. I don't mind. I am sustained by a deepening of the glimmer. So I slide the book into its place on the shelf that holds my father's work, waiting for the next time.

4

Writing Together

t wasn't until I had been writing collaboratively with my husband for a number
of years that it dawned on me that one reason why writing this way felt so
natural, so normal, was that I had grown up with the example of my father,
who had written books with various of his colleagues. This chapter looks back
on what I had witnessed—but not fully understood—as a child, and how my
early observations sustained me through a buoyant yet often stressful ten-year
writing project.

Writing collaboratively can break friendships and end marriages. It can
dissolve, after years of work, in failed projects.

What is the secret of successful collaboration? You're asking two or more
people to work together to create art on the page, people who, quite naturally,
have differing ways of writing, thinking, and organizing. Each, at any moment,
could offer some other valid approach that could foment turmoil of conflicting
ideas and opinions.

Looked at this way, successful collaborating seems almost impossible. Collaborators are, after all, dealing with their own egos and human feelings. To make it work there has to be, on the part of each person, utter dedication to the project. A solid belief in the work itself. Respect between all members of the collaborating team is crucial. As is trust. Ideally everyone enjoys spending time together. A lot of what looks hard, the thorny stuff, will just work itself out if you can gain a little objectivity. Humor helps here. It's important to laugh!

Ideally, each collaborator should have an area of expertise that's uniquely theirs, that they can be responsible for. There should be a leader who acts as a kind of chair of the board, with an eye on agendas and deadlines. All should be good listeners.

Basically, collaborating is like a marriage. At times you will find yourself relying on your collaborating partner(s) even though you're not convinced or even sure in which direction the ball is bouncing. Try to be patient. The surface should clear. If it's not clearing, if the muck is growing thicker and sludgier, well, it's time for you to bring your concerns to the table. But please don't speak harshly or point the finger. That will only make things worse.

Sometimes years roll by. It's easy to lose heart. And that's when the optimists come to the fore, as well as an unwavering belief in this project that drew you all together in the first place.

The surprise comes at the end. When the book is published it's like child birth. This baby is beautiful! The dust jacket is a perfect fit. There is a name on the cover—in fact all your names. The skies have cleared. The pain is in the past and, if not forgotten, at least slinks quietly away to take a seat in the back row, to be replaced by sheer joy of what you're holding in your hands. In fact, you are all so elated, and in retrospect you've had so much fun, you wish it weren't over. Amazingly, you're already talking about the next project.

~

As a child, I was fascinated by adult conversation. Some children are like that. Their adult world, to me, was an exciting and mystifying place, its conversation punctuated by laughter. The particular adults I knew, and who knew me, were part of the Lawrenceville School community where my father was head of the English Department. On dinner party evenings, when the fathers and mothers gathered in our living room, there was a lot of laughter. I understood their words but couldn't make sense of what made them laugh—the voices of the mothers light, high, flutelike, rising to the ceiling, the fathers' low, growly, cellos and double-basses, plunging down to the basement. On these festive nights my younger brother and I, if we behaved ourselves, were allowed to hang around the edges—my elected place for listening was on the stairs. But though I concentrated as hard as I could, unable to make what they laughed about be funny to me, it made me happy to be there.

During summers, starting in 1945, the last year of the war, we lived in the camp on the shores of Lake Raponda, near Wilmington, Vermont. My parents welcomed many visitors, most of whom were colleagues of my father. Four of the men, counting my father, were hard at work, writing an important book that recounted America's literary history.

There, on a sparsely traveled dirt road, was life at its simplest, best defined by what was missing. The one thing that we did have in the line of mid-twentieth-century comforts was electricity. But it was not, we learned, grounded; during electrical storms, lightning would spark out of the wall sockets. For some reason this was not something to be alarmed about—that is, my parents did not appear to be disturbed by this electrifying display—until after one particularly violent thunderstorm that produced a fireworks of sparks. The electrician arrived and instructed my mother to turn on the water at the sink, put her hand under the flow, and, with her other hand, pull the cord attached to the overhead light bulb. My mother quietly inquired if she might electrocute herself, whereupon the electrician assured her not to worry, that he was standing by to, as he put it, "pull her off." Memory falters as to whether my mother went along with the experiment, but my father told the electrician to go ahead and ground the system. Gone was the excitement of watching lightning spark out.

As for refrigeration, we had it, but the "icebox"—a small wooden chest, half the size of the white, upright refrigerator in our winter home—was located in its own special house, a small shed that was a short walk from the back door. The exciting part for my brother and me were the once-a-week visits from the iceman, who carried, with giant tongs, a huge block of ice slung onto a rubber pad that covered his shoulders and back. You could tell it was heavy by his wide-legged lumber as he climbed from his truck up our steep drive, and our mother's firm voice instructing us to keep out of his way.

We had running water, too, but it ran only cold and came out of the lake. My mother had to heat water for washing dishes. For drinking, it was my brother's and my responsibility to prime the pump at our well and fill our jugs. We loved wrapping our small hands around the pump handle, a great long curve of iron. We pumped briskly, and watched the water pour out in a cold, clear, bright, and wholesome stream, a miracle from underground.

We had an oil stove with only two burners that came with an oven the size of a small square suitcase, which could be set on the surface, covering the burners. My mother's kitchen was equipped, as well, with a woodstove, an iron beast that took up more than its share of the room. Only on particularly frosty mornings did my father fire it up. For heat we burned wood in a spacious fieldstone fireplace that we gathered around when we made popcorn, our parents guiding our hands as my brother and I took turns with a wire contraption that held the kernels. To keep them from burning in the open flame, we had to shake them without pause, a tough assignment for a child, but one that made us feel very grown up.

We had no telephone.

We had a radio, and on August 6, 1945, we heard that an atomic bomb was dropped on Hiroshima in Japan, and that the war was almost over. I was five. What I remember is the look on my parents' faces at the calamity of the destruction of an entire, thickly populated city, combined with the joy that World War II was ending. I found this completely puzzling: two emotions pulling me in opposite directions.

We swam in the lake every afternoon, a short hop down our woodsy path and across the dirt road to our dock, with the rowboat tied up alongside. Our mother taught us to swim, and it was as well that she did because otherwise she would have been heating a lot of water on her two burners. Swimming was a lot more fun than taking baths! We did admire our picturesque bathtub, however—a great white whale with claw feet that could have held our entire family, and that took up space in a bathroom that our parents speculated had formerly been a bedroom. "Formerly" meant, my mother explained, before the camp was modernized by plumbing.

In the mornings, we played in the forest. Our camp was surrounded by mostly evergreen woods, the forest floor thick with the needles of balsam fir and red spruce, cool and moist, good for digging and getting dirty in. Bob Spiller, my father's great friend and colleague, assured my mother that this was good, healthy Vermont loam we had ground into our blue jeans and under our fingernails, not *dirt*, the kind you'd find in cities.

Bob was Robert E. Spiller. He had arranged for us to spend the summer here. This made sense to me because my father was from Vermont. Of course he would want his children to experience his native state. This was our first of eight Vermont summers. Bob wanted my father close by so they could work on what they called "the literary history" together. This idea didn't come out of the blue. There had been other histories on books that had been written by Americans, namely the *Cambridge History of American Literature*. There had been pamphlets and articles on this subject. Now it was time for something more comprehensive, more cooperative. Bob had been steering those conversations from the beginning. He saw this undertaking not just including a complete history, but a bibliography of all America's literature as well.

Bob, and his wife Mary, who was a very good friend of my mother's, already had been bringing their family to Vermont for many years. Their house—a farmhouse with an attached woodshed, and beyond that an outhouse, also attached, but no longer in use since they had indoor plumbing—was situated at the end of a long dirt road that wound steeply uphill through woods, tall and dark, and then more gradually down until you broke out into a sunny clearing and there was the house, with a roofed-over front porch and chairs for everyone. Bob and Mary called their place High Valley, which, indeed, it was: a shallow bowl, with the fields spreading out down to the trout stream, the wooded hills rising up on all sides.

That first summer, the last of the war, we had arrived by train, and Bob and Mary met us at the Brattleboro station. This meant we had no car and there was a lot of walking of the mile or so between our two houses. On Sunday mornings the ritual was that my father and Bob walked to the nearby Haynes Farm to buy a chicken each, our Sunday dinner, and my mother would pluck and cook our chicken in her primitive oven, placed on the top of those two burners.

As summers passed and my brother and I grew older, we were allowed to walk up to the Spillers', scaring ourselves, when we passed the tar-paper shack where Ira—Iry he pronounced it—Butterfield lived. Would he spot us and come out? He was grizzled and hunched. He liked to talk but we couldn't understand him. Because, my mother explained, he chews tobacco and his accent is pure old-time Vermont. My brother and I, in a state of induced terror, ran up the steep hill overhung with branches reaching out from the dark forest. Cresting the crown, we tore down the other side yelling out in our relief, until we hit the grassy strip that separated the wheel tracks and were safe in the Spillers' open clearing, an ancient apple tree with a swing waiting for us. The sun was always shining on High Valley.

Bob taught at the University of Pennsylvania. I had picked up that the feeling was, at least in some European countries, that America had no literature, to speak of. But Bob and a number of other professors of his acquaintance were convinced that America had a fine literature.

So this was an important time for new beginnings. By 1945, they were well into this work: Bob Spiller and my father, along with Willard Thorp and Henry Canby. Years and years later, when Guy and I were sitting on the Spillers' porch after Mary's death, when Bob himself was past eighty, with High Valley looking just the same, he turned to us and said, "The *Literary History* was written on this porch." I could only nod in agreement: these words spoke to me so tellingly of the importance of their collaboration, a close drawing together of intellects at their finest, at work in service to America's literature, and, equally important, the deepening of friendships.

Willard Thorp taught English at Princeton, just five miles away from us in Lawrenceville, and when he came to talk with my father in his study, he might bring his wife, Margaret, to visit with my mother; they would sit in our living room where I could be beside my mother on the couch and listen in. I liked Mrs. Thorp very much because it seemed that I had reached an age that (some) adults could find interesting, and Margaret Thorp would talk to me. She was very learned, a quality for which I had immense respect. She was also, I could see, amused by me and my questions. What were they? I now wonder. Probably not about her work, though my mother told me Mrs. Thorp had written a book on Margaret Fuller, a friend of Emerson and the Transcendentalists, and a Transcendentalist herself, who was recognized by the men of her generation; she had not been spared by their poisonous tongues when she wrote reviews in *The Dial* critical of their poetry or prose. So these two Margarets became joined in my mind. They seemed so alive, as alike as sisters.

Henry Canby was twenty years older than the other three, who were within a few years of each other, their birth dates crossing from the nineteenth into the twentieth century, my father being the youngest, born in 1902. Willard, born in 1899, was swept up by Melville, a then-neglected American writer, and had made all sorts of discoveries that appeared in the book he had published in 1938.

Henry Canby knew all the writers because he had founded the *Saturday Review of Literature* back in 1924, and had published their articles and reviewed their books. He had written, himself, on Thoreau and Whitman. It was Canby who, when my father was working on "the Dickinson," said—I remember this scene taking place on our Vermont camp's porch, though more likely it was our living room in Lawrenceville—"Did she, or did she not, have carnal relations with that man?" This brought on a rumbling roar of shocked, excited laughter that, this time, I "got." The "man" in question was the Reverend Charles Wadsworth, a clergyman from an important pulpit in

Philadelphia, a well-married family man, twenty years Emily's senior. Only Henry Canby, in *his* senior status, could have gotten away with springing this irreverent question on my father, who was making it clear from his work that in Emily Dickinson, America had a poet the equal of any of the great poets from any century. Despite her greatness, *that* was the question on the minds of each one of those scholarly men.

At five years old, that first summer, I was hardly aware of what they were working on. But when they got together at our camp in the woods, sitting on our porch in conversation, my brother and I took up a position on the steps. As their conversation flowed along over before-dinner drinks, we—my brother and I—spread cocktail peanuts up the six porch steps to entice chipmunks, but listened for the adults' laughter. Great peals of it from Willard Thorp swelled out into the forest and over the lake. It was their work—not consciously did I know this—that made them laugh. What else could it be? That was why they were here. Was my brother picking this up, too? His eyes were glued on a chippy that was sitting on our favorite rock, only twenty feet away, shy of adult laughter, remaining aloof.

My mother and Mary Spiller became expert at producing gourmet meals on that two-burner oil stove. These dinners were served on a mixture of crockery, mismatched and chipped, wine glasses of various sizes and colors, coffee cups with missing handles, an assortment of silverware or steel cutlery. This elegant inelegance seemed only to spark the conversation to greater intensity, judging from the ripples of their laughter. And when my brother and I were trundled off to bed, I coasted to dreamland on the easy flow of their talk around the dinner table.

The way the *Literary History of the United States* worked was that Bob was in charge. He was the one who had pushed the whole idea forward, and he meant to carry out his vision, a vision shared by the four of them. They all took a part in the writing, but they would also approach others—together they knew everyone in the field—to write a chapter on what they were expert in, either an author or a specific aspect of American literature: humor, for instance, or writers from the South. This turned the project, as Bob Spiller intended, into a true collaborative effort. It had, in fact, expanded it into a team undertaking of fifty-five collaborators, those involved in American literature across the country, a branch of academic study that at the time had stagnated.

Willard Thorp remembered how, when he was in prep school, he read in his English class only one American work, Lowell's *The Vision of Sir Launfal*. In Hamilton College he fared worse with the English Department's curriculum of British writers. Why, he had wondered, was there no course in American literature? Even at Harvard, where he went for an MA, determined to study his own nation's literature, there was only a single course, a yearlong survey that met three times a week with a lecturer who droned on until Thorp stopped attending.

Despite the mighty task ahead of them, the four men had assured themselves that, start to finish, it couldn't take more than three years, at the most four, when they'd begun during the war, in 1942. Now war was ended, and some of the chapters were still being revised, while others had not even been written. After I grew up and began working with Guy on a book, a big project, the length of which we had woefully underestimated, I could imagine how Bob, my father, Willard, and Henry Canby must have lost a lot of sleep over the tardiness of some of these fifty-five collaborators. Macmillan, the publisher, adjusted the publication date as needed, but by 1947 the editing and revising was still going on.

More to the point for my father, whose work included his own chapter on the colonial luminaries, he was responsible as well for the bibliography. He had the gift for meticulous attention to detail needed for bibliographical work that had revealed itself in the care he'd displayed with his work on the poetry of Edward Taylor. For the *Literary History*, my father wanted to write bibliographical essays for each author or topic that would give background to the works written on the subject. He was most delighted that Macmillan had granted him a whole separate volume, volume 3, for this. But he needed, of course, the finished chapters to be able to proceed.

Well, big projects can come to happy endings, and when a copy of the newly published *Literary History* reached the home of Willard Thorp in Princeton, he wrote Bob Spiller on November 8, 1948, "Such fun we have had! And what a wonderful editor, guide, taskmaster, Spiller is. . . . You seemed to feel that the answers were there and that they would come out, if we would only keep talking and thinking. Working with you & Tom & Henry has been one of the happiest experiences of my life. I wish we were beginning all over again."[1] When I began writing myself, years later, I realized what I had learned from them was how much fun it all was. To be involved with work that meant everything was like dining at the table

---

1. Kermit Vanderbilt, *American Literature and the Academy: The Roots, Growth, and Maturity of a Profession* (Philadelphia: University of Pennsylvania Press, 1986), 511. I have drawn on Professor Vanderbilt's work for the details and background of the writing of the *Literary History*.

of princes every day, a rich diet that you could live on forever and never grow fat. Always, the muscle of your mind strengthened, and on this you were sustained for a lifetime, or could be, if you were lucky.

I learned about what collaboration among friends meant from my father and his colleagues in the *Literary History*, and, without thinking about it, because it came so naturally, I easily moved into a long period of collaborative work with my husband, Guy. Later, I collaborated with a few others, in particular my literary agent, Craig Kayser, with whom I found it was easy, and an enormous pleasure, to conduct back-and-forth conversations about my current writing projects. We revised a whole novel this way, over the phone. Fun? You bet!

And hard work.

When I started writing with Guy, I was not a writer. Being a book editor in New York City does not necessarily mean you can write them. Guy, on the other hand, had been writing for years. He liked to say he'd written speeches for three presidents: Dwight D. Eisenhower, Richard Nixon, and Gerald Ford, though, he added with a sly twinkle, none was president at the time. Being adept at any kind of speechwriting meant he could turn out thoroughly researched work with lightning speed. He was good at synthesizing, nailing down the salient points, homing in on the telling facts, and cogently wrapping up with convincing points. He relished tight deadlines and thrived on working under fire. He was at his best with short projects, finishing up one and, without missing a beat, moving on to the next. That was exciting for him. He didn't enjoy revising, though he liked working with others, meeting with the senators for whom he was writing to discuss the current speech. He was good at collaborating.

It turned out that we were pretty nearly direct opposites in our approach to writing. This wasn't something that became apparent right away. I was too much of a beginner for that.

When we moved from the city to the country to take up life as homesteaders, the hoped-for plan was to earn a modest living through writing. We got off to a good start when the editor of *Backpacker*, William Kemsley, asked us to write some articles for him. Our first assignment was an analysis of freeze-dried food, breaking the project down into categories of taste, price, weight, packability, ease of preparation, and so forth. Taste, obviously, was the crucial category. A number of new brands had recently come on the market and, as Bill put it, "You have to eat, right?" It was true, but we hadn't anticipated that testing freeze-dried food would go on for two years! Bill knew we'd be camping out on our land when we built our house that first summer, in 1973. So, the conditions were right, and we began to masticate and slurp our way through dinners, desserts, breakfasts, lunches, snacks, and drinks. This led to more writing assignments, including a couple of feature articles that involved backpacking trips that we made with Bill.

As I remember, I did very little of the actual writing on any of this. The collaboration, on my part, came through our conversations on how to organize the food testing. If you're confronting six beef stroganoff dinners—we were testing six companies and their dinner choices were similar—how can you be fair? If we ate one dinner a night, how could we remember, by the sixth night, what the first night's beef stroganoff tasted like? Besides, how could we eat six dinners of any sort a night? (Burp!) To see how we resolved this, check out the early issues of *Backpacker*.

My turn at the writing came when we were asked to pen a column on hiking and camping for *New England Outdoors*. The founding editor, Mike Pogodzinski, was determined to have his magazine match the *New Yorker* for quality of writing. He gave us a free rein, and by this time we were heavily involved with hiking in the Northeast, not just as hikers, backpackers, and climbers, but also as trail workers, and citizens who put a high value on the stewardship of our wild lands. For Guy and me, writing a column on camping and hiking came at the cross-hairs of an important moment.

The backpacking boom of the late '60s and early '70s, which had unleashed an unprecedented number of folks into the mountains, had the consequences of eroded trails, expansion of clearings around shelters as hatchet-bearing campers scrounged for firewood, polluted streams, damaged alpine tundra with boot traffic, and, of course, the accompanying litter on trails and at campsites. Public agencies like the White Mountain National Forest and the Department of Environmental Conservation (DEC) in New York, as well as hiking clubs like the Green Mountain Club in Vermont and state parks like Baxter State Park in Maine, were doing their best to educate these new hikers. Equipment manufacturers were seeing opportunities in offering camping stoves to replace the traditional wood fires, or hammocks to get camping off the ground. Signs appeared at trailheads and shelters, all in an attempt to awaken outdoors lovers streaming into the woods to be aware of our individual impacts. Rock climbers switched from metal pitons to a device known as a "nut" that could be inserted and removed with just one's fingers.

Addressing these issues, spreading the message of stewardship became our mission. We never used that word, but that was what it was, a deeply felt responsibility for the mountains we loved. In the process, I began to learn something about writing.

For our first column, titled "The New Ethic," Guy and I made a list of the topics we wanted to include, all of which addressed how to mitigate our previously outlined impacts. Guy asked me to choose what I wanted to write about. He'd cover the rest. We split the list in half, which was easy, as I had strong, firsthand feelings about all of it. I'd seen the trampled, compacted ground around shelters with the accompanying forest of hacked-off stumps. I'd seen, above treeline, and in particular on the narrow Franconia Ridge, the many braided paths through the tundra that had crushed alpine vegetation. I'd walked on trails eroded to the point where the original ground surface level was at my knees, or even my waist, my boots navigating a trench of unstable rocks—a condition that occurs on heavily hiked steep trails where the soil is loosened by boots and the rain washes it away.

That first morning, after we'd received the go-ahead from Mike, we sat facing each other at our small table in our cabin, scribbling away on our topics. Then we would read what we'd written aloud. Guy did a bit of connecting of the paragraphs to improve the flow. This was the routine we followed for all our columns. We could write a column in a morning.

We were very happy to have this opportunity to help spread the word. The mountain world was changing. The old ways of fires and bough beds and bathing in streams and walking on the tundra plants could not withstand the much too many of us seeking the mountains now.

We had made a list of what we wanted to write about for the next twelve months. Some of our topics took research, the kind that took us to mountains we had not climbed, or trails new to us, or to a particular person who was involved in the current issues, professionally or as a volunteer for a trail club. All this, deciding what to write about and ferreting out the material, was a collaborative process, as much as the writing was. I found it immensely satisfying, great fun, and hard work (though never "hard" in the sense of being onerous or something I wanted to put off). It was a good kind of "hard," of finding the right words, words that rang true for what I was seeing and feeling, that could reinforce the imperative for all of us to become mountain stewards. Our work together on the column led to our first book, *Backwoods Ethics*, in 1979.

Somewhere in those years, I began some writing projects of my own. I had become interested in women climbers—our part in the history of mountaineering—and ended up writing several articles that saw the light of print in both magazines and anthologies. Annie Smith Peck had made first ascents in the Andes in the early years of the twentieth century, while, at the same time Fanny Bullock Workman had scaled peaks in the Himalayas and the Karakoram. These two women became rivals, each determined to claim the honor of attaining the highest altitude, Fanny going so far as to underwrite a team of scientists to triangulate Annie's claim of Huascarán's summit in Peru. What a shame, I thought, that these women's great accomplishments turned them into fighting cocks, as aggressive as men. My own climbing at the Shawangunks and in New Hampshire had led to connections with the women who had pioneered on these cliffs, some of whom, like Miriam Underhill, had climbed in the Alps, inaugurating the frowned-on practice of leading her own climbs with only another woman as her partner. At that time—late 1920s and early 1930s—climbing without guides, let alone without a man in the party, did more than just raise eyebrows. It took strong women to stand up to the slings and arrows, sneers, and condescending comments that "manless climbing" provoked.

On these projects, Guy and I worked together in the sense that he took notes for me on my interview trips, and we worked together in the libraries I visited. He read my drafts. It was a collaboration, a step beyond our columns, since these articles were my idea, and Guy's role was supportively editorial. Although I was not fully conscious of it at the time, all this was an important step in becoming a writer.

We began work on *Forest and Crag* in late 1979 with a weeklong trip to the Dartmouth College Library, thirty miles down the road from where we lived. We'd been asked by the Appalachian Mountain Club's publishing arm to write it: a history of trails, hiking, and climbing in the mountains in the Northeast. Dartmouth housed a first-rate collection on the White Mountains. When we walked into the book-lined, comfortable office of Walter Wright, Dartmouth's Special Collections Librarian, and told him of our hope to write a history, a social history, of people coming to the mountains—how and why and what they did—he was kind enough to take us seriously.

We jumped at this chance to explore the history of our own mountains. We knew it extended back to 1642, when Darby Field climbed Mount Washington, at 6,288 ft., our highest. The history of our Northeastern mountains is connected with people: the ones who made the first ascents, the ones who built accommodations—like the Crawford family and their inn in the notch that bears their family name—who welcomed the early botanists, artists, and mountain tourists who came to climb, the ones who built the trails, and the ones who began the conservation efforts when the impact from logging became a grave concern.

Our plan was to compare and contrast mountain histories across the Northeast, from Maine to New Hampshire and Vermont, to New York's

Adirondacks and Catskills, and down into Massachusetts and Connecticut. All these mountainous areas, no matter how small in size or height, were beloved by the hikers who lived in their foothills, or who traveled from the cities to climb them. Each had its own story to tell.

We wrote in our preface, when *Forest and Crag* emerged in 1989, "We thought it would be a long job, that it might take as long as three years. Ten years later, here it is." The glory of this project was that, like our column, it took us to the mountains. The difficulty was that we had no idea what a wealth of mountain history lay in wait for us. All this was, of course, wonderful, a great climb in and of itself, but just as on a first ascent when all is unknown, you are feeling your way, and the summit seems unattainable, so was this the case as the years rolled by. Our book did not appear.

We wanted to write history, not just an anecdotal chronology. We wanted to generalize, synthesize, and analyze the major shifts in the 400-year span of the mountain recreation history of the entire region. We devised, for the research, a three-pronged campaign. We visited libraries, historical societies, and the archives of the hiking clubs. We corresponded with and interviewed the people who had cut trails, run hiking clubs, made early winter ascents, or engaged in particular conservation efforts. We went to the mountains themselves, sometimes with the people who had cut the trails, or to duplicate a notable first ascent of a major peak, or to celebrate an anniversary like the 150th of the original ascent of Mount Marcy, the Adirondacks' highest peak. All three of these efforts played out simultaneously over the next decade.

It was essential for us to start writing, though, and we did, right after that weeklong trip to the Dartmouth library. We began at the beginning, with Darby Field's 1642 ascent of Mount Washington—not called that then—which was at the time "as noteworthy a mountaineering achievement as any other in this history." We moved quickly on to any climbs that we could find information for that dated from the colonial period. There turned out to be a lot more than we expected. That became our first hurdle. Each of those early climbs was exciting to us, each had been buried in some dusty archive, and each cried out to be included. But Guy and I saw that if we continued to work at that level of detail we'd be writing the book for the rest of our lives, the resulting book would be too bulky to publish, and we'd never have time to go climbing again. Guy, in particular, found this last thought untenable. He needed to be in the mountains, not just for fun and exercise, but for his own well-being, his sanity.

Hitting this roadblock with the colonial ascents was the first time *Forest and Crag* felt like a monster. A panicky moment: What had we gotten ourselves into? I thought of the boy in the fairy tale, who, upon encountering the giant, lops off an arm. Another immediately grows in its place. Identifying what was essential (in the sense of original, watershed, or landmark) took us up a steep and stony slope. Along the way, aside from colonial ascents, we lopped off other topics, all of which could have made books in themselves: a history of summer camps, for instance, or the origins and histories of all the major hiking clubs, or the Appalachian Trail Conservancy. The organization of topics became an ongoing conversation between us. We drafted countless tables of contents in an attempt to cope with the amount of material flowing into our cabin from our research trips, responses to letters we'd written, and interview notes, as well as from our own climbs. Boxes of files began to reduce our floor space.

Right from the beginning, with those colonial ascents, it became blindingly clear to Guy, and to me as well, that I was not going to be a full partner in writing *Forest and Crag*. It would not be the kind of collaboration we'd had on our monthly columns. This was not only disappointing to me, but hard on my tender emerging writer's ego. It also came as something of a surprise. But it was the case. I could see it. What *Forest and Crag* needed, if it were ever to become a book between covers that didn't take the rest of our lives to write, was what Guy had been trained to do as a speech writer: someone who could digest huge amounts of material at breakneck speed. Writing fast was not my strength. I wrote slow. Many drafts. Much thinking and much, much rewriting. Too much for this book! And not just that: this wasn't writing I particularly liked, either. We'd tried dividing up the material as we had with the columns, but it didn't work. I thought working on a chapter would be similar to my articles on the women climbers, which I'd greatly enjoyed, or somewhat like a college paper. But what I needed was something more personal, less concerned with a historical assessment, and more about, well, emotions—people's intentions and motivations. And that's where, as a writer, I ended up, though it took years to figure out.

What Guy and I were good at together was talking about it: making the connections that dug into the meaning or importance of particular events: how people viewed the mountains and how that evolved over the course of the eighteenth, nineteenth, and twentieth centuries, at a decade-by-decade level. That was the heart of the book—an evolution of changing perspectives as people came to the mountains throughout the region, and moved from seeing these hills as "daunting terrible" to places to recreate, and how that recreation evolved as trail systems got built and changes in transportation made the mountains more accessible. This is what made *Forest and Crag* different, since it had not been done before.

In the spring of 1981, Guy received word from the National Park Service that his son Johnny, one of Alaska's best young climbers, had died on Denali (Mount McKinley). It looked like a suicide. We were well into the book now. I thought it would be possible that Guy would slow down or even suspend the project after this devastating news. But I wasn't surprised, either, that his reaction was to plunge into the work, to absorb himself in this task, that, in itself—the sheer length of it—had almost become too great to bear. He was up against the life-changing death of his son and our monster book project. At least the second he could wrestle with in a concrete way.

It's strange how a project that can be so wonderful and give such joy, that can hold you in its sustaining grip to the point of obsession where, no matter what life throws at you, you can't imagine not doing it, is, at the same time a cruel, dispassionate taskmaster that cracks the bloody whip. You wake up every morning knowing you're going to do the work—you can't not—because you want it to end, and if you miss a day you've only added to how long the imprisonment will go on. Training in writing speeches does not prepare one for this. That's what I think Guy felt. He never slowed down. Though I palpably felt his sadness over Johnny's death, I did not think of his low state of mind in terms of depression. It was Guy's energy that carried the book forward.

My feelings were different. I had grown up with my father's book projects, all of which took many years. I was undaunted by long projects. If you kept at them, they concluded themselves. I knew Guy would keep at it because he had said to me that if he quit he'd be letting down all the wonderful librarians and archivists, hikers and climbers, trail builders and mountain club folks who had given us so much of their time and encouragement. If he used our drafts for fire-starter, as he was tempted to do, he'd disappoint them. His acute sense of responsibility let him know he couldn't abide himself if he did that.

My collaborative role was to offer the kind of support that let Guy know I knew he'd keep writing. This wasn't something we talked about. Did Guy connect my ability to handle big projects with what I'd grown up with? I don't know. I didn't myself, until much later. And it's funny how when you come out on the other side—when you've descended from the top of the mountain—the tough days fade away. The mountain *did* have a summit, you reached it, and, you're at basecamp again, safe and sound. As Guy wrote in the concluding paragraph to our preface: "Enough preamble. Let's go to the mountains. We immensely enjoyed writing this book and we hope you enjoy reading about these wonderful forests and crags, the 'sun-flecked narrow paths' that wander through them, and the energetic and colorful, sometimes eccentric, often marvelous men and women who shaped the modern hiker's mountain world."

He meant every word of it!

The collaborative process. We ran the gamut from the low points to the high, and there were a few Eureka moments mixed in. The big one was Darby Field. Our information on his climb of Mount Washington is second- or thirdhand, and sketchy. Field, an Englishman, was illiterate. Most of what we know comes from Governor John Winthrop of Massachusetts, who kept a journal, but Winthrop's entry does not make clear Field's route. The ascent was so important that we, and many other White Mountain history buffs, wanted to be able to state with some exactness how Field reached the summit. It didn't look like that was going to happen until a letter dated June 29, 1642, was called to our attention in 1984 by White Mountain hiker and Vermont history professor Gary Thomas Lord of Norwich University. Though the letter does not pinpoint Field's route, it gives us enough information to believe that Field went up the ridge the Crawford Path now ascends, and that he made his way over the Southern Presidentials to Lakes of the Clouds, where the Appalachian Mountain Club's hut is today, and so up the summit cone from the southwest. This was truly electrifying. The Winthrop source had Field ascending from Pinkham Notch, possibly going up Boott Spur.

We drove over to Northfield, and Gary Lord filled us in on how a Maine magistrate, Thomas Gorges, serving as deputy governor, wrote to his cousin, Ferdinando Gorges, in England, who had received a charter for Maine in 1639, relating what he knew of Field's ascent. The letter was lost, but Ferdinando made a practice of drafting his letters into copybooks. These, in 1948, came to the City Library of Exeter, in Devon, England, "in a sorry state, having lain neglected, exposed to water and rats. . . . water-stained, blotted, frayed at the edges, matted together, disarranged."[2] More time was to pass before the Exeter Library notified the Maine Historical Society of this obscure information on Field's climb. Colonial historian Gary Lord had only recently read the Gorges letter in the Maine Historical Society's *The Letters of Thomas Gorges*, published in 1978. Now we could

2. Laura and Guy Waterman, *Forest and Crag: A History of Hiking, Trail Blazing, and Adventure in the Northeast Mountains*, Excelsior Editions (Albany: State University of New York Press, 2019), 11.

write, on page 12 of *Forest and Crag*, "342 years after the event, a second source—and probably an even more direct one—on Darby Field's climb had come to light."

Small revelations like that happened every time we visited a library, from tiny libraries like the one in Chocorua, New Hampshire, to the vast reading rooms of city libraries like the Boston Public with its card catalog in wooden drawers that we pulled out from the wall to thumb through the entries. In this space, illuminated by electric and natural light, we sat beside each other taking notes from material the librarians brought to us. Long tables with comfortable wooden chairs, the air smelling of the dust contained in the many volumes opened and closed by diligent workers on their own projects: we sat, all of us in a great cathedral—a cathedral to books and learning. When Guy and I broke for lunch, we took sandwiches—peanut butter and jelly brought from home—out into the open air, in search of a garden, and excitedly exchanged what we'd so busily taken notes on: what we'd learned, the connections we had made, the original documents it was our great pleasure to handle. These research trips were joyously collaborative, a true highlight of our years spent working on *Forest and Crag*.

When I think back on the history of great collaborations, it's Wordsworth and Coleridge who come to mind. And I like to include Dorothy, too, Wordsworth's sister, who brought their days to life with vivid intimacy in her journals, a brother and a sister and the great friend of each. They were young then. I'd contend that neither Wordsworth nor Coleridge went on to write better poetry than they did in *Lyrical Ballads*, the volume that came to fruition while the three of them lived in close proximity. Their library was the out-of-doors, the rugged and wild heights around Grasmere, where, on long walks, they reveled in the natural scene that suffused the writing of these three friends who lent their inspiration freely. Perhaps more than friends! Dorothy stayed in the house the morning her brother wed Mary Hutchinson, distressed that another woman had moved into the front and center of William's life. That life bore out the promise of *Lyrical Ballads*, and he died, revered, at eighty. And Coleridge? Poor troubled soul, an opium habit broke his health, and his collaborative years were quickly spent. Through much of his later life—he lived on into his fifth decade—he was supported by friends who had not forgotten his early greatness.

And Guy and me? We were friends as well as a married pair. *Forest and Crag* would not have seen daylight without both of us. Neither of us could have managed it alone, for different reasons. Again, isn't that the real definition of collaboration?

Recalling again those four men who wrote the *Literary History of the United States*, each offered a distinct talent. That's what the work called for to see it through. Each must have been aware of that. But at the heart's core of their success was their friendship.

This kind of friendship—I remember their laughter, which I took such pleasure in as a child—carried both Guy and me through to a happy ending when we held in our hands a mountain of a book about the mountains, a summit that had cost us tears and given us joy in the ascent.

II

The Homestead: Barra

5

Making the Break

Falling in love simultaneously with rock climbing and the rock climber I married might not cause most people to lose their jobs and become homesteaders. But it did me. Add in the changes sparked by Earth Day and a turning toward the world of Nature that outdoors lovers of the late 1960s and early 1970s encountered gave us reason enough to go to the mountains. As writers, this allowed Guy and me to be part of a national movement that was turning climbers and hikers into caring stewards of the wild places we all loved.

We cannot predict the paths our lives will take. I'd grown up playing outside: in the woods, in vacant lots, in the brook behind my house, biking everywhere, climbing trees, baseball and football as the only girl on our dead-end street in a small town. That was growing up in the late forties, early 1950s, when supervised activities for children were decades away. No one was talking about how playing outside was good for you—physically and most important mentally—and that encounters with the natural world could sow seeds for future directions.

After four years at a college where the Appalachian Trail traversed the back campus, I moved to New York City and immediately felt hemmed in, assaulted by noise, crowded sidewalks, bus exhaust, shrieking subways. Central Park really didn't cut it. I went to a beach once, a subway ride away, on a sweltering July day. Throngs of human bodies lying cheek by jowl on beach towels, the cooler within arm's reach. Respite from the city for some, but not for me. A tough transition, but turning my back on it didn't enter my mind. It took a good year to learn to love the rhythm that was New York, and now, looking back I see that decade as a formative time of character honing, eye-opening of my young self in ways that only being on one's own, paying the monthly rent, and managing a social life can do. I wouldn't have given up New York for anything. There was, though, I see now, a piece missing, and that was a free-ranging embrace of Nature and the outdoors.

But it worked out. Events transpired to send me headlong into the woods as a homesteader, and to the mountains as a hiker and climber. Most important for my emerging life as a conservationist and a writer was my commitment to become a champion for the wild, to lead others who loved wild places to learn to care for them too.

Guy and I lived in a hand-built cabin in a clearing for close to thirty years, and with his death my life changed. Yet, not as much as you might think. I left our homestead, moved closer to the center of our small rural village, closer to our library. Here I found plenty of walking and wild places to explore that Guy and I never bothered with, being intent on the highest peaks, the alpine terrain, the stony steep trails.

You might say I'm back where I started, a lifetime ago, completing a circle that's still brimful with learning and exploring. We begin the long walk facing an unknown future, and we might, as I did, surprise ourselves even as we daily experience confusion and uncertainty, or delight as we scan for the waymarks that teach us our best selves.

~

At 5:50 a.m. my power cut out. I had finished my breakfast but was continuing to read when the room turned black on this late October morning. I was not surprised. We'd had ample warning of a storm, of high winds and beating rains that had careened in during the night. It was very dark. I got up, my fingers felt their way along the mantlepiece for the box of matches. I struck one, located the candles, lit two, then two more. Tried to continue to read, but without much pleasure. My eyes require brighter light, which they weren't going to get until the power came back on. That meant I wasn't going to make much progress on writing projects today.

I was annoyed. Not with the storm, not with the (apparent) slowness of the power company—I knew those men and women were doing their best out in the rain and wind—but with myself. My husband and I had lived without power for nearly thirty years. After Guy's death in 2000, I went back on the grid and have been living this way since then. I'm used to the occasional power outage, but, over the more than twenty years, I have never stopped being annoyed at my own reaction to the inconvenience of losing power, a reaction that had me fiddling with candles and a battery lantern that really did not do the job of the power source. I've grown accustomed to living with electricity and find it inconveniencing when it goes out. *That's* what I found so annoying!

Yes, I've made the adaptation from kerosene and candles and flashlights to an electrified house. What I never foresaw was how living with electrification makes it difficult to step back into living without.

I had brought one of our kerosene lamps from Barra with me to my new home, and set it up once or twice when I lost power, but was rather put out by how difficult it was to go through the tasks of rolling up the wick, lighting the lamp, being vigilant so that the mantle did not flame up and char. It could take five minutes of slowly adjusting the flame to burn off the char. A tedious process! A process we had mastered—that is, we had mastered kerosene lamps. I had lost a skill once second nature. After I'd stepped from the nineteenth century into the twenty-first, I could not easily step back. The door had closed. I'd slipped through the warp of time, and the fabric had sealed itself behind me. I knew what I had lost.

When I graduated from college in 1962, aside from getting married, there were three career paths, as I saw it, open to those of us women who had majored in English: teaching, being a librarian, and publishing of some sort. The first two would mean more education. Not an option. I was ready to move on from school. Publishing appealed, though I found out that more schooling was indeed necessary, so I enrolled in the Radcliff Secretarial Program to spend that summer in hot, humid, noisy, smelly, crowded Cambridge to beef up my typing to the minimal requirement of thirty-three words per minute, and to become proficient in shorthand. Having spent all my previous summers outdoors in the countryside, this was—I still feel—the worst summer of my life. I was in some sort of transition and had difficulty concentrating on anything. Normally a voracious reader, it took me the whole summer to read one book: Ayn Rand's *The Fountainhead*, which did little to dispel the gloom.

But good things came out of that summer other than mastering the required skills without which no publishing company would consider me. I met Annie Barry, a Radcliff graduate, an English major who, as I did, had her heart set on going to New York and finding employment as a book editor. Annie had grown up on the Exeter Academy campus, our childhoods were similar, we knew some of the same teachers in our fathers' prep schools. So, New York City it was!

Annie ended up working as Norman Mailer's secretary, typing the author's manuscripts and using that shorthand as he dictated his letters. I bounced through the humiliating experience of being "let go" by Grolier—they published encyclopedias—which was cutting down their staff. When my boss called me in to his office to give me this news, he, as I look back on it, must have been inexperienced at firing new young hires. He appeared genuinely sorry, taking a while to get to the point. As I was packing up my desk, a slightly older sort-of-friend kindly invited me out for a drink and advised me to go to the employment agency the next day.

Good advice, and I ended up in the small editorial office of the Bobbs-Merrill Company, whose headquarters were in Indianapolis. I remained there for the next five years working on books in nonfiction, mostly as parts of series in literature or history or philosophy. There were five of us, all young, though I must have been the youngest, and an assortment of freelancers—copyeditors and book designers—who wandered in and out of the office. When our boss, Bill Hackett, made periodic visits to his New York staff in our building on Fifty-Seventh Street west of Fifth Avenue, he'd take us to lunch—two hours, well lubricated—and not much work got accomplished back in the office.

This was New York in the 1960s, feeling the effects of Woodstock, the Summer of Love, the Beatles, marijuana, Women's Lib, the Vietnam War, and the assassination of John F. Kennedy. The liberal, John Lindsay, was mayor. This was publishing before corporations began swallowing the small, privately run houses, and while editors still had working relationships with their authors, the way fabled Maxwell Perkins did with Ernest Hemingway and Scott Fitzgerald. My work day began at nine and ended at five o'clock. I never needed to take work home. Looking back I feel lucky to have experienced that moment in publishing that marked an end of an era.

In the beginning, Annie and I moved from one sublet to another, short-term rentals found for us by Annie's mother. We spent a part of that first winter with a friend of mine on Thirty-Third Street, between Lexington and Third Avenue, and then Annie struck out downtown to locate on the fourth floor of a tenement in Little Italy. Artists occupied a few lofts there, though we were unaware of them. And we had moved on before the area turned into SoHo and rents skyrocketed. Little Italy was a different universe from Midtown, but when Annie let me know that an apartment—rent controlled—had opened up on the top floor, I moved into 161 Prince Street located between Thompson and West Broadway. The Vesuvio bakery was across the street and I could look down from my large window on Mrs. Dapoletto, who dressed in black and sat in her broad streetside window where she could keep an eye on the neighborhood. Yes, this was a neighborhood. Our "super," a Puerto Rican named Mike Torres, ran the bodega on the corner along with his wife and two young daughters. The butcher and the barber—the Massimo brothers—were on the other side of No. 161. We paid our rent to Mr. Tursi, the slumlord. On Sundays, the street featured a bevy of Cadillacs—Mafiosos—we heard, driving in from New Jersey to have spaghetti dinner with Mama. That presence was why the neighborhood was so safe. And indeed—it was true! Once I had arrived back after a weekend spent with my parents to be told that a thief had tried to rob my apartment. But, I was gleefully assured, we ran him off.

I loved my apartment, a sixth-floor walk-up. A building of red brick, lintels over the windows—a decorative note—an iron fire escape attached to the front. Annie and I affectionately referred to the building as Tenement Hill. I was the possessor of four small rooms, a kitchen, living room, my bedroom, and a room that I equipped with shelves for books and my typewriter, a daybed that also served as a guest bed. My rent was $64.00 a month. This matched my weekly pay check, so easily affordable. The bathroom housed the toilet with a pull chain for flushing. The kitchen sink did double duty as the bathroom sink, and the bathtub (no shower) was in the kitchen and could be turned into a counter with a piece of plywood. I took my weekly laundry to the Chinese laundry one street away where they ironed my sheets and couldn't have charged more than a few dollars. Like Mike with his small grocery store, the entire young family was at the ready to take my laundry when I came in.

Annie took the subway to Brooklyn Heights where Norman lived. I caught the BMT line at Spring Street up to Fifty-Seventh. About twice a month Annie and I took the subway to the Old Met, located around twenty blocks south of its present Lincoln Center home, in what was an old brewery. No broad plaza with a fountain, no fancy lobby sweeping up a grand staircase overhung with chandeliers. Tickets for the Family Circle ranged from $2.00 to $3.00. Here I heard Leontyne Price for the first time, as well as Joan Sutherland, Birgit Nilsson, Franco Corelli, Jon Vickers, and Renata Tebaldi. Yes! It was the best of the best back then.

Meanwhile, back at 161 Prince Street we became friends with two young men who shared an apartment on the fifth floor. Barry and Larry. Barry was moving up the ladder at the *New York Times*, to eventually find his niche in labor relations. Larry was going for his PhD in English at New York University. For a while Larry and Barry shared their apartment with a young Egyptian named Omar, the devoted owner of an elegant Afghan, a golden color with long silky ears and sweet disposition. Omar, at eighteen, seemed to know more about the world than the rest of us. He possessed both sophistication and class.

Larry and I became good friends, in part drawn together by what he was studying. Especially, he was excited about the course in modern poetry with Prof. M. L. Rosenthal. When I exclaimed how I envied him, he offered to bring me to his next class—classes were in the evening. He introduced me to Professor Rosenthal, adroitly adding something about my father's work on Emily Dickinson's poetry. So I became a shadow student, and a routine evolved. Larry and I ate our dinner together—cooking separately— but alternately eating at the other's table. Then a ten-minute walk down Thompson Street to the NYU buildings near Washington Square. There were a few poems I had grown up with and liked—Coleridge's "The Rime of the Ancient Mariner" or "Kubla Kahn." I liked Emily Dickinson because of my father's work making her a presence in our house. But I had not taken any poetry courses in college—if you don't count a full year of Shakespeare. So what Rosenthal was teaching was enlightening and new to me. That winter of sitting in on his classes, the pleasant routine Larry and I had fallen into is one of my fondest memories of those New York days. M. L. Rosenthal's *The New Modern Poetry* sits in the poetry section of my home library.

You are probably asking yourself, did these two young people become lovers? The setting of the tenement dwelling, I much later came to equate with the garret, high above the streets of Paris where Mimi, the little seamstress, meets Rodolfo who writes for a literary paper, and they fall in love. But real-life adventures are generally more mundane. I was neither romantically carried off by tuberculosis like Mimi, nor did I fall in love with Larry. Though he might have wanted that part of the story to come out some other way. Perhaps more important, he was a dear friend who played a stellar role in my early life where, again like Puccini's opera *La Bohème*, all of the principals were on the brink. Yes, Annie and Barry formed a close connection too. The four of us were stretching our wings and learning to fly.

Then Annie moved east to St. Mark's Place. She had stopped typing Mailer's manuscripts and had taken up editorial work with Grove Press. Change happens. I, too, felt the need to upgrade my life from Tenement Hill and found an apartment on Seventeenth Street between Lexington and Third. It was double the square footage, had a real bathroom with a shower, was on the first floor, and had a garden, of sorts. I say that this building was on Seventeenth Street, but, in truth, I'm not sure. It was near Gramercy Park where I occasionally walked around this small open space. It didn't take me long to realize what I had lost—the neighborhood—the importance of that to my life, was gone. No Mike adding up my purchases in pencil on the paper bag. Now I shopped at a faceless supermarket. I wouldn't hear about the progress of his eldest daughter who had gotten into a top-flight science and math high school. No Chinese family. Now I took my weekly wash to the laundromat. What had happened to Barry and Larry? They had moved on as well. Larry to an apartment in the Village I had seen a few times. Barry might have moved closer to his work at the *Times*. Annie gave me news of him now and then. But the connection was broken.

Then in March 1967, the Indianapolis headquarters of the Bobbs-Merrill Company closed its New York office. I would be looking for another job. Hey! Wait a minute I told myself. Take a break! For the past few summers I had traveled first to Italy and next to Greece for my two-week vacation. I wanted more. I had heard about traveling on freighters.

So I booked passage on a Greek cargo ship that took passengers. This dream trip entered the Mediterranean to make stops at most of the coastal North African cities, then glided up to Athens and over to Istanbul to enter the Black Sea and stop at the Romanian port of Constanza, which at that time was behind the Iron Curtain. I disembarked at Genoa, the last port of call before the freighter steamed back to New York. I spent several weeks in Rome with a fellow passenger who had become a friend and had come to the Eternal City to study opera. I ended my sojourn with a mountain walk in Bavaria with a college classmate.

In September I was back in New York and the world of publishing. I had lined up employment with Oxford University Press before I had left, but had trouble settling into city life. Someone at Oxford told me about the Appalachian Mountain Club, and I began going on their hikes, up to Harriman State Park and Bear Mountain and the gracefully rounded summits along the Hudson River, Storm King and the Breakneck Ridge.

At some point during that winter, an editor I knew at Atheneum offered me a job and I took it. I was happy at Oxford, but I liked the idea of working for this smaller, fairly prestigious press founded by Alfred Knopf Jr. and Michael Bessie. I continued to get out of New York on weekends and discovered I loved walking in the winter woods. It took me another year to find out that the Appalachian Mountain Club offered instruction in rock climbing at a place called the Shawangunks, near the town of New Paltz. I didn't know what rock climbing was, except that it had to do with mountains.

For some reason I could not explain, I had always been drawn to mountains. I'd been born in a flat state, New Jersey, but my father, a Vermonter, packed his family off to the southern Vermont town of Wilmington beginning in 1945, the last year of the war. He wanted his children to know Vermont. We spent eight summers there, in our rented camp in the woods, on Lake Raponda. Whenever we drove to Brattleboro or Bennington on Route 9, I looked with fascination out the windows of our black Chevy, craning my neck, trying to figure out how mountains were made. What, exactly, was a mountain? My parents tried to explain, but all I saw were tall trees—evergreens, mostly, that seemed to grow on top of each other. Yet, I knew that wasn't possible. It was frustrating to me that the far-off view of mountains didn't look anything like the close-up.

At twelve I read Maurice Herzog's *Annapurna*, about the first 8,000-meter peak to be climbed. That was quickly followed by *The Conquest of Mount Everest* by Sir John Hunt. Those books came out in the early 1950s. I didn't see why I couldn't climb mountains like that, and finally, in my late twenties, I saw my chance: rock climbing must be a way to larger mountains.

With that first climb, "Easy Overhang," in the autumn of 1969, I entered a new world. Being high up on the face of that cliff—way above the tops of the trees—exhilarated me. It was beautiful to reach up for the next handhold, the roughness of the rock under my fingertips, my feet on an inch of ledge, miraculously moving upward through the atmosphere. Or so it felt. At the belay stance I could pause and look out over the valley, not quite seeing the Hudson River, but knowing that from those Hudson Highlands ridges I had hiked, you could see, on a perfectly clear day, these cliffs—a great escarpment three hundred feet high. Poised on a foothold between earth and sky, I felt a freedom new to me. It wasn't just the physical aspect of climbing, or even the glorious beauty, it was the climbers themselves that drew me. They were doing something they loved and I was loving it, too. It was as if we all shared this secret that was not a secret at all, that, through climbing, you could turn your life into anything you wanted.

It wasn't until that next spring, the spring of 1970, that Guy Waterman—a climber, part of the AMC group—and I began to talk, and I found out how much he disliked his own job and his life. He was going through a divorce. He had three teenage sons. "I thought you had four sons," I said. He gave me a quizzical look. "John and Jim," I said. I'd seen those boys at the cliffs.

"And Bill," he said.

"How about Ralph?" I asked. From the surprised, humorous look on Guy's face I began to feel I'd just said something a little silly.

He laughed. "Ralph is our dog!"

Climbing together is a good way to get to know someone fast.

Except that spring I wasn't climbing. I had severed my Achilles tendon in a skiing accident at Taos, New Mexico, that February and was sporting a knee-high cast and Canadian crutches. But the climbing friends I'd made that previous autumn had offered to drive me up to the Shawangunks anyway. I had a tent, so I camped out on a piece of land owned by one of these climbers. That's why I was grounded at this first beginners' weekend of early April, and Guy Waterman was grounded, too. He was in charge of pairing up beginners with leaders, which meant he was tied to the Überfall, the area in the Gunks where all the climbers gathered, a place under the cliffs where you could leave packs, eat lunch, make up climbing parties, and talk about climbing. It was an energizing, happy social scene composed of men—and women, but mostly men—who were corporate types like Guy, scientists and engineers at the well-known labs in the New York/North Jersey area, university professors, lawyers, college and high school students. There was a fellow who ran a salvage operation in Camden, New Jersey, who brought up his workers. There was a dedicated couple who drove up from Washington, DC—every weekend. All of them were technically smart, but all displayed a degree of humanity, and not a few were downright eccentric in the way extreme intelligence can reveal itself. To climb at all demands a certain obsession. For all, their weekends were sacred. Climbing was central to their lives, and most were intimately acquainted with the mountain ranges around the world.

It was here at the Überfall—sitting on the boulders beneath a climb called "Ken's Crack," a forty-foot impressive-looking jam crack, meaning you climbed it by jamming in your hands and feet—that Guy and I began our first real conversation. I never tired of our talks that began under that quartzite conglomerate, the white-gray rock of the Shawangunks, and lasted for the next thirty years.

He was telling me he was desperate to get out of New York. He'd already managed to move out of the city to the off-the-beaten-track Hudson River town of Marlboro, just a thirty-five-minute drive to the cliffs. "And two-and-a-half hours back to the General Electric building," he said. I kept looking at him. He was sitting a few feet away on a rock, chin in his hands, a thoughtful, rather disgruntled look on his face. But this long commute, he said, was part of his plan to earn a living connecting with what he really loved: mountains, climbing. He wanted them to be the same—or feel the same. Work and play, that is earning a living, both equally rewarding. I was listening. This sounded like an ideal life. Mainly, though, I was focused on his thick reddish-brown hair and gray eyes. He was not at all tall, about five feet six inches with a compact athlete's build of wide shoulders and narrow waist—like those Greek statues at the Metropolitan Museum of Art that give a sense of both solidity and grace. I liked the way he looked, and, again, over the next thirty years I took a deep pleasure in just looking at Guy Waterman, at how he swung his double-bit ax—the concentration that took—or at the care he took planting carrots, that despite his large hands and thick fingers, he got those impossibly tiny seeds spaced just right.

He was seven and a half years older than me, and with so much more life experience. Closing in on divorce. Three sons, the youngest, Jim, living with him along with Ralph, their dog, a golden-collie mix. This was new territory for me. I could see how much he loved climbing, how good he was, how much others enjoyed his company. How he liked to laugh, and by telling stories, cause others to laugh, too. There was a lot of laughter at the cliffs.

At last I was out of that confining cast. We were climbing together every weekend, and I was making that two-and-a-half-hour commute with Guy into New York City. I was twenty-nine and had not met anyone I could imagine spending more than a weekend with. But from our earliest conversations, I knew I wanted to spend the rest of my life with Guy Waterman.

We talked on the Carriage Road beneath the cliffs that gave access to the routes, we talked on the commute, we talked in bed, and what was happening to me between Guy and climbing felt like a new world, as indeed it was. I learned our fathers were both teachers who went on to become famous. Alan Waterman, a physicist, was appointed by President Truman to head the National Science Foundation—the first director. Mine was approached by Harvard University Press to be Emily Dickinson's editor. Strong father figures, each of whom, I much later came to see, left their mark on their children's psyches.

While the pattern in the Waterman family was for its progeny to graduate from Ivy League colleges, Guy broke the mold with George Washington University, putting himself through in three years, Phi Beta Kappa, by playing ragtime piano with Scotty Lawrence's River Boat Trio in the hot spots around DC. When I met him, his Steinway grand was sandwiched into his small Marlboro apartment. He played often for the climbers who came for a pick-up dinner on Sunday nights before heading back to the city. Guy's playing was infectious. He could spark a room, and I loved listening. I always felt so proud of him. The way he sat with absolute command of the keyboard, his large hands dancing the ten-note spans, bright-eyed, enjoying everyone's pleasure in this music he loved. This was his way of communicating. Like his stories, here he was his best self: easy, relaxed, confident, wrapping up the room in his own energy.

He was never a showoff at the keyboard, though the music itself was often showy, catchy, wildly upbeat, and finger-snapping happy. He played to honor the song itself, to communicate the emotional heart that he knew with his musician's instinct could find its way to his listeners' hearts. This was his way of letting everyone know he loved them. Yet, Guy wrote in his unpublished memoir, "I left jazz piano playing without ever finding out whether or not I might have had something important to contribute there." He wrote this having already made a contribution by writing articles on early jazz and ragtime for the *Record Changer* that were later anthologized.

He had married Emily Morrison, a fellow student from Sidwell Friends in DC, at eighteen and was nineteen when Bill was born. He had majored in economics. He studied in his car. The contrast with my college years, and years in New York, was so different. Marriage, for me, had only seemed possible since meeting Guy. Yet he was comfortable with this offbeat path. He never talked as if he regretted any of it. Rather, its unconventionality, as he told me the stories, seemed to please him. Despite his present employment at GE, Guy Waterman would have never fit into the "gray flannel suit."

After college, now in his mid-twenties with three small boys, came a handful of brilliant and exciting years as a staff aide on Capitol Hill writing speeches for the leading senators of the mid-1950s: Everett McKinley Dirksen, at the time Minority Leader; Paul Douglas of Illinois; Kenneth Keating of New York; Gerald Ford, then a fast-rising member of the House of Representatives; and—the grand finale—Richard Nixon during his 1960 presidential campaign. These were flashy names. But Guy never talked to impress. The idea was to fill me in. To let me see what kind of person he was that I'd gotten myself attached to.

He had loved this work that placed him right on the Senate floor. As he described it in an unpublished memoir, "We'd sit at the right hand of the Senator who led our side in debate, be involved in cloak room huddles to decide strategy, be responsible for quickly digesting amendments as they came up so as to explain them and their implications to Republican Senators, and of course write short speeches setting forth our position."

It turned sour all too soon.

When he became the chief speech writer for the Republican senator from New Hampshire, Styles Bridges, Guy's eyes were opened to what could go on behind the scenes of those corridors of power. From having seen Bridges as a principled individual, it became clear to him that the senator's primary concern was maintaining his own power. To compound matters, Bridges had a staff director who, by devoting himself to ensuring Bridges maintained that image, manipulated Bridges's staff in ways that kept that staff in turmoil. No one knew who the staff director would turn on next, and when Bridges tried to manipulate Guy, Guy's reaction was: *no one does this to me.* "I knew I was regarded as a comer," he wrote, "as a bright-eyed young man, very capable and in demand by senators, and it went to my head." He had walked into Bridges's office and announced his resignation. "I actually had some sort of notion," he continued, "that I was so valuable Bridges would agree to my being assigned elsewhere in the Senate staff hierarchy. What nonsense on my part: in fact, the staff director simply dogged Bridges into firing me rather than allowing my resignation. The old crafty pros easily disposed of the foolishly ambitious renegade. End of promising career."

Over our thirty years together I heard this story many times. And every time I could feel Guy's sorrow that things had turned out this way. But I never felt that he regretted his actions. He'd caught on to Bridges and he could not have behaved other than he had. Bridges was scum, though Guy never used that word. He was deeply disillusioned that this man he'd seen as "principled" was motivated solely by power, meaning in Guy's book that working for good, for the happiness and well-being of the American people, was never on Bridges's agenda. This wholeheartedly resonated with me. I could not have cast my life with anyone who felt otherwise.

Well, it was not quite the end. Dirksen and the senator from Hawaii, Hiram Fong, were willing to sign Guy on, but both shortly reversed themselves rather than cross Bridges "over a matter of such little importance as my future," Guy said with a wry smile. "I was left feeling that while I was seen as brilliant, by my action, I was also judged unpredictable, unreliable."

"Surely," he later wrote in his unpublished memoir, "the destructive impulse of the Caliban within me had triumphed over the public service impulse of Ariel. . . . In many ways, thinking of the public service aspects of my work in Washington, I think the most useful thing I could have done with my life would have been to remain in the center of staff work there—I might have contributed in important ways to the nation's business."

Disillusioned, Guy transplanted his family to Stamford, Connecticut, within commuting distance of New York, still in the same trade: speech writing, but this time for the corporate executives at General Electric. Yet, the urgency, the privilege of writing the words that a senator would speak that could influence policy and make a difference in world affairs, was gone. Lost to him was the feeling—the ability—of devoting himself to a cause he believed in. It had all turned boring, tedious. "Who really cared about profits raising a quarter of a percent?" he said. "I turn out this stuff with very little effort and no real thought, and," he paused, looking me straight in the eyes, "I was drinking too much."

He had time on his hands. So he started hiking on weekends in the woodlands near his Connecticut home, where he had hiked with his own family when he was small and his father was teaching at Yale. The Sleeping Giant made a nice walk, but he wanted more and began exploring the hilly terrain to the west, with its attraction of the Appalachian Trail, with his two oldest boys—Bill and Johnny—and Ralph. "They loved it and so did I," he told me. When his two-week vacation came they spent it in the real mountains, up above treeline, in New Hampshire, reveling in those steep rugged trails that shot up from the great glacial cirques in the Presidential Range. "We met some hikers," he said, "who told us if we liked scrambling, we'd find plenty of that at the Shawangunks—the 'Gunks' they called it." In 1963, Guy signed up for the training program offered by the Appalachian Mountain Club. "Pretty soon I learned enough to bring up Bill and John. Johnny got very good, very fast."

By the time I came into the picture, Guy had gotten control of his drinking and had filed the separation papers in the state of New York. According to New York statutes, it would take two years before his divorce would come through.

He'd investigated working for college administrators so that he could have the summers off for climbing. But that led nowhere because in his line of work—speech writing—he wouldn't have summers off. Then our climber friend, Brad Snyder, told him about a book by Helen and Scott Nearing called *Living the Good Life*. He read it—we both did—and it opened up a path. The Nearings' book was about sustainable self-sufficient living. They called it *homesteading*. By becoming homesteaders, we could better align what we loved—climbing mountains—with a way of living that felt a lot more real than what he was doing now.

I had no idea what a homesteader was. It was another new word like "belay" and "pitch" and "rappel"—the climbing terms I was absorbing. But the more we talked, the more such a radical change seemed possible. For Guy, the plan had become lifesaving, and he began to use our commute to draw house plans, calculate how to make it work financially, and read *Organic Gardening and Farming* we'd just subscribed to.

Not far into that spring of 1970, my boss at Atheneum, whom I liked very much, let me know that I was turning in sloppy work. I didn't see it coming. I couldn't figure out what had gone wrong with my editing. I tried to do better, but the thing was I really didn't care anymore.

Climbing can do this. Even climbers say that climbing has no social value. It is, however, very real. It requires utter concentration, a heightened awareness of where you are both physically and mentally. A great deal of rapid reasoning goes into each move up the rock. This thinking—or processing—is all connected to the physical movement. Without doubt, the risk is an attraction, and this risk is constantly calculated. Climbers, contrary to opinion, are not risk-takers. They are careful planners. They have placed themselves in what appears to be—in fact *is*—a risky situation, but with intelligence, training, and physical skill, they work to keep a safe passage up the rock. Climbing can change lives because the very nature of the risk can call into question what's not working in your life. You can't hide from yourself the marriage that's gone sour or a job that no longer fulfills. In my case I fell in love with climbing *and* with Guy, and had no wish to defend myself from either. Both had come to feel a lot more real, more meaningful, to me, than my job at one of the best publishers in New York.

The upshot was, I was fired. Well, it wasn't quite that brutal. My understanding boss arranged for me to be let go from Atheneum in a way that allowed me to collect unemployment compensation while I looked for another job. I applied to a few publishing companies and got hired, but when I thought of myself sitting at a desk editing manuscripts I knew that history would only repeat itself. I wouldn't last a week. I was finished with publishing, with all desk jobs, and wasn't sorry about it. But I needed to find some kind of work, meaningful or otherwise. I wanted something that would keep me outside.

I ended up working for Camp and Trail Outfitters. This first store in New York to sell climbing and camping equipment dated back to the late 1930s. I was hired to put together their catalog. But what I enjoyed most was helping to make the equipment. Ben Siminow had a little factory of two or three workers on sewing machines making packs and sleeping bags, gaiters and tarps. Once a week we all stuffed the bags with goose down and fastened, with a machine, grommets on the other equipment. It was a lively place down on Chambers Street, a different world from Midtown Manhattan, and I thoroughly enjoyed it.

What did my parents think of all this? I'd just burned through a promising career in publishing that had certainly seemed to suit the book-loving person I was. They understood that world. My dad was not only a teacher, but a writer. My mother was a part-time indexer for Princeton University Press, and an occasional critic for my dad. (I could hear them debating the changes she suggested while doing my homework upstairs, his voice raising, hers firm, neutral, and unyielding. Him losing his temper and storming off. Much later she told me, with some satisfaction, that when she read the published product, she saw he'd taken her suggestions.) Now their daughter was calling herself a rock climber and working in a climbing store! She was involved with a divorced man, a father of three teenagers! This must have caused come concern. What was happening to their sensible daughter? Whatever they thought, they never verbalized it to me. They asked a few questions about rock climbing. How safe was it? What kind of people did this? I did my best to assure them on both points. Perhaps they saw that, yes, Laura's life was changing, in ways they didn't understand, but she seems happy. My mother told a neighbor, a good friend of mine, too, who years later said that my mother had said she had never seen me happier. She meant about Guy.

One day, when I came back from lunch, one of my coworkers, a young climber named Tom, said, "Laura, there's a man here who says he's starting a magazine for backpackers. You should talk to him. He's over there. Looking at tents." That was how I met Bill Kemsley, a climber and hiker who ran a small company that published annual reports for corporations. He was gearing up to publish a magazine for hikers and backpackers using his office staff. He needed someone for the editorial work, he told me, when I introduced myself.

"I'm what you're looking for." I said, "I'm a book editor who spends all her weekends at the Shawangunks."

Bill smiled and we launched into a conversation about climbs, naming our favorites. Bill Kemsley was well acquainted with the Gunks.

A few days later he formally interviewed me in his office, and I became his editor for *Backpacker*. It meant returning to Midtown Manhattan, but this job suited me. I worked for Bill for one year, and then he kept Guy and me supplied with writing assignments when we later made the break. I had told Bill of our plan to homestead, of our hope to draw what we loved, mountains, together with how we made a living. I had also arranged that I could leave work on Fridays at noon—to go climbing. Being a climber himself, he understood.

Bill Kemsley's sense that outdoors folks were ready for his magazine was right on the mark. The backpacking boom that had begun in the late 1960s was in full force: people, especially young people—back-to-nature types—were streaming into the woods. The impact resulted in overfilled shelters that were surrounded by a forest of stumps where young trees had been axed for firewood, the ground compacted and muddy. Trails were eroding, with the heavy use. Streams were at risk of pollution from so many of us bathing and washing dishes in them. Above treeline, trails braided through the tundra destroyed alpine plants. Litter was everywhere. Bill wanted *Backpacker* to carry the environmental message of stewardship in a persuasive way that had hikers opening their eyes to their own impacts. He wanted his magazine to get across the message that had us caring enough about the woods to do something about our own actions. He asked me to critique each issue to make sure the magazine was staying on the high ethical track he had envisioned.

Already, at the Gunks, we climbers were aware of our impacts on the cliffs. The problem was the manner in which climbers protected themselves from falls by pounding pitons, metal wedges, into cracks. Especially, the way pitons were removed, by pounding them back and forth, chewed the edges of cracks, causing them to widen. A movement had started in Yosemite that encouraged climbers across the country to transition from pitons to a type of protection we called "nuts"—they looked like machine nuts—that we could slot into cracks and remove with our fingers. No hammering necessary! This was revolutionary and the change swept through climbing areas with amazing rapidity. In less than a season the sound of a piton being hammered into a crack was gone from the Gunks.

It was a matter of education: educating hikers and climbers to take care of the places they loved. That's what Bill Kemsley hoped to do with *Backpacker*. As did the hiking clubs like the Appalachian Mountain Club, the

Green Mountain Club in Vermont, the Adirondack Mountain Club in New York, and the state and national agencies like the Forest Service. Another new word—stewardship—had entered my vocabulary, and the vocabulary of outdoor lovers everywhere, as we learned how to "steward," to nurture and care for, by our actions, the woods and mountains, cliff faces and rivers that enriched our lives. Reciprocity! Giving back. This was a new language for all outdoors lovers.

While this, a national movement on the part of those committed to caring for the outdoor places they loved, was going on, Guy and I were moving forward with his plan—now our plan—to find a life out of the city. In the summer of 1971, we scoured the Northeast for land: acreage that would include a house site—we would build a small dwelling; a space for a garden—we would live on its produce; room for an orchard and berry bushes. We needed a stream for water, and a woodlot, a mix of northern hardwoods and evergreens, for firewood and building projects, with enough sugar maples to supply our sweetening needs in maple syrup.

We found this land in Vermont, near the state's eastern edge, the White Mountains of New Hampshire and the Greens of Vermont in reasonable reach, a rural setting, a small village nestled into a narrow river valley, not on the road to anywhere. No ski areas of any size nearby, or cities, or even large towns. And we settled in to make it work.

Bill and *Backpacker* were good to us. More important, the underlying cause that was changing the world of all outdoors lovers gave us a subject we could give ourself to wholeheartedly. We were in the right place now to be in the mountains, to see what was going on there, and to write about it.

Shortly before his death Guy wrote in his unpublished memoir: "A few people have said some very nice things about our books, but on the whole they and our ideas about eastern wildness seem to be sinking into oblivion unnoticed. All this is accompanied by the feeling that I could have done better." But that was in the future. The decade of the seventies as homesteaders and writers, Guy penned, was "the happiest in my life."

The morning's power outage continued all day, and into the next. All told, I have been without power for forty-eight hours now. It is inconveniencing, as losing power tends to be, but by the second day I've found that I've sunk back into my old Barra habit of carrying a small flashlight in my pocket. As the outage goes on, I've begun to use the flashlight less as I become accustomed to darkness that really isn't that dark. I'm learning, again, to feel with my fingers, to rediscover that kinetic sense of which drawer contains my favorite paring knife. I am back at Barra, almost. By tomorrow morning, when the power will suddenly announce itself with the hum of the refrigerator restarting—well, that will be fine, too. I will be back in my present chosen life again.

6

The Adirondacks 46 in Winter!

Adventure stories can turn into published articles or books. They can also quietly sit in diaries, until the moment comes and you find yourself rummaging back through the years to find that diary entry that will refresh your memory as you commit that long-ago time in the mountains to the page.

 Much of our reading—Guy's and mine—was of books or magazine articles on mountain adventures, and polar ones, too. Names like George Mallory of Everest, or, half a century earlier, Edward Whymper on the Matterhorn, or jumping to mid-twentieth century, Tenzing Norgay on Everest, sprinkled our conversation. We read Alfred Lansing's Endurance *about Shackleton three or four times. Apsley Cherry-Garrard's* The Worst Journey in the World *recounts the Winter Journey—Cherry's mission to locate the Emperor penguins' breeding grounds and return with their eggs, set against Robert Falcon Scott's ill-fated march to the South Pole—has been called the greatest expedition story ever penned. Why? Because Cherry takes us there. You are in the tent, hammered by hurricane winds and searing cold. You're resenting your bagmate for taking up more than his share of the room. When I turned my hand to an American Arctic expedition of the 1880s, also ill-fated, I took* The Worst Journey *as my model. I wrote to experience with those twenty-five men the state of mind when you're hungry, facing starvation, fearing cannibalism, suspecting abandonment.*

Every expedition book I had ever read, every winter trip I had ever been on, I drew upon to put me there, in a starving camp of men losing their minds, losing hope. How would I react? That's what pushed me to write Starvation Shore. *It all started on those early 1970s trips to the Adirondacks in winter.*

∾

Goal setting was how Guy Waterman operated. He did well when being driven by a goal. Naturally, peak bagging appealed to this aspect of his character. In the late 1960s and early 1970s, a few hardy souls became somewhat obsessed with bashing off the list of forty-six peaks in the Adirondacks that were over four thousand feet—in winter. As with any list of mountains, the calculation of elevation can change. When this Adirondack list was first established by the Marshall brothers, Robert and George, with their friend and guide Herb Clark in 1924, it was later found that four peaks were below that magic mark. However, in honor of the Marshalls—Robert in 1935, spearheaded the founding of the Wilderness Society, and later, the Bob Marshall Wilderness in Montana was named for him—it was decided by the peak-bagging group, calling themselves the Forty-Sixers, who followed in the Marshalls' footsteps, to keep those peaks shy of four thousand feet on the list. Of those four, three are still ascended by unmarked paths, making them a more challenging climb.

Guy had never climbed in the Adirondacks and so had the brainstorm that he would climb all forty-six peaks in winter before treading over even one in the nonwinter months. Winter, to peak baggers, is defined by the winter solstice to vernal equinox. During the winters of 1968–1969 and 1969–1970, Guy made numerous weekend drives from where he lived near the Shawangunks to join in with a small group of men, and, occasionally one or two women. Most of the men worked for General Electric in Schenectady, as Guy did at the corporate headquarters in New York City.

There are no easily reached summits on this list, especially in winter, unless you put up an argument for Cascade and Porter, short climbs close to the road. When the winter of 1970–1971 rolled around, Guy was ready to take a break from his group of male partners to invite me to climb those two peaks with him on January 1, 1971. I was brand new to winter climbing and to snowshoeing. I could trudge uphill since that was merely a matter of putting your head down and placing one foot in front of the other, that is, acquiring that kind of attitude.

That day on Cascade and Porter I learned some essentials: how to keep my water bottle from freezing by placing it in my shirt, not in my pack where it will not only freeze but be hard to get at. Staying well hydrated in winter is important. I learned how to regulate my temperature by shedding clothing to keep from sweating. Once you've soaked those inner layers you're chilled enough to be at risk for hypothermia. I learned how doffing your wool hat (we dressed in wool in those days) cooled you; likewise, putting on your hat restored heat.

I was not completely ignorant of how to keep myself comfortable in winter, having gone on some of the "cold weather" backpacking trips in the Catskills offered by the New York Chapter of the Appalachian Mountain Club that past autumn. But November in the Catskills is a different world from January in the Adirondacks. Cascade and Porter were the real thing, or a stepping stone in that direction, and under Guy's patient tutelage I discovered how much fun winter hiking could be.

We made slow and steady gain of elevation up Cascade. Leaving the deciduous trees behind, I moved into the world of spruce and fir, branches bowed down by the mighty weight of snow. The snow, in those years of the early 1970s could be counted on to be of great depth, and if you were breaking trail, you had your head in the branches. Naturally, one's instinct was to reach out with your ice ax and bat off the snow to clear the way forward. Timing, I discovered, is everything here, if you want to avoid covering yourself with snow.

That New Year's Day was cold and cloudy. No views from the open summit of Cascade. Yet, as I stood with Guy in the wind, crunching gorp and drinking water, this easiest of mountains felt like Mount Everest to me. I had learned how difficult it was, if you are going first, to break trail in deep snow. There was the challenge of picking up the blazes since the tree trunks themselves were often plastered with snow that obscured the blaze marks. On Cascade, Guy had introduced me to the pattern of changing the lead every ten minutes, an exercise in teamwork that avoided exhaustion. In those days, with so few other hikers out there, you had the pleasure, privilege, and the glory of hard work!—breaking trail from bottom to top of any of those forty-six peaks you'd set your heart on.

We began spending nearly every weekend that winter of 1971–1972 in the Adirondacks. That meant Guy's VW bug was packed with camping gear and food, ready for a quick getaway on Friday when we returned from our two-hour commute. We hurtled up the New York Thruway, then the Northway in the dark, a four-hour drive. Guy, when I met him, had been amusing himself by memorizing *Paradise Lost*, and it became my pleasure, on these drives, to listen, book in hand, as he practiced reciting, ready to supply a helpful nudge with the forgotten word, if needed. I was tremendously impressed by this. I had not enjoyed Milton in college, but by listening to Guy recite, some passages many times, I began to understand what had drawn him to the poetry: ". . . when straight behold the throne/ Of Chaos," he declaimed, "and his dark pavilion spread/ Wide on the wasteful deep; with him enthroned/ Sat sable-vested Night, eldest of things,/ The consort of his reign, and by them stood/ Orcus and Ades, and the dreaded name/ Of Demogorgon." I laughed. I couldn't help myself. Guy looked at me, eyebrows raised. By this time, he was well into book 8, only four left to go. Yes, it does seem that Guy's quest to memorize all of Milton fit in with the kind of obsessive drive that prompts a desire to climb a list of peaks.

We ate our dinner of sandwiches in the car, and another of my duties was to supply the two of us with hot drinks. We had brought along a small butane stove for this purpose that I could set between my legs. We had a small pot I filled with water, added a tea bag, and turned on the gas. This worked beautifully until one stormy, snowy dark night—Guy had reduced his speed to 40 mph—the tan bug slid into the guardrail on the Northway. The guardrail itself was buried in snow, making this a comparatively soft landing. It was, however, too much for the butane stove and its pot full of water. Both took off for the interstices of the back of the bug. When we had ascertained that we were both fine, if a trifle jostled, we began an immediate search for the stove. It was not alight, having by some miracle extinguished itself, and the water had disappeared. Disintegrated into droplets, perhaps, since neither of us, nor our gear of sleeping bags and tent, were wet.

Guy pulled out of the snowbank and drove on at a sedate pace to the next exit. We did feel we should have the car checked out, if possible, it now being around ten thirty. By a stroke of luck we found a service station open, but about to close up. The owner assured us he'd be back at 7:00 a.m., if we could find a nearby place to spend the night. We suggested setting up our tent in back of his garage. He generously agreed. At 7:00 he returned and pronounced the car safe for travel. We thanked him and continued on, and after that close call did some of our best climbing ever on steep slopes in high winds. We remarked to each other, and to the friends we climbed with, that we felt immune to accidents, having already just survived one.

Normally, for a Friday night, we would have pulled into the small roadside parking lot at Chapel Pond on Route 73, only a few miles from the village of Keene Valley, located in the very heart of the Adirondacks High Peaks, at midnight. We would have set up our tent on the pond, staking it to the ice with an older version of the ice screws we used for climbing.

We had never known the pond to be unfrozen, except once. We were already camped on it when a massive thawing rain occurred in the night. The ice remained firm, but around 5:30 a.m. we realized that the floor of the tent was awash in water, and any loose items were floating on the surface. We, on our sleeping pads, had turned into islands. But this by no means demanded retreat, and the climbing continued as usual.

By early March the official season for bagging winter peaks was closing in. Guy had saved for last Mount Marcy, at 5,344 feet the Adirondacks' highest. We'd set the date for the weekend of March 15th, but as the Fates and weather gods dealt the cards, that weekend presented the worst driving conditions of the winter: freezing rain for Friday night going into Saturday, too hazardous even for us. Everything rested on the next weekend, which marked the vernal equinox.

Mount Marcy demands much from hikers, especially those who ascend its flanks in winter, with its eight-mile approach and its open summit with the last half mile in the arctic-alpine zone. A small group of friends joined us at the trailhead that included our most frequent hiking companion, Will Merritt. All went straight forward with the trail breaking, and I carry no particular memory of the climb except the wild beauty of being on Marcy's windy summit, huddled down among the rocks, munching carrot cake I'd made especially for this celebration of Guy completing his crazy goal of not just hiking the 46 in winter, but having never hiked even one in summer. And, now, said my husband with a smile, after we had returned home, let's see what progress you can make on the list.

I had already climbed eleven peaks of the required forty-six. Guy proposed that a good way to knock off a number of them—seven total— would be to do a backpack over the Great Range. This, I knew, would be a challenging trip. To add muscle to the trail breaking we invited our Gunks climbing friend, Mike Fye. The mountains that make up the Great Range resemble the teeth on our crosscut saw: steep sided with deep cols between. I would be carrying around forty-five pounds, and Guy and Mike much more. I was doubtful that any of the trails would be broken out, and this turned out to be the case. It would be a three-day trip, meaning two nights in the woods.

The three of us, and our gear squeezed into the VW bug, arrived at Chapel Pond at 9:30 p.m. When we crawled into our sleeping bags, the temperature was a reasonable fifteen degrees.

∾

> For over 100 years, a traverse of the Great Range has been considered a premier challenge for Adirondack hikers. The views along this spectacularly rugged route are some of the best in the Adirondacks; but . . . nearly every foot of this route is on steep terrain with very rough trail for most of the distance.
>
> —Tony Goodwin and David Thomas-Train,
> *Adirondack Mountain Club High Peaks Trails*, 14th edition

When we awoke on Friday morning, February 8, 1974, it was minus fifteen degrees. My thought immediately went to our root cellar at Barra. Hoping against hope that by some stroke of luck, it wasn't that cold at home. Since we heated our house entirely by our woodstoves, we always took a chance leaving those fires untended in the winter, but we made sure that our root cellar's temperature was on the high side before we left. Our root cellar contained the food we'd grown that summer and stored for winter use: potatoes, beets, carrots, onions, and rutabagas. We closely monitored the root cellar's temperature, holding it to forty-three degrees. Before multi-night winter trips we kept the trapdoor open to allow the warm air of the cabin to boost that temperature into the upper forties. We could not allow those vegetables to freeze! But I soon let the root cellar go since there were many more immediate issues to occupy my mind.

We hoisted our packs at the Garden parking lot and began snow-shoeing into the Ranger's Station, a relatively flat approach of several miles as is typical for the Adirondacks High Peaks. We found the path trodden out, not surprising since it leads to a building where hikers could spend the night in some degree of comfort. And, sure enough, we passed two of those hikers who were walking out. Also not surprising, we knew one of them, a young man I had worked with in a climbing store in New York. There were so few people tramping the winter woods then that if you crossed paths with someone chances were you knew them.

No one had snowshoed beyond the Ranger's Station. So we mentally prepared ourselves for the ascent of the Wolf Jaws, breaking trail. This was our easiest day. Well, not really. We had no easy days. But when we had reached Wolf Jaws' Notch we could off-load our packs and climb Lower Wolf Jaw without them. One summit down. Only six to go! We descended, shouldered our packs, and broke trail to the summit of Upper Wolf Jaw where we did not linger but slid down the other side to confront the steep ascent to Armstrong.

On all our ascents we rotated the lead among the three of us, the steepness of the trail forcing us to kick steps into the slope, creating a ladder for the followers. We were using the long-handled ice axes of the day, and the approved technique was to plunge the shaft of the ice ax into the slope in front of your nose, then haul back with a leg and slam your snowshoe into the snow, step up, and repeat the process. Slow and exhausting work, but somehow immensely satisfying. Good, among other things, for getting out any aggressions that might be lurking. The skill involved was not to collapse your own step as you stepped up.

On the summit of Armstrong we tramped out with snowshoes a level place to pitch our tent, sticking in stakes and securing the tent with the guylines to the nearby firs. Ours was a generous two-person tent. With three of us in there, down sleeping bags fluffed, our bodies generating heat, our tent became a cozy haven. We always kept track of the temperatures, and I recorded in my journal entry that the maximum that day was eleven degrees. That might sound cold, and it is cold, but when you're breaking trail, as I described, up a precipitous incline you are working hard enough to sweat if you're not careful to regulate your clothing. Merely removing your hat will do wonders in cooling you down.

On the morning of the ninth we were greeted by a brilliant sunrise. The thermometer had settled at minus six degrees, so we wasted no time in eating our oatmeal and drinking orange Jell-O. High in sugar, this drink is not recommended in civilization, but it becomes just the thing on cold backpacking trips. We broke camp and descended Armstrong to turn our attention to Gothics, at 4,736 feet, one of the Adirondacks most prized mountains. There is a slide on its North Face that Guy and I had climbed with our friend Art Fitch two years before. We reminisced about that with Mike as we moved upward to encounter winds gusting on the Gothics ridge that Mike clocked at 30 mph. Here we were in the alpine zone, unprotected by the trees, so we didn't stop long on the summit, though the view was worth admiring. Crossing over the ice-covered rocks, we avoided stepping on the plants as much as we could with our snowshoes, to encounter the kind of steep descent the Great Range is famous for. So steep, that I found I was best off facing into the slope, the snow nearly in front of my nose, which, of course, made it only more fun.

At the Gothics Col we gathered our breath.

The steep snowshoe up Saddleback verged on the vertical. Perhaps because of the excitement of that I remember feeling some kind of reserve of strength kick in at this point. We were in the heart of this great mountain range, a crown jewel of the Adirondacks. The snow was bottomless, the evergreens draped with it. Clouds scudded by casting their shadows over us like a benediction. No sign of other humans, though we did pick up the tracks of hares. We longed to see one but never did. Hard work as it was—or because it was hard—all of us felt that there was nothing else at this moment we would rather be doing. The descent of Saddleback was steeper yet.

Now for Basin, a big mountain at 4,800 feet and our hardest climb. Psychologically hard. Basin has two peaks with a col in between. It can be demoralizing to reach a summit that isn't *the* summit, which meant we must climb back up another three hundred feet. This was our last peak of the day and we made a rapid descent to camp at Snowbird lean-to, at that time one of the few high-elevation lean-tos in the Adirondacks. They have since been removed when the numbers of hikers increased and caused environmental problems. A tough decision, since these deeply loved, charmingly primitive shelters in the spruce-fir belt defined the heart of a quintessential Adirondacks backpacking experience. We had climbed four peaks that day and had to fight for every yard of the four miles we walked. Our tent, sheltering three tired people that night at 3,500 feet, was, we all agreed, the coziest place on earth.

For February 10th, I wrote in my journal: "We thought it was going to take us a long time to pack out so got up and started climbing Haystack in the dark. Haystack, at 4,960 feet, is the third largest 4,000 footer. Made good time to the col. Dumped our packs and took off for the summit. Wanted to see the sunrise and were on the summit at 8:10 watching the sun come up over the Dixes. Marcy and Skylight behind us were aglow." We stayed on Haystack trying to take in all that was happening around us. We were on top of the world for the start of a new day. We would be descending now, for the last time. No more peaks to climb. And we felt a bit of the sadness of that, even though we'd be back to the mountains by the next weekend. Still, we were closing down on one of the Great Trips. All three of us were aware of that, so there was an overlay of goodbye mingled with the extraordinary good fortune of our success.

We covered the nine and a half miles back to the Garden in half the time it took us to do our four miles of the day before. Not counting a good half hour we spent sitting on the porch in the sun at the Ranger's Station polishing off the remainder of our sandwiches and the chocolate. We sat on the railing without hats or gloves or wind shells, awash in the sunlight, and when Guy read the thermometer he had hung on a branch, it read fifteen degrees, our highest reading for those three unduplicatable days.

7

Discovering the Spirit of Wildness

What I wrote titled "On Writing Wilderness Ethics: Some Further Musings on the Spirit of Wildness," for the August 2003 International Journal of Wilderness, *lay at the heart's core for Guy and me. We focused our trail work and our writing to serve and preserve the wild spirit of the mountains. It was eye-opening for me to build the bridge that connected our work with that of conservation officer Erick Kasana and the Masais' concern for their cattle—their economy—whose intensive grazing can create a threat to wild flora and fauna.*

Building bridges is a useful skill that we do all the time without much conscious thought. It can happen when a friend introduces us to someone she wants us to meet. You immediately try to find common ground, or mutual friends. You want some way of looking at the world you can compare and share. It's human behavior and it can lead to productive places, or, perhaps, nowhere other than a pleasant few hours.

I like to think, however, that even the most minimal bridge-building adds to our lives in some way. For example, I am unlikely to cross paths with Erick Kasana again, but the time we spent together broadened my thoughts about the threats to wildness. It helped me to think more deeply about how best to protect the wild places that I call home.

In dealing with such threats, the importance of maintaining wildness on an increasingly populated and industrialized planet is a hard-sell vision. We, as humans, have trouble visualizing what will be lost, until it is gone forever. The hut built on a formerly pristine ridgeline; a trail constructed on a mountain that had never seen a trail before. What is the impact of that hut, that trail on that (formerly) wild place? One of our better human traits is the impulse to share. But the downside is that it's easy to ignore that that urge might lead to the desecration of wild nature. We tell ourselves it feels selfish to exercise restraint.

Yet, if we turn our minds to how our actions can affect the lives of the bears and the moose, the beaver and the water birds for whom this wild land is their only home, that can be the jolt we need to say a resounding NO to adding more infrastructure that only diminishes the heart of why we seek days in the mountains. Whether consciously or not, we go for the renewing wildness.

When we've built a bridge with Nature itself, we've reached the point in our thinking that opens a path to new ways of seeing, new ways of cooperative caring, new ways of marshaling the cohorts to become stewards for the wild.

~

For my husband Guy and me, it started at the Shawangunks in 1970 when climbers were making the transition from pitons to nuts. Pitons damaged the edges of cracks; nuts, camming devices inserted into cracks and removed with just fingers, solved the problem. This revolution in how rock climbers protected themselves tore across the country from Yosemite to the Gunks in a little more than a year. It was a transition, built on reciprocity: climbers loved their home cliffs and that love ensured protection from their own impacts.

At this same time, hikers and backpackers were coming to the mountains in greater numbers than ever before. The mountain clubs and public agencies were straight-out trying to mitigate the damage to tent-and-shelter sites, trails, and streams. "Pack It In/Pack It Out," and "What If We All Built Fires" became the slogans of the day. Hikers got the message, as did equipment manufacturers, and backpackers began using lightweight stoves for cooking, ground pads instead of fir boughs under their sleeping bags, and hauling water away from the streams for dish washing. New techniques evolved for trail work to accommodate the increased numbers of hikers, whose impact was eroding trails. Above-treeline alpine stewards, employed by the mountain clubs, opened eyes to the low-growing tundra plants, remnants of the Ice Age that were being ground to pulp under hikers' boots.

At a time when Guy and I were looking for income to supplement our homesteading, the editor of *New England Outdoors*, a fly-fisherman named Mike Pogodzinski, offered us a monthly column on camping and hiking. This continued for the next five years, beginning in 1976, and our subject was these changes, spreading the word about our own human impacts and how we could clean up our act. Publisher Henry Wheelwright read our columns and contacted us about a book. Stone Wall Press released *Backwoods Ethics: Environmental Concerns for Hikers and Campers* in 1979.

In 1993, Carl Taylor of The Countryman Press asked us to write a companion volume. We called this new book *Wilderness Ethics: Preserving the Spirit of Wildness*. Roderick Frazier Nash, professor of environmental studies and history at the University of California, Santa Barbara, wrote the foreword to its first edition. *Wilderness Ethics* came out in a second edition in 2014, with a foreword by Ben Lawhon of the Leave No Trace Center for Outdoor Ethics.

For the second edition of *Backwoods Ethics* (1993), noted environmentalist Bill McKibben wrote the foreword, as he did for the third edition, which The Countryman Press released in 2016, changing the title to *The Green Guide to Low-Impact Hiking and Camping*.

I wrote an introduction for *The Green Guide* that updated the book, with special attention to what I saw was the greatest game-changer in the backcountry since the book came out in 1979: handheld digital devices that enable us to communicate with the frontcountry while we are in the backcountry. (This was not of environmental concern, but could, I felt, compromise our relationship with the mountains, and being fully in them.)

The coronavirus pandemic of 2020 unleashed an unprecedented surge of people into the woods and onto the heights, many of whom were newcomers. It is essential that those unfamiliar with the backcountry be given the opportunity to learn environmentally low-impact hiking and camping practices. This education should come naturally as they build a connection with mountains and the wild.

In that 2003 article I penned for the *International Journal of Wilderness* I wrote how I had recently been introduced to a Kenyan of the Masai people named Erick Kasana. He was a conservation officer visiting the United States to attend a conference at Harvard University about creating solidarity at the community and grassroots level. My friend, Kate, a Harvard student who had helped to organize the conference, brought Erick up to Vermont to experience snow for the first time. Following an afternoon of sledding, we settled in at my house for dinner.

"Here's Laura and Guy's book I was telling you about," Kate said, handing Erick *Wilderness Ethics*.

During dinner, Erick explained to me the complex situation of land pressures the Masai now feel as a result of colonialism. "Our economy," Erick said, "that is, our cattle, needs a natural resource base."

"You mean grass? The grasslands?" I asked.

"Yes," Erick said. "And grazing creates a pressure and threat to wildlife and flora. But it's more complicated than that. What appears as overgrazing is the result of complex pressures from people that have forced the Masai onto marginal land."

When we said good night, Erick took *Wilderness Ethics* with him. I noticed his light was on for some time. But what can he be finding in our book, I wondered? Our focus was the northeastern US. Our forested land, our mountains, were so unlike his grasslands. Then I began to think about what had caused us to write the book in the first place.

Like Erick, Guy and I spent a lot of time on the ground. In our columns we had written about what we observed on our trips to the mountains. Often, it seemed to us, values were in conflict in the backcountry, just as they were in the lands of Erick's home country. Here are three examples.

1. On a hike in to a lean-to beside a mountain pond that we'd recalled as being an idyllic spot just a few years earlier, we found a crowded and heavily used site. Wood railings had been erected to discourage hikers from cutting through the woods every which way, and a board pathway was laid down on the wet trailbed around the pond; the managers were trying to "protect the resource" here but, in the process, had turned this beautiful place into a woodsy suburbia. It struck us that the same results could have been achieved by blocking off access to the trampled spots with boulders or rotten logs and using rough-hewn planks, not store-bought lumber, to create a treadway over the muddy path skirting the pond.

2. Once, on a bushwhack up a stream valley, we came across a flattened clearing with a network of trampled paths and the

charred remains of numerous campfires. The woods appeared denuded of downed trees, and the spruce and fir stripped to head height of all their lower branches. Along the stream we saw evidence of heavy tramping, with some of the banks caved in. We later learned that this was the location used by a wilderness course from a nearby school. Every November, for the past twenty-four years, about one hundred students, in groups of ten with two adult leaders, had come out backpacking for two weeks along a craggy and forested ridgeline. At the end of the course, each student was sent off into the woods alone for three days to experience the solitude. Students were expected to keep a journal and take a close inward look at themselves, while keeping outwardly warm with a campfire. The twenty teacher/leaders also camped and kept a campfire going. It was seen as a priceless experience for young people, but on our hike we had stumbled across the price—its impact on the forest.

3. With a few friends we had climbed to the summit of a remote New Hampshire 4,000-foot peak by a steep, trailless route. The hike proved harder and longer than expected, and we arrived on top late in the afternoon. The plan was to take the trail down, but we'd have to move fast to avoid being benighted. We all felt the thrill of climbing this isolated peak by a route that took all our skill with map and compass, not another party in sight all day. The view before us showed only mountains. So we were a bit taken aback when a member of the group pulled out his cell phone. "Hi honey, just calling to let you know I'm safe," he said. "We're on the summit and are about to take the trail down. Guess I'll be late for dinner though."

Taken aback is not putting it strongly enough. We were aghast! That single call smashed through the fragile fabric of wildness. In fact, that phone's presence made a travesty of a climb during which we had felt committed, on our own in the wild.

From these, and many other similar experiences, we began to see that highly desirable goals like education, safety, and protecting areas from impact could have adverse effects on other, equally important, and sometimes fragile or vulnerable values. We began to realize that what was most at risk was a spiritual quality. We began to call this elusive value "the spirit of wildness."

Our thoughts about the spirit of wildness grew when we began a tenure of trail maintenance on a 1.8-mile trail section of Franconia Ridge that traverses several White Mountain summits and lies entirely above treeline. Guy and I were privileged to have this responsibility from 1980 to nearly 2000, the year of his death. Our main concern was to take care of a popular trail in such a way that would protect the precious alpine plants yet not interfere with a hiker's sense of freedom. We thought it essential that our trail work not stand as a barrier to hikers experiencing the wildness of this ridge.

Reading Aldo Leopold's *A Sand County Almanac* (1966) also influenced our thinking. Leopold's cry is that only when we stop looking at land as a commodity will we see that it has value in and of itself. Only then will we treat land with true respect. Leopold called this new way of seeing a *new land ethic*. We sought to carry this a step further in relation specifically to wild land. In *Wilderness Ethics* we proposed that some rough-hewn ethic was needed that spoke for the spiritual side of the wild. The intangibles, the subjective elements we saw in the wild, were even more fragile and threatened than the physical ones. We were pleading for respect for the mystery of wildness.

Our question to readers was this: Once the land has been saved from development—the strip mining, logging, dam construction, and second homes—then what? We continued:

> Profound theorists, we are not. We're just two people who spend a lot of time in the woods and on the mountains; who have observed a few things and asked ourselves a few questions about wildness, and who would like to invite you to share our thoughts and think about some practical questions yourself:
>
> • What are we trying to preserve?
>
> • What are the threats to the wildness in wilderness?
>
> • What can we do about it?

We wanted to write a book that alerted readers to the fragility of wildness and how easy it was to erode it by building, say, a hut at some quiet view spot, or locating a trail up a hitherto pathless ridge, or constructing a bridge where none has been deemed needed before, or calling in helicopters, or traveling in large groups, or whipping out a cell phone. Wildness can be easily overlooked by hikers and managers alike; wildness is expendable, and once spent, we can rarely call it back.

It seemed to us a question of values. We were asking hikers and managers to think about what was important. What was at stake? What mattered? If wildness was an important value, we could view through that lens questions ranging from whether to construct a new trail to whether we should tramp through the woods in large groups.

Another way to approach thinking about what kind of backcountry we wanted was from the standpoint of a love of land. We hoped hikers and managers would be guided by a concern for the land's well-being and would approach the care of land with a spirit of humility. That, too, was a way to keep the spirit of wildness alive.

It seemed to us that this meant a real change of thinking if we were to exercise restraint, respect, and responsibility. It was more than a question for managers—the hiking clubs, the Forest Service, and the Park Service—to grapple with. We were asking all outdoor people, every hiker, backpacker, climber, fisherman, and hunter, to think about backcountry in terms of values and ask themselves a question: What kind of backcountry do we want?

One of our favorite quotations is often attributed to conservationist Geza Teleki: "Everything is less important. Career is less important. Science is less important. Fame is less important than doing the right thing when you're dealing with the natural environment."

Guy and I admired Teleki's words for their humility. In learning to put them into practice, we turn ourselves into stewards of the land in the sense Leopold had hoped for. Humility seems key to how we relate to land. If we were more humble, all of us, wouldn't the spirit of wildness stand a better chance?

Much has changed since Guy and I wrote our early columns for *New England Outdoors*. Land managers have come a long way toward learning how to "protect the resource" in ways that are in keeping with the quiet nature of the woods. Schools and clubs that offer outdoor programs are learning how to clean up their acts. But many threats remain, such as cell phones, radios, video drones, and the persistent use of helicopters. Managers still upgrade backcountry facilities in ways that seem out of step with a wilderness experience. And more people keep coming. With *Wilderness Ethics*, we hoped to begin the conversation. Now it depends on the hikers and managers to keep that dialogue alive as we make decisions for the future.

It seems to me that Erick Kasana was facing many of the same issues we do here in the Northeast. For us, the land feels the pressures of people—of us, as hikers and climbers. For the Masai people, pressures came from their colonial legacy under British rule, from present-day tourists, as well as from their own growing population that results in increasingly crowded conditions for their cattle, leading to overgrazing.

Erick and Guy and I looked for a response to land issues—as well as solutions—from those to whom the land mattered most. Our hope was that grassroots efforts could have that ripple effect, like a large stone dropped into the center of the pond: we wanted to see the rings widening out and out, far beyond the point of impact, far beyond the limits of our vision.

We desired to make room for the spirit of wildness. That was our message, one we tied around the stone we dropped in the pond. Giving room to what nurtures our spirits when we go to the mountains is, it seems to me, the ultimate challenge for those of us who seek the wild in the twenty-first century.

We need mountains and wild country now more than ever before, and more pressures are being put upon the land as people crowd there, looking for solace and solitude, for spiritual renewal and strength, for exercise and just plain fun. We wrote *Wilderness Ethics* because it seemed to us that it was terribly important to save an elusive thing we could not see, a spirit of wildness essential to our human souls—the underlying reason, whether we are aware of it or not, why we seek the wild places.

I would venture to say that Erick and Guy and I were all concerned with both the physical and spiritual aspects of the land ethic. The Masai have an immediate need to address the physical, but I would guess that a spiritual ethic is critical to them as well and that their own culture is grounded in a spiritual connection to the land. Whether Masai or American, we all need a land ethic that includes both the physical and spiritual, and as a community of people on the earth we need to think about what that means, defining it for ourselves (there is no formula, no easily applied blueprint) whether we live in the Northeast, the West, or in the Kenyan highlands.

8

Seasons of Sugaring

The whole time I was writing this chapter, I smelled raw sap thickening, its sweetness permeating my clothes, and felt my hair stiffening in the sugary steam while my hands were growing dirtier as the weeks passed from handling the wood as I stoked the fire with its accompanying ash and smoke and soot, and from the inevitable arrival of Vermont's mud season.

An excerpt from this chapter appeared in Vermont Almanac, *December 2020, entitled "The Trees Called the Dance." This was, as far as I was concerned, a felicitous arrangement with Dave Mance, a sugar maker himself, and one of the more gifted editors I've had the pleasure to work with. Hannah and John Narowski of Maplestone Farm were my guides about how to run an up-to-date commercial sugaring operation.*

Distilling the sap of the sugar maple into syrup, at least the way Guy and I were doing it, more closely connected us with nature than any of our homesteading yearly rounds.

Sugaring, the process, grew on us season after season. The trees, because we had named them, became themselves, that is, revealed themselves to us in a way only naming can do. These trees we tapped became personal for us and we kept a close eye on their health—as a farmer would with his animals—on the lookout for wounds, insect damage, or soft spots in the bark.

We had not expected this to happen. A tree is a tree after all. The naming started as a game, a way of referring to these trees we were picking up sap from. But this is only one of the mysteries of sugaring. When we were in the forest selecting trees to take for our wood supply, in other words when we were in the mindset of loggers, we were looking at our trees through an impersonal lens. Though we knew a logger who would inform the landowner he would not cut a certain tree the owner wanted cut. When we questioned him about this, he said he just couldn't bring himself to chainsaw the tree down. This didn't happen often. He wouldn't have been in business long if it had.

I like to think that, for those who work on nearly a daily basis in the woods, if you are open, the trees begin to speak. Meaning, mainly, that we begin to listen. We are not aware of this; it happens through living with trees over years. It's like developing our human friendships: It takes time. It takes patience. It takes forbearance. It takes reverence. It takes love.

∾

How many of our neighbors, getting on into their seventies, have declared their intention, year after year, of making this time the last sugar season. Then, as winter rounds out into the following spring, the fever grips their blood and with the first warm sunshine they are out in the sugar lot scattering buckets, tapping, gathering, and boiling, and telling endless yarns of the wonderful sap seasons in the days of their youth and early manhood.

—Helen and Scott Nearing, *The Maple Sugar Book*

Sugaring, Guy and I agreed, demanded more of us than a whole season of winter climbing. Climbing in winter, we said, put us in good enough shape for sugaring.

How could this be?

Sugar makers typically use black polyethylene tubing to connect their maples, and these lines carry the sap directly to the sap house or to roadside receptacles where the raw product can be easily delivered to storage tanks. Sap can literally travel several miles through pipelines.

Few sugar makers cut their own wood these days. They use oil or some other fossil fuel to stoke the fires that boil down sap from sugar maples, *Acer saccharum*, into that golden syrup sold in gallons, quarts, pints, even half pints. When you walk into that quaint Vermont country store, you'll see, if you've got your eyes about you, that the smaller the container, the higher the price per fluid ounce. This is smart Yankee trading. It's been going on for as long as there have been Yankee farmers making maple syrup in that fallow time between the end of winter and spring planting.

As the sun strengthens, anyone with a backyard sugar grove is lured out into the fresh air to tap a few maples. It's healthy, it renews one's connection with the land, it's exciting to watch that sap drip into a bucket—if you're using buckets—or pour in a continuous stream through your pipeline into your evaporator. It's a family activity, and it's just plain fun.

Much of the romance has gone out of sugaring: no one is working with horses to bring in the sap anymore, and few are using buckets. For the commercial operators, it's all automatic.

But there are still a few folks who carry on as if the times haven't changed much; we were a part of that breed.

Here's how turning sap into maple syrup works. It's very simple. Nothing is added—no additives! None. Whatever the size of your operation we're all doing the same thing: evaporating out the water content from the sap.

For a commercial producer, a top-end small rig measures 4 ft. by 10 ft. It's a rectangle of steel that can hold two hundred gallons of sap coming from more than six thousand taps drilled into maple trees that grow up to 120 ft. high and are anywhere from fifty to over two hundred years old. A rig of this size can "draw off"—that is, produce—forty to fifty gallons of syrup an hour. Large evaporators can handle two to three hundred thousand taps. Some of the largest sugar makers power their evaporators by generating electricity with solar panels, a clean and environmentally sustainable way to go.

Generally, two people, though sometimes just one on a small rig, can be handy when the sugar maker is drawing off two hundred gallons of prime quality maple syrup a day. Or night. (Often sugar makers have day jobs and fire up their evaporators when they get home from work.)

Bear in mind, it takes forty gallons of sap to make one gallon of syrup. The sugar maker controls the heat under the pan and so regulates the rate of evaporation. As the water content is evaporated, the maple sap thickens and sweetens. When the correct measurable viscosity is reached, the sugar maker declares the syrup done. Twenty or so years ago, sugar makers found a way to remove a good percentage of that water content in a process called reverse osmosis. This shortens the boiling time, but they are still confronted by the tricky part: managing the continual feed of raw sap into the pan at the same time the finished syrup is drawn off.

Every sugar maker's greatest fear is scorching the syrup and burning out the pan. This can happen with amazing swiftness if the raw sap coming in is not regulated to compensate for the finished syrup exiting the evaporator. The sugar maker is dealing with a frothing foaming bubbling mass of syrup on a large flat surface intent on evaporating water at what can feel like the speed of light. The depth of sap in the pan is generally kept at one inch or less. That leaves very little margin for error. A burnt-out evaporator means not just a costly replacement, but the loss of many gallons of finished syrup. This would take time, and the sugar maker could lose days, even weeks, very likely the entire sugar season that is confined to—discounting tapping and cleanup—around one month.

Guy and I, being noncommercial and not overly concerned with efficiency, kept our sap level at around four inches. Even so, we needed to be vigilant, especially when closing down for the night. The fire, even reduced to a bed of coals, continues to evaporate the sap. We learned this the hard way early on when we came down one morning to a pan half blackened with overdone sticky syrup. It took us a good part of that day to scrub out our evaporator.

The time for making maple syrup is prescribed by the time it takes for the season to change from winter to spring. As the day warms, the sap moves out of the roots of the maples and up into the topmost branches. At night, as the air cools, sap moves back down to the roots. Thus is developed a pumping action. How this pumping action actually works is only one of the many things we don't fully understand about sugar maples.

At some point, as the days and the nights warm, the quality of the sap turns to what's called *bud sap*. The trees are budding! Anyone looking upward into the canopy can see that faint, alluring greenish/reddish haze that signals full-on spring and the end of the sugaring season as the sap coming out of the trees turns cloudy. Sap at the beginning of the season is as clear as a rushing mountain stream and tastes as pure—cold and refreshing—hardly any taste, though when we sugar makers taste it we're sure we can detect the promise of sweetness. Indeed, the promise is genuine and can be measured in individual trees with a hydrometer at 2 percent or even 6 percent of the sap, according to botanist Donald Peattie.

~

DESCRIPTION: *Bark* of old trunks brownish or grayish and finely scaly, becoming deeply furrowed. . . . *Leaves* thin, dark green above, paler green or whitened beneath, 3-lobed or 5-lobed with a main nerve running to the tip of each lobe, 3 to 6 inches long and broad. . . . *Wood* very tough, strong, medium-hard, medium-heavy (44 pounds to the cubic foot, dry weight).

—Donald Culross Peattie, *A Natural History of Trees*

Guy and I were rank beginners when we started sugaring. This would have been in spring 1975, our second upon moving to Barra. We couldn't have gone about it more inefficiently, but every sugar maker has to start somewhere. We used the same small fireplace made of a few rocks with an iron grill on top that we cooked on for most of that summer when we were building our house. We placed two pots that could hold a few gallons of sap on the grill and began the deceptively beautiful, simple process of evaporating water out of sap.

Like those Yankee farmers, as well as the commercial sugar producers, we were filling in the month or so before spring planting when winter recedes. The imperative of warming days, longer daylight hours, drew us outside to renew our connection to the land.

We sensibly decided to start small and tapped only nineteen trees. All these maples were a good distance from our cabin: a walk down to the bottom of our clearing, across our stream, and uphill into the sugarbush. Sugaring begins in early March, still winter, so we wore snowshoes. Our largest maples—the 200-year-old trees—were a good tenth of a mile from our primitive seat of operations. A long walk, yes, and uphill, but downhill on the way back with the full buckets. We just couldn't resist seeing what these magnificent gnarly giants could produce. These were trees that two people couldn't join hands around. It required three good-sized people to encircle a trunk.

We soon discovered that not all the trees we'd tapped that first year were sugar maples. Of the nineteen trees, sixteen were sugar maples, one a red maple (which also produces sugar sap), and two were elms (which do not). We made seven quarts of syrup. We knew we could finish off the syrup inside, on our cookstove. But we had also heard that the steam could peel off wallpaper. As we didn't have wallpaper, we gave this a shot. An unsuccessful shot. Yes, we could take the mostly boiled sap down to the finished product. But somehow the fun, especially the mystery, vanished by turning sugaring into an indoor activity.

Fun? What was fun about conditions that had Guy continually cutting and splitting wood, and me continually stoking the fire, hovering over two pots that refused to boil on a fire being blown sideways in the March wind? I can't explain it. It makes no sense. But once you've poured off that golden-hued end product made from merely evaporating water out of sap that comes from a *tree*, a maple tree, a true monarch of the Northern Hardwood Forest, which gives us, aside from its sap, about the best firewood you can burn in the Northeast, you forget all about the pain and suffering. Despite the long tedious hours of boiling, the back-breaking labor of hauling sap, the fact that you're getting very little sleep, what you've just made at merely the cost of your own human labor feels like a miracle, and tastes like one too. That first sugaring season we fell in love with the glorious process.

The next season we sensibly moved down into our woods, judiciously placing ourselves on a small knoll, in the heart of our maple grove. In every direction we snowshoed out paths to our tappable maples. We constructed a larger fireplace on which we situated an evaporator measuring 3 ft. by 4 ft. that we'd purchased for $5.00 from a friend who had upgraded his equipment.

Sugaring, however, overlapped with the tail end of winter climbing. It didn't take long to discover that the two activities could not be carried on at the same time. This hit hard when we returned from a winter trip—only one night away—to find overflowing buckets. Our sugarbush was in the midst of an insane run of sap, a great deal of which had spilled out of the tops of our buckets to be absorbed by the snow.

As we snowshoed madly around the sugarbush that late afternoon, the sap wasn't just dripping, it was close to running—each spile[1] had become a very leaky faucet. We counted the pings: *ping, ping, ping*, a glorious steady beat, like a metronome set at a quick tempo. In awe we listened to our trees perform as we scrambled to empty buckets into our galvanized gathering

---

1. Spiles, metal spouts, are hammered into the tree after a small hole is drilled—we used a brace and bit—through the bark and into the cambium layer, often called sap wood. Spiles are now made smaller, an intentional change so the tap hole drilled is less invasive.

pails and lug them to this place in our woods consecrated to the rite of sugaring. No sap house yet, no woodshed built—all that came later. Just a small evaporator on a rectangle of stones. We lit the fire, piled on the logs and began to boil.

So, we made a compromise. The winter climbing season ends on the spring solstice, March 21st (that is, if you're a peak bagger counting mountains climbed in calendar winter). The sap begins to drip, generally, several weeks before that. We were willing to lose the first run, or even the second to the mountains, but as the years unfolded, and sugaring seeped into our blood, our souls, and our biological clocks, it edged out the last week or two of winter climbing.

It wasn't just that we used maple syrup for all our needs requiring sugar, consuming about fourteen gallons a year in pickle and jam making, and general household uses. Or that syrup made excellent gifts. Or, according to Donald Peattie, that maple syrup is the only sweet, excepting honey, which contains the bone-building phosphates that cause calcium retention. No, it wasn't the practical use of syrup that had us so fiercely looking forward to each season.

We had discovered something we'd never suspected that came only from the repeated pattern of one sugaring season following another. It didn't take long before we realized we had bonded into a working relationship with these amazing trees.

Since we worked with buckets, not pipelines, we were in a position to become acquainted with the dripping patterns of more than 250 maples. As early as that first season we had begun measuring how much sap we picked up each day from each bucket. We kept those records for all twenty-seven of the years that we sugared at Barra. Of course, if you are working with pipelines, as most sugar makers do, how much sap any one tree produces is not available, nor is it vital to the mass producers running a commercial sugaring operation.

The records we kept on our sugar maples moved us into the kind of working relationship with our trees that the logger must have felt for his draft horses, or the dairy farmer for his cows, or the hunter for his hunting dogs. It's a reciprocal arrangement with a living nonhuman organism. Guy had, with his tendency toward obsessive record keeping, opened a passage into the secret lives—the dripping habits and patterns—of our maples, tree by tree. It moved both of us into a state of reverence.

From chapter 10, "Counting our Accomplishments," you will see that Guy was no stranger to statistical record keeping. When he began climbing mountains he noted the name of the peak, the date, and who he climbed with, or noted a solo ascent. He did the same for rock climbs. I did, too. This is not unusual; many climbers keep track of their climbs. Later, much later, after Guy's death, our climbing records proved invaluable to me as an aid to memory that ensured accuracy. Guy's lifelong and consuming interest in baseball was also statistically based, and he published his findings in *Baseball Digest* from time to time, and also in *Nine: A Journal of Baseball History and Social Perspectives.* His love of the game went back to his boyhood years in Cambridge, Massachusetts, where his father took up teaching duties at MIT. Here's what Guy wrote for *Nine*, volume 7, issue 1, about a magical wartime summer:

> For me, in 1943, there was only Boston Braves baseball. I suppose I took in a few Red Sox games when the Braves were away, but Braves Field was closer to where I lived than Fenway, and I distinctly recall attending 53 of the NL entry's 77 home games that summer. These were the Braves who had, for four years in a row, avoided the cellar only by sagaciously playing in the same league as the Philadelphia Phillies who had taken out a long-term lease on the NL basement.

He walked to the stadium with his friends, he told me, along the Charles River, tossing a baseball back and forth. I liked to picture that. He would have turned eleven that season.

"They argue over which were the golden years of baseball. To me," Guy continued, "there's one obvious answer: the years when you were age 10 to 12. Before that you were too young to appreciate the grand sweep of the game and its traditions. After that came distractions like girls and other adolescent torments. But from age 10 to 12, for the fortunate, there is only baseball."

When we went out to collect sap, we carried with us, along with our gathering pails, a three-by-five index card with each tree's name listed on it, a pencil for recording the number of quarts picked up, and a stick marked to measure quarts. Our guests, many of whom returned year after year, became well acquainted with the game, shouting out how many quarts a tree gave along with that tree's name. We entered the number on the index card for posting on the grand tally sheet at the sap house.

We had numbered our trees that first year but soon decided we could remember them better as individuals if we named them. Some names grew directly from the physical characteristics of the tree (Old Burrface), others from location (Swamp Fox), at least one from its extraordinary output of sap (Mad Dog). Gradually we got to know their dripping habits. A handsome, tall tree, Mordred, in the part of our sugarbush named for characters in the Arthurian legend, gushed sap early in the season, then suddenly tapered off. Swamp Fox, dwelling deep among the hemlocks, a shady place, meaning he got off to a slow start, we discovered could be counted on to produce at the end of the season, after the temperatures had moderated and his roots had warmed. The part of the forest we called the Highlands, where we had made those repeated trips during our first season to our biggest, best, and most magnificent maples, named after the Himalayan 8,000-meter summits, kept us busy without letup, season after season. Inevitably, some trees were not worth tapping but were so conveniently located to the sugar shed that there was no point in passing them up, such as Ozymandias. As with his namesake in Shelley's poem, when we removed the lid from his bucket we "looked on his works and despaired."

Building on Guy's love of baseball, this record keeping quite naturally led to a Tree of the Year race. Everest, one of the giants in the Highlands, won the first year, and in fact went on to become Tree of the Decade for the 1970s. But Mad Dog, a tree that had three large trunks and dwelled near our stream, won Tree of the Year eight times and was named Tree of the Century. As you can imagine, this race added tremendous zest to the sugaring season. It provided so much entertainment for us, as well as the folks who visited us year after year, that we soon came up with a Rookie of the Year award. It was not surprising that Everest and Mad Dog were Rookie of the Year winners. In fact a number of Rookie winners went on to win Tree of the Year: Annapurna, Lancelot, and Black Sheep, to name only three.

At the end of collecting the day's sap I would read off the numbers of quarts gathered, and Guy recorded the amounts next to each tree's name on the chart posted at our sugar shed. He added up the total number of quarts produced that day, and every few days he tallied up the Top Twenty Trees to see how the race was shaping up. We learned that the big trees were not always the biggest producers, though sometimes they could be. We learned—to our surprise—that Voltaire, who was a Tree of the Year, was not a sugar maple. (You would have thought we would have learned our trees better by now.) This news hit us when we had the pleasure of introducing this noble maple, which, to judge by his wide branching low down on his trunk, must have spent his early life growing in a clearing, to Sumner Williams of the University of Vermont's Proctor Maple Research Center. Sumner knew as much about sugar maples as anyone in the state, very likely the world. We pointed out a large area of rot and proudly announced that despite Voltaire's health problems, he was still Tree of the Year. This astute judge of maples eyed us, a little peculiarly we thought, and said, "I thought you were going to tell me this is a *red* maple." We blushed.

~

It has even been asserted by doctors that certain New England farmers and their families could do twice or three times the work performed by others because of maple sugar in their diet.

—Donald Culross Peattie, *A Natural History of Trees*

The work and excitement of sugaring lent itself to visitors. Family and friends came to Barra for the pleasures of gardening and wood collecting, but sugaring was in a class by itself. It underlined as nothing else could the change of seasons. For us, the great pleasure was in being outside from dawn to dusk, living, on a daily basis, with the lengthening daylight, the gradual warming that had us pulling off hats, mittens, and discarding layers until we were working in shirtsleeves. We witnessed the snow pull back from the base of the trees. Ground appeared on south-facing hillsides. Yet, our well-snowshoed paths retained their snow, and, for a short while, we were walking on a snow-packed ridge until this gradually diminished in depth and firmness and we weren't wearing snowshoes anymore.

This was the pattern: sugaring began on snowshoes and ended in bare boots. We always hung our buckets as low as possible, just above the snowpack, because if we didn't, by the end of the season we'd be struggling to remove full buckets a couple of feet higher than where we'd started.

But to every hard and fast rule, there is always an exception. This occurred a few years after Guy had died and I was sugaring with the stewards who were, at that time, taking care of our homestead. They had never sugared and I was spending every day with them, starting with tapping the trees. "We're on snowshoes now," I said, "but by the end of the season, you'll be walking on solid ground." I went on to rhapsodize about the glory of being a witness to the season's change, how sugaring involves us in that change itself! "Keep your tap holes low," I instructed, "around hip level, or by the end of the season, you'll be reaching up to shoulder height to lever off those buckets."

You can always count on more snow during the month of March and even into early April, but this particular year, the snow level stayed constant. It was not receding as the world moved toward spring. In fact, the snow was creeping up the outside of the buckets themselves, making them harder to remove. By the end of that season, as the trees were budding out and we were pulling our taps, we were still wearing snowshoes. So the last laugh was on me!

One year a pair of pileated woodpeckers decided to take up residence in a tall beech tree about one hundred feet from where we were boiling sap. Pileateds are spectacular birds: as large as crows, with a conspicuous red crest. It was always exciting to see them flying overhead, easy to identify with their sweeping wingbeats and flashing black and white coloration. Their loud calls rang out over the forest, to us sounding more than a little demented. Their drumming, unlike the quick rapid taps of the hairy and the downy woodpeckers, is a deep, slow beat that tears out pieces of wood two or three inches long to mound up at the base of trees. Despite how pileateds draw attention to themselves, these birds are shy.

But not this pair that were working on the beech, digging out a cavity for a nest. At first, we tried to be as quiet as possible, not wanting to disturb them. We were concerned about the weekend coming up when a troop of friends would arrive to participate in this spring ritual, and to glory in the season's change that the flow of sap means. Sugaring would be a buzz of activity. But how about these woodpeckers? Wouldn't they be driven away? As it turned out, those birds completely ignored us. We, of course, were fascinated by them. The weekend was spent with all of us—birds and humans—carrying on within sight of each other the imperative demands of the season.

The sugar shed we built was a three-walled shelter made of logs. We placed the evaporator in front, out in the open, set on a fireplace of rocks. A step or two away, we constructed a woodshed, roofed over, that held four cords, stacking the wood in four-foot lengths, leaving an alleyway down the middle where we could saw and split under cover. A big part of each day was keeping up with the wood. That, along with the tasks of bringing in the sap, keeping the fire stoked to the maximum, monitoring the evaporator by adding sap as needed, and tending to the small fireplace next to it on which we finished off the syrup, could engage many willing hands.

How busy we were was dictated by the flow of sap. If it was light, say the buckets were at most only a third full, it didn't take us long to zip around the sugarbush. We had settled on tapping eighty-eight trees, in large part because eighty-eight names could be fitted conveniently in three columns on both sides of an index card. One year, however, we expanded to one hundred trees because we were curious about so many trees we hadn't yet tapped. It turned out to be an overabundant yield of sap that year, and many of those trees were a good distance (uphill!) from the sugar shed. A visit to just two trees could fill our gathering pails. Of course, this was wonderfully exciting, but it was also exhausting. We made twenty-two gallons of syrup that year, and the next year backed down to a more sustainable eighty-eight trees.

While we loved a spirited day of overflowing buckets, it was often a relief when a run petered out and we could catch up with wood. There was a rhythm to the sap flow, and just when we were congratulating ourselves that we had it figured out, it would surprise us. I recall a morning when we awoke to a temperature that had sat at thirty-three degrees all night. It looked like we'd have an easy day of it, just picking up what had dripped late yesterday's afternoon. The temperature had not dropped low enough to get the pumping action in the maples started again. After breakfast Guy thought he might amble down to check a few buckets on our more vigorous maples. I was mentally planning my day when I heard Guy sprint onto our porch shouting that the trees were dripping like maniacs, must have been running all night, some buckets *already* close to overflowing. How could that be? What prompted that pumping action? This was only one of the unexpected mysteries of sugaring, reasons known only to *Acer saccharum*, that had us shaking our heads and putting on our boots, happy servants to the flow of sap.

∾

. . . a period following the close of the winter tree-cutting and preceding the barking season, when the saps are just beginning to heave with the force of hydraulic lifts inside all the trunks of the forest.

—Thomas Hardy, *The Woodlanders*

Sometimes overflowing buckets meant we'd be boiling all night. Sugar makers are well advised to boil down their sap as quickly as possible. Cool temperatures can keep raw sap, but when the thermometer crests in the fifties and stays there, the sap will grow cloudy and the syrup will lose its maple taste. The commercial folks have huge refrigerator tanks, temperature set to thirty-three degrees, where they can hold the sap for as long as they want. But those without that option must move fast and, in our case, all-night boils were often a necessity when our sugarbush was in a state of eruption. Such events were unplanned on our part; they happened at the whim and will of the trees. That's what made them so energizing and delightful—the trees called the dance.

One of us would dash up to the cabin for sleeping bags, grab something for dinner, and breakfast, too. (We often used the fire to heat food. We were expert at toasted cheese for lunch and offering our guests tea with maple syrup for sweetening.) Meanwhile one of us was madly sawing and splitting wood while we still had daylight, enough wood to carry us through the night. Then we settled in, knowing the night would be clear and cold, but knowing as well that we'd be perfectly comfortable with the advantage of the evaporator directly in front of the shelter—our stone hearth not so enclosed as to prevent it from throwing out a good deal of heat. Inefficient for boiling down sap, but well suited to keeping all sugar makers comfortable throughout the season.

Guy and I divided the night into shifts, and if we made sufficient inroads into the glut of sap, we could stop stoking the fire and crawl into a sleeping bag.

These were magical nights. One of us, on watch, sat on the edge of the shelter in the dark, listening to the fire burn—big logs that crackled and popped and sparked and shifted, hard at work consuming themselves. You were alone with these sounds, and in the dark you found yourself paying attention to the hissing, sloshing, churning of sap at a rolling boil, with the kind of attention you didn't give to it during the business of the day. Every now and then you'd stir yourself to check the level in the pan with a stick marked for inches to see if you needed to add sap. If the answer was yes, you went into a side bay of the shelter and scooped out a pailful from the tubs. Adding the cold sap cut the boil, changing the sound coming from the evaporator. But the roiling soon returned, a reassuring sound that signaled all was right in your world, deep in the forest, participating with these trees in the acknowledgment of the earth's inevitable turning toward the sun, once again.

We witnessed, over the years, on these nighttime vigils, several eclipses of the moon, and, in 1986, the appearance of Halley's comet, coming into view on his seventy-five-year rotation. In early April 1997, our all-night boiling corresponded with the appearance of the comet Hale-Bopp, who remained in the sky for several nights. And we could track the stars. There was rarely a breeze. These were cold, still nights with the temperature dropping below the freezing mark.

I remember how, at the beginning of my watch, the time seemed just to creep along. It took my mind and body awhile to adjust to the slow pace—little to do other than adding wood and sap. Not enough light to read by. As the night progressed, I found myself taking in all the information I needed through my senses: the sound of sap busily bubbling, evaporating off that water, the sweetness of the air around me as the sap thickened, and the smell of smoke, too. The syrup we bottled carried that smoky sweetness, preserving those days, and especially the nights, of our lives spent sugaring. When I was to awaken Guy, I would find myself giving him another fifteen minutes, and then another, not wanting to end this suspended state fueled by the sounds and smells the sap and the wood made, not wanting to break out of a world created by these elements that seemed to close down the passage of time.

This weird and wonderful suspension, Guy told me, happened to him as well. And he, as I had, extended his watch, not wanting the spell to end.

But dawn, inevitably, pushed away the darkness, making room for day. The tree shapes grew visible, the maples we knew by name, sporting their buckets that we had painted green. No pinging, ringing drip of sap yet, still too cold. But we were up, one of us sawing wood, the other adding sap to the evaporator, stoking the fire, sparks flying upward. All of us in the routine: Mad Dog, Everest, those faithful sugar maples, and this year's rookies, Black Sheep and Galahad, all of our sugarbush swept up in the urgent work marked by the season's change, partners in the ancient golden harvest of sweetness and miracles.

9

Of Time and Mountains

I imagine there will always be divided opinions on how to relate to time when we go to the mountains. On the curve of lenient to obsessive, Guy and I kept a vigilant eye on the passage of time—not that we constantly referred to our watches, more that we stayed clued in to the path of the sun, or lengthening shadows, or other hints that the day was running its course. Whatever camp you're in, you probably have a strong opinion. We used our column in New England Outdoors *to express ours. Twenty-nine years later, I was delighted to write again on this perennial subject at the request of Christine Woodside, Appalachia's most able editor, for the Summer/Fall 2007 issue, in an essay titled "Giving Ourselves Time to Track Time."*

Keeping track of time seems to be something we humans need to do. For better or worse it's how we run our lives. Guy told me of a favorite uncle whose casual relation with time had him missing his steamship for Europe. This was a funny story that typified this uncle and went around the family. This would never happen to most people, certainly not to Guy, who knew how to make time work for him. He used clocks and three-by-five index cards to keep him on track. The word "downtime" was not in his vocabulary.

I have a looser connection to time, but not by much. This, I suppose, was fortunate in terms of our marriage. Interestingly, I've found during these last two decades without him, that keeping track of time is a high priority for me in terms of daily living. Does it make me more productive? That's the object, but who can say? Downtime? If you count reading as downtime it's a necessary part of my life. The point is, I guess, finding our own comfort level with this universal construct called Time.

~

As if you could kill time without injuring eternity.

—Henry David Thoreau, *Walden; or, Life in the Woods*

Basically, Guy and I wanted to present the other side of an argument going around in the late 1960s, early 1970s, that people should get away from time when they went to the woods. Leave the watches at home, the argument went, because here was a chance to be "spontaneous"—a word carried over from those years—and turn our backs on the time pressures and clock watching of the workday life.

Thinking about this caused us to ask ourselves a question: How do we want to relate to time when we go to the mountains? It seemed to us that how we keep track of time affects our relationship to the land, and to wildness itself.

Isn't this a worthwhile question to ask ourselves again with each generation that looks to wild places? Certainly those who came of age in the horse-and-buggy days had a different relationship to time than did the 1960s generation that grew up with traffic jams, television, transistor radios, and the telephone, and the 1980s–1990s generation that grew up with Internet access, iPods, cell phones, text messaging, and ever-speedier highway systems leading to the mountains.

Back in the 1970s, when Guy and I wrote that piece in *New England Outdoors*, we understood how a timeless Edenic innocence could be an appealing notion if, on the job, you felt beaten down by the daily grind. But it made no sense to us why anyone should want to actually get away from time when on weekends in the mountains. On our hiking trips, there always seemed to be many good reasons to know what time it was: How soon should we start making camp if we didn't want to be cleaning up from dinner in the dark? Have we got time to take that side trip over to the other summit? How can we be sure to get up early enough to be on the trail at first light, so we can be above treeline to watch the sun rise? In winter—days are short then—when should we set our turnaround time so as to have the steepest part of the descent or that dicey stream crossing behind us in daylight?

All these seemed like practical situations (and goals) we would need a clock for, but, as it evolved, neither of us wanted to keep track of time by wearing a watch. I wore a watch during the week—we were working in New York City at the time—and kept it stuffed in my pocket on weekends. Was it that wearing a watch in the mountains pushed time front and center, in our faces? Whether this was so or not, Guy tended to break watches. One was ripped from his wrist by a stub of a stunted spruce as he glissaded down a steep snow slope on Mount Clay. Another suffered a smashed crystal in a climbing fall in the Shawangunks. Keeping track of time in the mountains, for Guy, was getting to be expensive, but then he had always been hard on equipment.

After fooling around with pocket watches he kept losing, Guy finally decided on an alarm clock and purchased the large, round, white-faced kind they sold in the dime store. Later, after the clock malfunctioned on a winter hiking trip and we slept through an intended predawn start to awaken in a sun-drenched tent, he bought a second clock as a backup. In winter, with those short daylight hours, it was even more essential to keep track of the time, so Guy carried both clocks in his shirt to keep their works from stalling out in the cold. At night, he slept with them in his sleeping bag. Eccentric? Well, sure. But it was a practical solution that worked for him, and he had no trouble working such eccentricities into his personal style. For instance, if a hiker stopped us to ask the time, Guy would obligingly dig a hand into his shirt and haul out the dime store clock—this in the midst of the snowy woods in January, miles from the nearest highway. The hiker would take a step back. Guy, eager to provide the questioner with more assurance, would rummage around in his shirt again and produce, with an impish grin, the second large, white-faced clock.

Though clocks had a bad reputation with the spontaneous set who went to the mountains to lose track of time in the 1970s, our various timepieces served us well. The problem of time, we discovered, was not with time itself, but how we treat time. That is, in our work-week lives we can fracture it, overfill it, break it, bend it, and stuff it with distractions, all of which can upset us, causing us to feel stressed and harried, and to chafe against the time.

Guy and I certainly found this to be the case when we first started climbing together while we both were working in New York City offices. Our lives were divided into workdays and weekends in a way that was creating split personalities. Each Friday, after work, we made the long drive on snowy roads through the night to get to the Adirondacks. We set up the tent in the dark and were in our sleeping bags by midnight. The alarm went off in the dark. We ate breakfast in the dark, made the short drive to the trailhead in the dark and were strapping on snowshoes in the half-light. We climbed everything in sight on Saturday and Sunday. Sped back home Sunday night in the dark, feeling great but exhausted until Tuesday, recovered by Wednesday, and were ready to repeat the whole process by Friday night. It was crazy, we said, but if we wanted to spend weekends climbing mountains we had no choice.

It was getting harder and harder, though, to show up in the office on Monday morning. There the time passed so differently. In an office, you were often just waiting, the meetings dragged on, the report you were working on was putting you to sleep, and you found you couldn't keep your eyes off the clock, whose hands hadn't appeared to budge for the last half hour. You wished time could just slip away. Then the boss walked in and dumped a job on you that jeopardized your weekend, which you weren't about to compromise, so now you were so busy that you were rushing from one task to the next. At the end of the day you were not sure where the time had gone, and you felt like you hadn't accomplished anything. As you packed up your briefcase to begin the commute back home, you were plagued with a nagging feeling that your whole life seemed to be disintegrating in a way that was tedious, unproductive, and, worst of all, totally unfulfilling.

In the mountains, we feel the opposite about time. We want it neither to slip away nor to speed up, and keeping track of it becomes vital in a very different way than in the office. Here we're aware of where we are in the passage of the day by the way the light changes. We're attuned to our environment, to the woods, to the wind, to where we are in space, and where we are in time too. Contrary to what we'd thought, which was that because we aren't in the office we can forget time, we find time becomes not less important, but if anything more important, even though we don't need a clock to track it. Perhaps we might refer to our watches, but we sense more from the quality of light whether we have time for another peak or whether it's time to find a camping spot and put up the tent. In the mountains, the clock no longer rules as it did in the office but takes its place as a useful tool for integrating the passage of time in a way that seems to positively inform everything we do. In the mountains we understand what poets mean when they write that time flows, that time is a river. Here time no longer feels split, and our lives have stopped feeling broken up into little bits.

In 1973 all that changed for Guy and me when we moved to Vermont and became homesteaders. When you've set your life so you haul your wood and water, your notion of time changes. You've changed your relationship to time when you can't drive quickly to your own front door. In fact, something you didn't expect has happened. Instead of having less time, you feel like you have more: you've planned in that extra half hour of walking time it takes to reach the car, and walking is all you do during that time. And thinking, and observing, and listening: that scratching in the leaves to the right is a white-throated sparrow; the ferns are uncurling (*note to self: pick fiddleheads*). You feel relaxed and very rich in time. And you feel a close connection to the land because you're experiencing time in a way that tunes you into the land itself, and wildness.

We managed to erase that boundary between how we lived during the week and what we did on weekends, the split that came from fracturing the time, chopping our lives into little bits in the office, and the even larger split we felt between our "working" lives and what we did for "play" on weekends.

By radically changing our lives, we had brought into alignment these two separate parts. Now they felt more of a piece, more whole. The mountains had become a natural extension that led from our cabin in the clearing, to our vegetable garden, to our woodlot, and beyond.

Time spent at home felt the same as that spent in the mountains—the split feeling was mostly gone. (I'll get to that "mostly" in a moment.) But, at its best, our life on our homestead felt integrated and real. It meant something to us to live in a way that made us solely responsible for growing what we ate, heating our house, and all the other daily tasks of keeping a homestead going.

There was nothing casual about how we treated time. The only major change was that Guy traded in the big white-faced alarm clocks for a small and silent travel model that he kept stowed in his pocket.

Thoreau said, "Time is but the stream I go a-fishing in," which conjures up for me all the mornings Guy and I spent in our garden. In spring we forked under the soil, laying out rows of carrots or beets or beans and taking time to get each row straight. In our woodlot, we took care to see how a tree would fall and made the notch just so, the ax blows precise—a solid *thunk*—not rushing the felling so, no matter how large the tree, by pacing ourselves through our two-person crosscuts we would be fresh at the end and ready for the next saw cut. It was like walking up a mountain trail: how you felt at the end of the day was set by the pace you established at the beginning.

It all comes back to time. We'd regulated the pace to the speed of Thoreau's stream when we'd moved to our homestead. On those mornings we spent a-fishing, the time passed in a quiet, gentle, unhurried way, and by noon we had a lot to show for our labor. By the beginning of June, the garden we'd begun at the end of April was planted and growing. By late fall, the wood cords behind our house were filled from the work in our woodlot that had begun in May.

On our homestead, we were living also by the broader marking of time: the seasons. The snow-free months were our busiest time, though we could always fit in the occasional day trip. We learned how to blend in the longer trips, too. We could be gone for nearly two weeks rock climbing in the Shawangunks after sugaring and return in time to plant peas. By the Fourth of July, the garden was fully mulched and growing well, so in the lull between canning the peas and canning broccoli we could take nearly a week in the White Mountains. In mid-September, after the early fall harvest and the first killing frost, we fit in, over a period of several years, hiking most of Vermont's Long Trail.

Even in the winter, when we spent more of the day inside, we were outside enough—in the light—to feel the natural flow of time. And since there was less to do on our homestead, we had more time for the mountains, needing only to return home after four or five days to warm up the cabin so as to keep the temperature in our root cellar above freezing.

"Remember that time is money," Benjamin Franklin famously advised a young tradesman. In a sense, he had it backward. Yes, we needed to earn money, but we'd cut what we spent money on to the bone. Reducing expenses meant the need for income was reduced, an important part of our plan as it gave us more time.

By starting small—articles for outdoor magazines—Guy and I moved on to books. We wrote about what we knew: environmental problems we saw in the 1970s and 1980s that resulted from the backpacking boom. Of concern to us was: the well-being of the mountains and how all of us who come to hike can play a part not only in their restoration, but in keeping them healthy. Our wage-earning lives—that is, our jobs—and our mountain lives had fallen into alignment. They weren't fighting each other for time. The time between them had smoothed out and overlapped. Each shared the other's time in a way that fed both. Neither wasted nor took time from the other but extended from it naturally, blending to make a complete life. It was a satisfying feeling and it had been our fondest hope when we made the big move from New York.

Yet sometimes, as I hinted earlier, we could get ourselves in trouble with time. This happened when we took on too much and over-heaped our plates and, to mix the metaphor, the waters of Thoreau's stream got roiled and the fishing lines snagged. Well, fishing lines do snag sometimes. And it's a tedious business to untangle them. When this happened, we found ourselves running from one task to another, as we had in our New York office days. "Multitasking" is the popular word that describes this frenzied state, and suddenly we were right back in that old disjointed, fractured feeling we thought we'd left behind.

Our homesteading life worked best if we did one thing at a time: spend one morning working in the garden, then the next in the woodlot, and the morning after that write a magazine article. When we tried, for one reason or another, to crowd the schedule, we were right back in the office, feeling we couldn't give anything the attention it deserved, feeling harried one moment and wishing time would move faster the next, having troubles with concentration because we were too distracted to give our full concentration to any one thing. Worst of all, we couldn't connect to what we were doing, not in a way that meant something. We couldn't connect with the birds singing in our clearing, or with the clouds sailing overhead, or even with each other. The small travel clock, which usually sat quietly in Guy's pocket, was being pulled out at increasing intervals. Our lives were no longer calm and peaceful but became controlled by a strange outside artificial manipulation known as "The Job." The clock no longer informed what we wanted to be doing but stood in its way. In these painful moments, Hamlet's phrase, "Time is out of joint," described our situation.

Hikers coming to the mountains these days are dealing with some very complex time issues. The temptation is to multitask. You're "just" walking up the trail, so why not pull out the cell phone to talk to your secretary or your business partner, or even your mother at the same time? Or, why not listen to your iPod? Well, sure. But if you do, you're no longer aware of the birds or noticing the undergrowth or paying attention to the play of light and shadow across the path you're walking on. If you're with others—your friends, your life partner, your children—you're not paying attention to them either. Even though you're at this moment walking through the woods and in nature, you're not part of it. You're disconnected. You're absorbed only in listening to the words, the tunes, coming into your ear, and you're missing all the wildness that surrounds you. You're disconnected from your friend, partner, child, too. In fact, you're disconnected from yourself: you're mentally in the space of the phone call or the iPod list, and only physically in the woods. You've split yourself.

Thinking about this makes me ask: How can we care for land, for wild land, if we disconnect ourselves from it—even when we're in it? How can we truly care for that to which we aren't connected? If we don't want this kind of disconnected relationship to land, what can we do?

We can stop. We can just stop!

If we don't want to disconnect and experience those fractured feelings that leave us unhappy, dissatisfied, then . . . just connect. Restraint is necessary here, even modification of habit. (*Memo: On the next mountain trip leave the cell, the iPod, etc., at home.*)

Now that we've put ourselves in a position to connect, we can feel respect for the woods, the land, wild land, wildness itself, for surely we can't care for that for which we feel no respect. We'll be giving ourselves time to be fully *in* it. We'll feel respect for time itself, because we're giving ourselves time to savor it.

And this leads to the most important thing of all. We can respect ourselves. We're no longer clumsily fighting time, but by gracefully being in ourselves, in the land, and in time, you might say we put ourselves in a state of grace.

~

Oh, my ears and whiskers how late it's getting.

—Lewis Carroll, *Alice's Adventures in Wonderland*

Guy was more time conscious than I was. Not that I was casual about time. I hated to keep friends waiting, so was generally early.

But Guy had a highly evolved sense of time. As I saw it, for him every second counted. Every second could be put to good use. Certainly this played out at Barra, but right now I'm thinking, particularly, about how Guy made use of time in the mountains.

I had not known him very long when he invited me to join him on a hike he had planned in the White Mountains over the Fourth of July. He'd be accompanied by his dog, Ralph, an experienced hiker who had already climbed all the 4,000-foot peaks at least once. There are forty-eight of them. I was not fully recovered from that ruptured Achilles tendon surgery. This would be a four-day, three-night backpacking trip. I had camped out, but not on a multi-night backpacking trip. I was thrilled that Guy had invited me, not just because I found him so fascinating and fun to be with, but this would be my first major excursion in the White Mountains that I had heard so much about from the Gunks climbers. I was most anxious to learn all I could about backpacking. Guy had already proved a skilled teacher on rock. Now I would develop mountaineering skills.

We left Guy's tan Volkswagen Bug in Crawford Notch and began the ascent of Mount Willey via the Ethan Pond Trail. We stopped at the junction with the trail leading to the summit of Willey and Guy proposed we'd drop our packs here for this quick steep climb. He pulled a three-by-five index card out of his shirt pocket, looked at his watch and assured me we were doing great. Whatever that meant it sounded good to me, and, without those heavy packs, we nearly flew up to the summit. Then tore back down to regain our loads and head for Zealand Notch on the Ethan Pond Trail. We camped that first night somewhere in there choosing a pretty woodsy spot, heating up our freeze-dried meal on Guy's compact backpacking stove. Ralph gobbled down his dog food.

As it grew dark we crawled into the tent. Guy explained to Ralph that there wasn't room for him, but Ralph was determined to be included, which he demonstrated by whining and refusing to budge from the tent's entrance. "Ralph has always slept with me, you see," Guy said, "but there is really not room for three." I assured Guy that I'd be delighted to share space with Ralph. I meant this. Ralph was a lovable dog. So Ralph was ushered in and was asked to stay at the bottom of the tent. During the course of the night Ralph managed to insinuate himself between us, so that his furry head was on a level with ours. He was very clever about this. We were never aware of movement, yet he moved. This was to be the case from then on with Ralph on camping trips. Ralph would obediently curl up at our feet and end up where he wanted to be—a cozy threesome!

On Independence Day we packed up the Zeacliff Trail and along the Twinway to Mount Guyot, then down to the shelter. We erected our tent and ate our sandwiches, sitting on the front edge of the shelter. Guy pulled out his index cards and said, "Good. We'll trot over to the Twins." He began getting ready by tightening the laces on his boots.

"You mean now?" I asked.

He just smiled and asked how I was feeling and if there was any reason I wanted to linger longer. There was no reason, I told him, other than I just was enjoying sitting here in the woods.

It was at this moment that I began to become aware of the use Guy Waterman was making of these three-by-five index cards. He had explained them to me when we were about to ascend Willey, but I wasn't paying much attention. Now he said, showing me a card, "I use these to schedule times, calculated against mileages, including rest stops." That hadn't made much sense then. But now the whole picture snapped into focus as Guy said, "If we don't leave now, we compromise reaching both Twins—South and North." He was looking at me closely. His eyes were a striking shade of gray. "It is unlikely we'll be back this way in the foreseeable future. That aside, it is most desirable to be cooking dinner in daylight." His boots retied he hopped to the ground. "When we return from the Twins, Laura," he gave me another of his dazzling smiles, "you can spend the whole evening right here in these woods." He waved his arm to show this view of evergreens and a mix of birches, an impenetrable forest of green.

I got the picture! This was my revelatory moment into the character of Guy Waterman. He lived a scheduled, planned life. I saw that if I chose to remain with Guy (for life, as I hoped to do) I would need to agree with the concept. I had always paid attention to the time, but this elevated time's importance in everyday life. Yet, I understood what such planning allowed, which was to make excellent and efficient use of *time*.

On the morning of the fifth we left Guyot shelter to pack over Mount Bond and Bondcliff, dropped down to the Wilderness Trail, crossed over to the Desolation Trail to ascend Mount Carrigain. The Desolation Trail is one of the steepest in the White Mountains. Guy said, "Why don't you go first and set the pace. That's what I had Bill and John do on steep trails. Until the day came when they announced that I should go first." He grinned. "We'll break it up with rest stops. Hike for twenty minutes, and then rest for five. Drink water, munch a little gorp. Take it in easy stages." This was another way to make time work for you, and that long ascent went by with surprising ease because, well, anyone can walk at a moderate pace for a short time period. Rest. And move on again. You benefit from the rhythm and, suddenly, you're on top of the mountain!

We set up our camp just down from the summit, then ran up the fire tower where Guy had stayed with Bill and John on their last and celebratory night of a two-week trip in 1966 on which they climbed all the White Mountain peaks over four thousand feet. Ralph was along on that trip, but now he was an old dog, and though we would have loved to have slept in the fire tower Ralph could not climb the stairs. Even if Guy could have carried him up—at ninety pounds—it didn't seem right to subject him, unable to descend, to that small space.

On our last day we packed down Carrigain and out via the Nancy Pond Trail—a long and weary slog. No summits. No excitement. It was an easy trail, but there was nothing to hold my attention or to anticipate. No views. No landmarks of special interest. Nothing to distract myself from how sore my feet were and how tired I felt. Ralph was tired, too, which he demonstrated by lying down in the middle of the trail. He did not respond to urging or coaxing or dog biscuits. So Guy said, "Let's keep walking. I think he'll be motivated by that." We kept looking back and calling him, and finally Ralph was on his feet, walking slowly, just keeping us in sight until we reached where we'd parked the Bug, at the Willey House Station.

Our itinerary had included seven summits. It was eye-opening for me in terms of the amount of ground covered. I felt great, that is, about what I'd accomplished. I realized I was at an advantage of not knowing anything. Meaning, I was not concerned about steep rough trails and whether I could do it or not. Climbing mountains was, basically, putting one foot in front of the other. Now that I knew what to expect, well, I had learned ways to manage pace, and time, too. It took several days for my Achilles tendon, swollen, to settle down. But before then I realized I'd loved this trip. I was back climbing with Guy the next weekend and it wasn't long after that I sublet my apartment and moved in, closer to the Gunks, making that two-and-a-half-hour commute into the city.

10

Counting Our Accomplishments

TEN YEARS Later

My husband loved numbers. Control was very important to Guy, so perhaps counting and numbering things at our wild homestead was a way to achieve that. In any event, we had been living happily at Barra for ten years, when, in his fashion, he summed up the decade by writing and lettering this document, which he titled "An Alphabet of Accomplishment." I created the text of this essay to fit around Guy's alphabetical calligraphy. It is published here courtesy of the Dartmouth College Library, where our papers are housed.

Reading through, in preparation for writing this headnote, I was struck, once again, by Guy's obsession with quantity and numbers. Yet, these numbers are anything but dry. They recall for me whole worlds and bring to life the nature of our work, our sheer enjoyment of it, and our pride in the accomplishment.

Starting with "A for Asparagus," I am amazed by the bounty of that bed: three rows twenty feet long that we kept well weeded, fertilized with manure, wood ash, lime, and, most important, maple leaves. We were told about the maple leaves by Lewis Hill, a great horticulturist and a great man from whom we bought our six apple trees and two pears and two plums. We raked up the maple leaves in the fall, in our woods, enclosing a great pile of them behind wire fencing wrapped around a few tree trunks. This was a seasonal job. Rain and winter snows settled the leaves and began their decomposition into an organic matter that we piled a foot high between the rows. Talk about satisfaction! The maple leaves guaranteed bounty and cut down weeding. We began eating those tender spears by mid-May—one of our first vegetables from the garden—and declared the Fourth of July the terminal date for asparagus season. From then on until the snows came we had the pleasure of watching the spears grow and branch, creating a fernlike effect, and giving us one of the most beautiful sights in our garden, especially when the early morning sun slanted through, sparking the dew into a sprinkle of diamonds.

Walking through our woodlot with ax and saw we could be surprised by an encounter with a red eft. This soft-bodied little creature, the eastern newt, in its innocence, its vulnerability, its adeptness at covering ground with its beautifully articulated limbs, always caused us to set our tools down and commune. There is something about the red eft that went straight to our hearts. Partly, I think, because they could be so easily stepped on. We could not help but pick them up. They, of course, seemed unperturbed and kept walking up our hands. We got the message, and set them down on the leaves out of the path, away from our clumsy human tread. But we didn't need to worry about them in terms of predators, since this newt carries a self-protecting toxin that tastes most unpleasant if bitten into.

Barra, the land itself with its three open acres surrounded by northern hard-
woods and a smattering of evergreens, struck us as ideal for attracting a great
variety of bird life. The flutelike notes of the hermit thrush could stop us in our
tracks. We would stand stock still as the bird began with the overture, a long
introductory key note, then came the body of his song with four or five phrases
in different pitches. That was the miracle of the hermit thrush, we said to each
other—to sing the same phrase but on different pitches. Guy could duplicate them
on his piano. We could also be stunned by the wood thrush's song, as clear as
a mountain stream, and by the veery, also a thrush, but a less common visitor,
who captivated us with his liquid and breezy downward trending whirring
whistle. These three birds were top contenders for the Medal of Mozart award
we gave out at the first of every month that they spent with us. We made a
small ceremony of these awards that included Bird of the Month and Bluebird
Award, by making an announcement from our porch after breakfast. It was
just silly fun, but it kept us tuned in. For instance, Guy noted we had heard
or seen the indigo bunting 396 times in that decade, most often making himself
known when we were working in the garden, causing us to stop work, and
Guy to take out his index card on which he recorded the birds heard or seen
daily at Barra, so as not to miss that flash of deep rich blue for which that
bird was well named.

Reading, that is reading aloud, held as important a place in our lives as gar-
dening or firewood collecting. The first a sedentary activity, the other strongly
physical. Both had their own mental component, though differing in nature.
The reading aloud entered our lives early, when it was discovered that Guy
and I ate at vastly different speeds. He could have won prizes among the fast
eaters of the world and I would have amassed a fortune in gold medals for the
slow masticators. The idea of Guy reading aloud while I consumed my dinner
not only solved this problem, but gave boundless pleasure of the sort you could
spend the day looking forward to. Our tastes in reading were similar, that is,
the English and American writers of the nineteenth century, novelists, that is.
Dickens, Sir Walter Scott, Hardy, Kipling for the English. Melville, Hawthorne,
Twain for Americans. Shakespeare, too, and books about animals, especially dogs.
In that first decade we read 979 literary works. We'd discuss what we'd read
while doing the dishes. As the years rolled by I discovered that this ritual formed
another purpose. If Guy's "demons" were plaguing him during the day, and I was
unable to help so felt the misery as well, somehow, the action of Guy's pulling
the book off the shelf and beginning to read seemed to restore his equilibrium,
or at least give respite to his raging moods. We both felt this, though we never

talked about it. It was relief enough to be back in sync, finding ourselves again united in the world of Oliver, or Ishmael, or Uriah Heep.

We were interested in the weather and kept close track of it as you will see under N: "Shivered through 32 Nights of 20 below"; R: "Measured 322.16" of Rain"; and S: "Shuffled through 806" of Snow."

There got to be a point in the winter when we'd raked enough snow off the north side of our roof that it was close to breasting the windowsills. We were always rooting for this, but to happen we needed winters of extra heavy snowfalls. One winter it finally happened that we had to shovel the snow away from the kitchen windows. We welcomed big snowfalls not only because we enjoyed snowshoeing, but because our small cabin became extra cozy with the wood fire burning—a true haven from that frigid air on the other side of the door. Aside from our mountain trips, we always wore our snowshoes when we walked the mile and a half to the village for our mail or to the library. We kept that path beat out, and the friends who came to see us considerately wore their snowshoes, too. So the path remained smooth. In a deep light snowfall you can maneuver almost without effort on snowshoes. Well, that's probably overstating it. We kept snow stakes—a yardstick attached to a pole—in three different locations. We averaged the daily depths and recorded them on the tally sheet. A big snow winter could mean thirty inches of snow on the ground. So if we were walking through the woods, our heads could be up among the lower branches. All this is what we found so exciting about big snow winters!

We kept track of rainfall as well. Adequate rain was always a concern for us since our stream was barely up to the job. So we worried when we were in a period of drought, and we worried when we got heavy, pounding deluges, too. We could be awakened by a storm of rain and lie in bed envisioning our road washing away. There was a notoriously steep hill that we had heavily water barred—that is, built drainage ditches. We kept these drains carefully scrapped out, a tricky job since it was important to keep the depth at a level a car could drive over. We'd listen to the rain pounding and felt the conflicting emotions: glad for our stream and concerned for our road. But that's how things are when you're living in a way that brings you close to nature.

If the temperatures in January and early February showed signs of going way below zero, we were always disappointed when it stopped the plunge short of twenty degrees below zero. Somehow nineteen below was not the same as a good solid twenty. We were treated to thirty below zero only once. And because this was so exciting we took the thermometer that was in the house and brought it outdoors—having dressed warmly for this experiment—for the thrill of watching the bulb drop from seventy degrees downward—a ninety degree plunge. WOW!

Barra was not a windy place, being protected by cliffy highland on the north side. We were glad of this. Winds can be tough on a garden. They can bend over corn and desiccate soils. We had several huge old ashes and red oaks near enough to the house that gave us concern for broken limbs that could land on the roof. This never happened. But on the first day of February 1974 a violent wind storm swept through the Northeast that caused a tree on the downhill edge of our clearing right below the garden to fall. We heard the crack at night from inside the house. We had noted this tree for its height and had speculated as to its years. We had named it the Empress Pine. In one way its death was well timed. We had just completed our first garden year and as yet we had not built our eight-foot fence. We had planted the posts but the wire was yet unstrung. That tree would have crashed right through that wire probably taking several posts with it. We also learned something about tree identification since we were newcomers to this. That lofty monarch we discovered was a spruce. But since we had begun by calling it the "Empress Pine" we continued to do so, just to memorialize that fateful windy night.

In the mid-1990s Guy began working on a map of Barra. His goal was to draw a map that showed our tree species in color: hardwoods in yellow made the dominant hue on the map. Sprinkled in were the evergreens (spruce, fir, hemlock, white pine) in shades of green and blue. He spent an hour or so on many afternoons tramping around with his compass and notebook. This was something Guy liked to do and was good at. I enjoyed hearing about his progress, and I believe his absorption in the work quelled his "demons." He took as his model the maps in Tolkien's Lord of the Rings trilogy, simple line drawings showing the natural features, roads and paths, streams and rivers, and other points of interest. The end result of Guy's map framed, measured seventeen by twenty-one inches with a key to the colored areas—not just the trees, but the open land around our cabin and garden, our orchard, and our sixteen blueberry bushes planted in a circle. Our sugar shed, a five- or six-minute walk from our cabin, was well placed in the center of our sugar bush on a small knoll. We had named various areas in the sugar bush to be able to refer to them when we were collecting sap: the Forest of Arden contained trees named for characters in Shakespeare. The Highlands was the location of our largest maples, named for the 8,000-meter Himalayan peaks, or Middle Earth, Tolkien again, with names drawn from those books. We estimated our forest had been logged about seventy-five years before we acquired the property, making it around the turn of the twentieth century. We could trace two of those old logging roads, perhaps six to eight feet wide, making a relatively flat surface. They became useful to us when we were first learning our way around our woods. We gave them names—Floating Birch Road for a yellow birch whose roots wrapped around a fallen trunk to reach the ground, and West Road for its location. They became the beginning of our path system. More paths grew as the sugaring became an important part of our lives. From the cabin there were several paths to reach the sugar shed; there were, as well, a number of paths to reach the maples we tapped. Some maples were right off the path itself or not far from it. We needed to make collecting sap as convenient and efficient as possible. Our land was hilly and we had tried to contour our paths as much as we could. It wasn't so much the paths that acquired names, as the places they accessed. So if I said to Guy I was going over to the sugar shed and then up to the Highlands, he would have an exact picture of where I'd be. In this way Barra became its own contained world. This can happen when you put down roots on the landscape. You find, as you go about your daily living, that you've grown into the land itself.

Using the letters—twenty-six in the standard English alphabet—Guy tallied up the thrust of our life—the decade from June 9, 1973, when we moved to the land and began homesteading, to June 9, 1983, ten years later.[1]

AN

ALPHABET of
ACCOMPLISHMENT

The ABC's of what we've been doing
for the past ten years . . .

of a lot of good friends (. . . with the help
in many cases!)

Laura and Guy Waterman
Barra - East Corinth Vermont
June 9, 1983

---

1. Note to readers: Please read with caution, bearing in mind that the images and the text do not always line up.

This alphabet includes counts of what we grew and harvested from our vegetable garden, starting with "A" for asparagus: that is, *exactly how many* asparagus spears we picked.

Since moving to Barra on June 9, 1973, we have. . . ⟶

We planted fruit trees and blueberry bushes. "B," for example, is for blueberries. In that ten-year period we picked 19,107 berries from our sixteen highbush blueberry bushes.

A

GROWN
1,356 A̲ SPARAGUS SPEARS

That's through 1982. To that,
add _211_ grown through
June 8, 1983.

A IS FOR ASPARAGUS

Yes, we counted individual berries, and we noted the name of the bush (blue ray, blue crop) that the berry came from. Our friend Chuck discovered this, much to his chagrin, when he showed Guy his box of berries and proudly announced how many he'd picked. Guy said (with a grin), "But from which bushes?"

PICKED
19,107 **B**LUEBERRIES

At Barra, that is... that's not counting uncounted blueberries atop Percy Peak and elsewhere.

B IS FOR BLUEBERRIES

I won't go into the explanation of why we counted individual berries. If inclined, you can read about it in my memoir, *Losing the Garden*. I'll just say it made perfect sense at the time.

CUT
68.7 **C**ORDS OF WOOD

with bucksaw and ax,
crosscut and peavey

C IS FOR CORDS OF WOOD

The canning of all this produce was, of course, vital to see us through winter months. You'll find the statistics on canning under "J is for Jars": quarts and pints.

CLIMBED

1 BLACK DIKE

. . . just once, on
St. Patrick's Day, 1975
. . . once is enough.

D IS FOR BLACK DIKE

Thoreau served as our model for keeping track of our lives on a daily, even hourly, basis. So you'll find here, alphabetically, records on birds observed as well as the other creatures who lived in our woods. You'll find what kind of weather data we collected: how much rain, how much snow in that ten-year period.

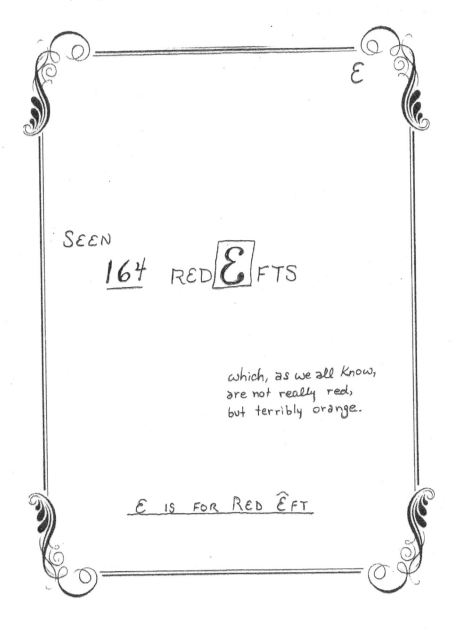

$\mathcal{E}$

SEEN
164 RED $\mathcal{E}$ FTS

which, as we all know,
are not really red,
but terribly orange.

$\mathcal{E}$ IS FOR RED ÊFT

(To add an aside here, I admit to looking at our minimum/maximum temperatures every morning on our master list—a list we maintained for just short of thirty years—along with our average daily temperatures. This ritual has impressed on me the presence of a warming climate, at least as observed in my corner of the world. Check out the letter "N," for "Nights at 20° below," and see what you think.)

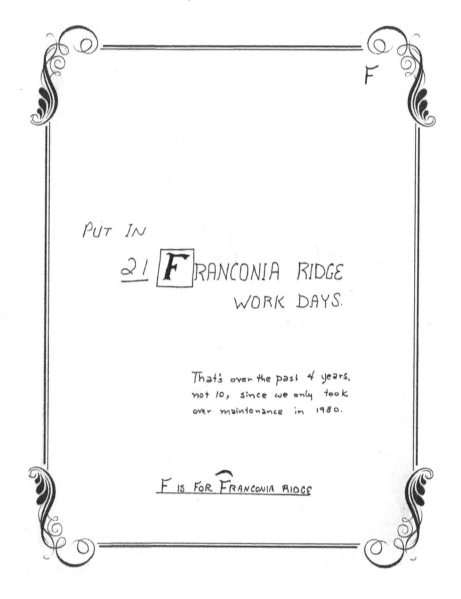

PUT IN

21 [F]RANCONIA RIDGE
WORK DAYS.

That's over the past 4 years, not 10, since we only took over maintenance in 1980.

F IS FOR FRANCONIA RIDGE

Guy had a lot to say about sugaring: for instance, how much sap we carried, from the trees to the sugar shed, in terms of weight, figuring eight pounds per gallon. We hung buckets on our trees, emptied them into our gathering pails, and lugged them by hand, wearing snowshoes.

WELCOMED

1,371 **G**UESTS

... OR RATHER
GUEST APPEARANCES, SINCE
many OF THESE HAVE BEEN
WELCOMED REPEATS.

(THIS TOTAL OMITS ONLY THE
BIG TRAIL RIDES CROWDS.)

G IS FOR GUESTS

Keeping track of how much sap each tree produced during the season was a high point of our year. Sugaring gave us such a close connection with our maples that it made a whole world in itself.

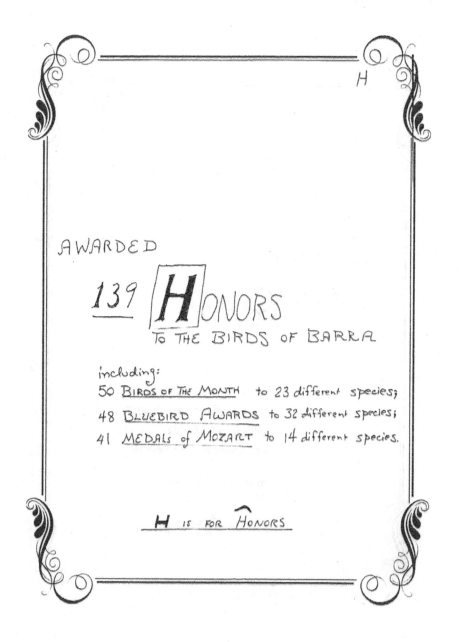

AWARDED

_139_ **H**ONORS

To THE BIRDS OF BARRA

including:

50 BIRDS OF THE MONTH to 23 different species;

48 BLUEBIRD AWARDS to 32 different species;

41 MEDALS of MOZART to 14 different species.

H IS FOR HONORS

We collected our wood for cooking and heating our house, and also for sugaring, with axes—double bit for Guy, single for me—and saws: bucksaws and crosscut. Motorized equipment required maintenance skills we lacked and was smelly and noisy, drowning out birdsong and the wind stirring through the trees.

HEARD

396 INDIGO BUNTING
SERENADES

THIS NUMBER IS THE TOTAL OF DAYS
ON WHICH WE'VE SEEN OR HEARD THE
INDIGO BUNTING, THROUGH 1982.

THROUGH JUNE 8, 1983, ADD __10__ MORE.

I IS FOR INDIGO

Was it only the two of us who did all this work? Oh, no! We had many visitors, many of whom were returnees, who came to help with garden work, sugaring, wood collecting, and even helping us to count a blueberry or two.

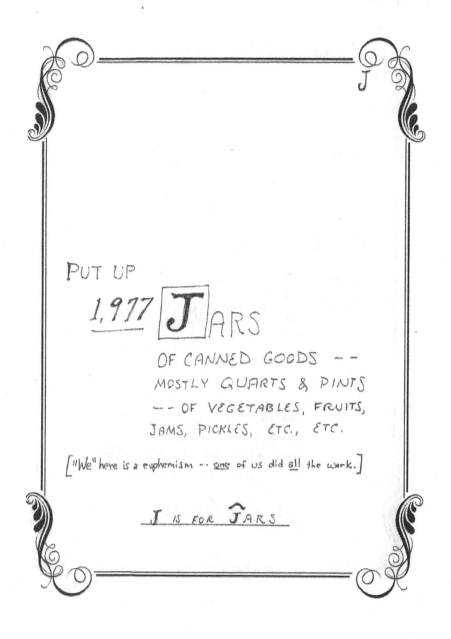

PUT UP

1,977 JARS

OF CANNED GOODS --
MOSTLY QUARTS & PINTS
-- OF VEGETABLES, FRUITS,
JAMS, PICKLES, ETC., ETC.

["We" here is a euphemism -- one of us did all the work.]

J IS FOR JARS

Since we climbed as much as we possibly could, and winter gave us the most time for climbing, check out mountain statistics under "M," for mountains.

K

EATEN

4 2 1 KOHLRABI

... ah, delicious Kohlrabi

K IS FOR KOHLRABI

Reading aloud: this was our nightly after-dinner ritual. Guy did the reading while I, a famously slow eater, finished my meal.

READ
97 *L*ITERARY WORKS
OUT LOUD TOGETHER AFTER DINNER.

L IS FOR *L*ITERATURE

Franconia Ridge trail work days are included, too, under "F," for the beautiful Franconia Ridge; because the work there required the same care and thought as our homesteading work, we considered it an extension of our "backyard."

BAGGED

<u>98</u> **M**OUNTAIN PEAKS

OF THE WHITE MOUNTAINS
IN WINTER TOGETHER.

A FEW IN THE ADIRONDACKS
PUT THIS FIGURE OVER 100;
AND OF COURSE IT DOES NOT
INCLUDE MANY CLIMBED SEPARATELY.

<u>M</u> IS FOR MOUNTAINS
(OF COURSE)

Music. We had Guy's Steinway grand piano. Guests came with their own musical instruments.

SHIVERED THROUGH

32 NIGHTS AT 20° BELOW

and 105 at 10° below,
and one at 30° below.

N IS FOR NIGHTS BELOW 0.

Our friend Nancy once strapped her cello on her back, wrapping it in her sleeping bag to protect it from the cold.

PUT AWAY
3,409 ONIONS

O IS FOR ÔNIONS

It was winter, so of course she snowshoed to our cabin. The violinists had a much easier time of it. As did the violists.

PROUDLY PLUCKED

89 **P**LUMS

... that's in just one year, so watch this figure grow!

P IS FOR PLUMS

The letter T needs explanation.

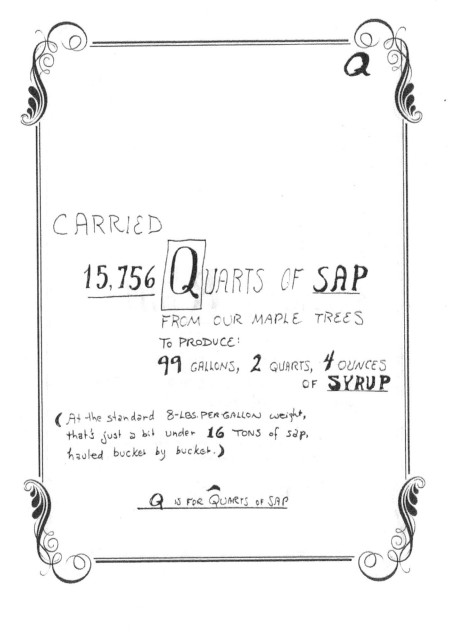

CARRIED

15,756 QUARTS of SAP

FROM OUR MAPLE TREES

To PRODUCE:

99 GALLONS, 2 QUARTS, 4 OUNCES OF **SYRUP**

(At the standard 8-LBS. PER GALLON weight, that's just a bit under 16 TONS of sap, hauled bucket by bucket.)

Q IS FOR QUARTS OF SAP

Since Guy pronounced "tomato" with a long drawn-out "a," and I was brought up to turn that "a" into "ah," and each of us refused to give in, we found a comfortable compromise by calling the tomato *Malawi*.

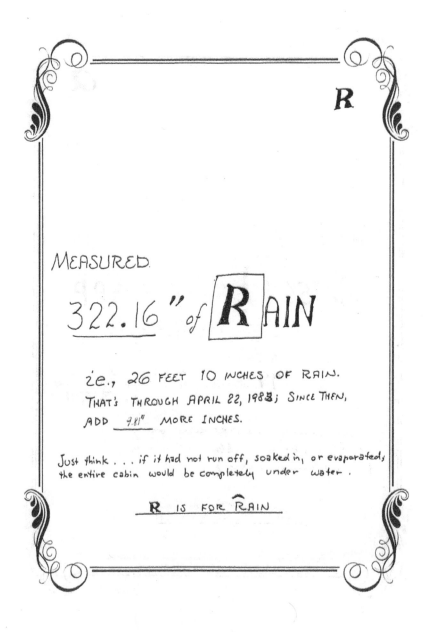

MEASURED.

322.16" of **R**AIN

i.e., 26 FEET 10 INCHES OF RAIN.
THAT'S THROUGH APRIL 22, 1988; SINCE THEN,
ADD 7.81" MORE INCHES.

Just think . . . if it had not run off, soaked in, or evaporated, the entire cabin would be completely under water.

R IS FOR RAIN

Guy chose this name.

SHUFFLED THROUGH
806" of Snow

ie, 67 feet --

wouldn't it be nice to get
that much every winter?

S IS FOR SNOW

We had a friend who was living in Malawi at the time. Well . . . silly, I know. Such was daily life at Barra.

NIBBLED

5,009 TASTY MALAWI

- all home-grown -

T IS FOR MALAWI ?

"U" is for hugs, *U*nlimited . . .

SHARED

. . . UNLIMITED HUGS

. . . UNNUMBERED

U IS FOR HUGS

Well, the point of this document was to include every letter of the alphabet.

V

PROUDLY PRODUCED

ONE VERY OWN - GROWN
APPLE

...not counting hundreds of apples
from the wild trees already here...

V IS FOR VERY-OWN

Now I'll step aside while you, dear reader, turn the page— . . .

SEEN

392 WHITE-TAILED DEER

392 sightings, that is . . . maybe
Some keep coming back again.

W IS FOR WHITE-TAILED DEER

PLAYED MUCH E|X|CELLENT MUSIC

together, separately, and
with good friends

X IS FOR EXCELLENT MUSIC

X

Y

TURNED OVER

$\dfrac{1 \text{ TRILLION}}{}$ **Y**ARDS of TOP·SOIL

... the whole garden, twice a year

Y IS FOR YARDS OF DIRT

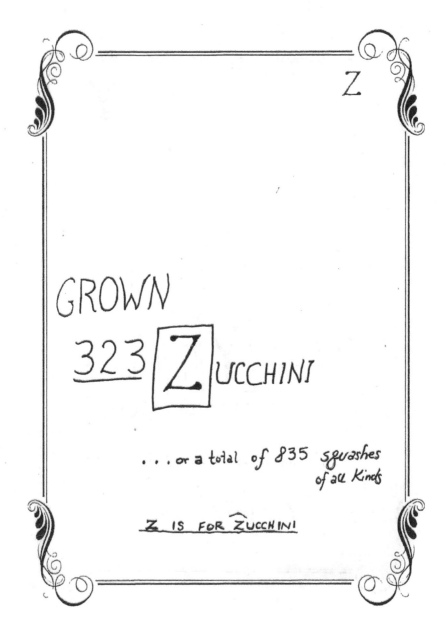

GROWN

323 **Z**UCCHINI

. . . or a total of 835 squashes of all kinds

Z IS FOR ZUCCHINI

AND NOW, FOR THE NEXT TEN YEARS,

THERE'LL BE MORE, MUCH MORE...

. . . more asparagus to grow,

more blueberries to pick,

more cords of wood to cut,

the black dike? . . . well, er . . . more day-hikes to go on,

more red efts to see,

more Franconia Ridge work days to put in,

more guests to welcome . . . .

11

From Climber to Mountain Steward

A phone call to the Appalachian Mountain Club's weekend leader to sign up for the club's beginning rock climbing course at the Shawangunks was the most life-changing call I've ever made. One result was that I had my eyes opened to our environmental impacts, the amelioration of which has given me a lifetime "cause." As John Glenn said to Ohio State University graduates in a 2009 commencement address, "We are more fulfilled when we are involved in something bigger than ourselves." And, oh, yes, I met the fellow climber who was to become my husband.

My thanks to the editorial skills of Paula La Rochelle and Katie Ives, who grasped what I was trying to express and set me on the path of discovery in a piece titled "On Becoming a Mountain Steward" for Alpinist, *volume 61, Spring 2018.*

I wanted this piece to cry out for wildness and the preservation of it. Especially here in the Northeast where we have so little compared with what lies west across the Mississippi River and the Rocky Mountains. A mountain cabin or even a hotel if built in those western ranges would probably not arouse the clamor that the Cog Railway's plan did here. But that doesn't mean we can complacently accept any building in a wild spot that's never felt a bulldozer.

Restraint comes hard for us humans. We want to share the wild places we've just discovered. Nothing wrong with that, until the trickle becomes a crowd, and then a hut is built with the rationale that it's better for folks to stay inside a building than to be erecting tents and trampling the ground to a muddy slough. At that point, where does the solution lay? Scrap the proposed building, ban camping, and give the forest a chance to recover? But often, depending on ownership, this is not possible.

I see stewardship as an educational tool passed on verbally perhaps by a caretaker at a shelter or on a summit. The message has to be felt deeply by the newcomer. It has to enter into their bones. This can happen easily when you're in the mountains, in the presence of the wild beauty, and the wild power of a mountain flower. When it happens, when you are a captive, you, too, are poised to take the next step to mountain steward, a missionary for wildness. At least that's how it happened to me.

~

There is nevertheless a certain respect, a general duty of humanity, that ties us, not only to beasts that have life and sense, but even to trees and plants.

—Michel de Montaigne, "Of Cruelty"

The best in nature, like the best in art, is sacred. Look upon it respectfully, reverentially, or not at all. Even the wild beasts know that much.

—Joaquin Miller, *Game Regions of the Upper Sacramento*

I was not held a willing captive, or mesmerized, or intoxicated by mountains until I'd reached my late twenties. It was a fresh autumn day in 1969, on a beginners' climbing weekend, that I was blindsided by the gleaming white and gray quartz conglomerate of Shawangunks rock. I stood at the base of a seemingly infinite line of cliffs that arched and angled away above the trees into the brightening sky. I was here to climb!

A year earlier, I'd joined the Appalachian Mountain Club and learned about a landscape above the treeline, an alpine zone that supported mountain-top gardens of small shrubs and flowering plants, called lawns or meadows. These were great open spaces that the wind kept mowed, perpetually open to the sky, that burst in mid-June into a lavish display of pinks, magentas, and whites. The Presidential Range of the White Mountains is crowned by eight square miles of alpine tundra, the largest swath south of Canada and east of the Rockies. The six northern peaks of the range are all above five thousand feet, and the path from peak to peak is along a broad, undulating ridge, a rounded crest eroded and ground down from Himalayan height beginning 440 million years ago, until the last glaciers of the Quaternary Glaciation retreated eleven thousand years ago, leaving only scour marks. Alpine azaleas, pink blossoms against tiny evergreen leaves, spread out like a mat over the rocks. The mountain avens bloom large, bright as a buttercup. Robbins' or dwarf cinquefoil is found only on Agiocochook (the Abenaki name for Mount Washington) and the airy, narrow Franconia Ridge to its west; the entire plant is about the size of a bottlecap, with yellow petals a quarter inch across. These flowers shelter among rocks that are themselves colorful with lichens of muted gray, pale green, and eye-catching orange. Rocky and exposed to the Presidentials' famous winds, the summits are bare and full of hazards in fog and storm, but they also afford breathtaking views of cloud-swept ridges and cool forests in summer. In winter, the peaks are buried by ice and snow.

During the late 1960s, AMC's Huts Committee revealed a plan to build a mountain hut in the Presidentials at Sphinx Col, the saddle between the two rolling uplifts of Mount Jefferson and Mount Clay. The AMC's hut system had come fully to life in the 1930s, a time when only a few hikers visited the chain of primitive structures that served meals and provided shelter. This new hut seemed to me a marvelous undertaking. I knew very little about the mountains then, and I only saw it as a convenience for my own interest of exploring the alpine terrain.

On my Gunks weekends, though, I quickly became aware that climbers from AMC's New York Chapter were vociferously against the new hut. The AMC already had two huts not more than eight miles apart, my new friends pointed out, at either end of the Presidentials. The proposed third hut would be located smack in the middle.

"Damn AMC!" these climbers growled. "They can't build a hut without wreaking destruction on the tundra. Those plants can't survive such trampling. Sacrilege!"

Fortunately, AMC management abandoned the Sphinx Col hut plans. I was learning that some hikers and climbers saw any building as a danger to the alpine terrain, as well as an intrusion on the wildness: a civilizing influence that had no place in the mountains. I was beginning to understand that enclosed structures in the wild can separate us from the place itself, and that the mountains would be better served with simple, open, three-sided shelters or campsites under the charge of caretakers. For the huts that already existed, I realized, their best use was to provide educational opportunities for newcomers to wild land, as I was then.

Meanwhile, through climbing, I was developing an awareness of my body in space: the way my callused fingertips grew sensitive to the myriad changing textures of the rock and my own harsh breath filled my lungs as I encountered a hard move; then the release of tension and surge of well-being as I climbed higher and became a part of the rush of a raven's wing, the shadows as a cloud dimmed the light, the first drops of summer rain. *Contact!*

On Shawangunk rock I'd found myself in another wild sanctuary that immersed me in the natural world. And, as I got to know the community of climbers there, I began to comprehend what it could mean to be a mountain steward—a defender of wildlife, plants and rocks, and of wildness, that intangible ingredient that made my experiences seem so precious and rare.

The responsible actions by backpackers and climbers around the nation that developed from the outdoors boom of the 1960s and 1970s—nothing short of a revolution—were in tune with a heightened environmental awareness generated by the first Earth Day, held on April 22, 1970. Our eyes were opened to our own impacts, and we could not look the other way. Among the particularly glaring signs at the Gunks were multiplying paths that led from the highway through a short strip of woods to the carriage road that circled the privately owned cliffs. The Mohonk Preserve, taking responsibility for its land, invited AMC's professional trail crew to give instruction in the art of building a rock staircase. As a result, climbers like me gave up some precious weekend climbing time to help. But we drew some satisfaction from moving big rocks with a rock bar, an effort that seemed to take the same physical precision and mental calculation as executing a difficult move. The result was a single path that could withstand heavy use. We'd sweated together building this! We'd learned something new about giving back.

By 1973, as I've said, I'd married one of those Shawangunks climbers, and we gave up the life of New York commuters to homestead in rural Vermont and arrange our lives so that we had maximum time for climbing. Because we spent so much time in the woods and hills, however, we were constantly in touch with issues of environmental concern. And by the mid-1970s we'd reinvented our skills as writers and editors to become advocates in the cause of mountains.

In our column for *New England Outdoors* we discussed issues that troubled us. For instance, we'd noticed how the growth in hiking had led to a rise in accidents, which in turn led to a demand for even more infrastructure. In the White Mountains, rescues were frequently carried out under the auspices of the Appalachian Mountain Club, and the college-age kids who staffed the huts were often first on the scene. During the late 1970s, an accident occurred near the Carter Notch Hut and the victim had to be littered down the 3.8 miles of rocky mountain trail from the hut at night. After the incident, AMC's Huts Committee proposed building a helicopter pad in the notch for the ease of rescues. This plan would involve decapitating some boulders and daubing concrete here and there to create a suitably flat surface.

Just north of the Presidential Range, Carter Notch is a boulder field situated between the rounded shoulders of the Wildcats and Carter Dome. Some of the rocks are house-sized. In 1959, as a camp counselor, I'd led my campers up those 3.8 miles to the hut. We went swimming in the frigid waters of the ponds, and after supper the hutmen—no women then—escorted us onto those boulders, where we sat in the evening shade of the looming massif and watched as the remaining daylight retreated toward the summits.

The dusk settled deeper into the notch and the boulders themselves took on the silent presence of sentinels, compelling us, as they darkened, to gaze out through the V-shaped notch at the lights of the faraway town of Berlin pinpricking the valley below. Our conversation turned to the separation between the inhabitants of those stuffy houses and the place where we were, perched atop boulders that had been shaken from the mountain at the beginning of time. The sky above revealed stars as the air cooled and breezes drifted, aimless and free. That exhilarating hour among the ancient boulders of Carter Notch must have been the initial spark that later, at the Gunks, ignited my love of mountains.

Guy, at that time, was on the AMC committee that had come up with this idea of the helicopter pad. It quickly became highly controversial, with pro-pad forces led by the helicopter pilot. We heard from a hut crew member—an inside source—of a certain rare plant that grew only in that boulder field, and we alerted a botanist to the possibility of using this plant to block the pad. "Your snail darter," sneered the pro-pad forces, referring to a victory achieved in 1978 by Tennessee environmental advocates seeking protection of a small mountain fish under the recent Endangered Species Act. Land managers with the White Mountain National Forest stepped forward and pointed out that the AMC, a club given maintenance authority over the national forest's trails, did not have the authority to knock over boulders. The club's plan would have to be approved by the forest supervisor and accompanied by an environmental impact statement. As Guy and I later recalled in *Wilderness Ethics*, we put our column at the service of the boulders, but we were uncertain how the AMC committee's vote would go. We thought it might be close. Fortunately, a vote of eleven to one permitted this rock pile—which had stirred the sensibilities of one teenage girl so long ago—to exert its mute power over others who might seek its wondrous company.

Climbers of every generation have had to face their own impacts, and the rise of sport climbing has soon led to new kinds of conversations. Before the proliferation of bolted routes, the few people who climbed at Rumney, New Hampshire, encountered quiet cliffs in a green untrammeled forest. On a trip there in the early 1990s, when I first looked up at a line of bolts next to a perfectly good crack, I could hardly believe what I was seeing. When I returned about a decade later, this accessible cliff had become so popular that there was a rabbit warren of paths up to the base and trampling of vegetation where the climbers clustered to belay. Trad climbers, who'd tried to combat the bolting, eventually bowed to the new local ethics or stayed away.

In 2005 the US Forest Service—the primary landowner with responsibility for the land's health—drew up a plan that included directions for climbing management. The plan ran into the problem that what worked for all other climbing areas in the White Mountain National Forest didn't work for Rumney: most of the walls were too blank, too devoid of cracks for climbers to rely solely on natural protection, yet the Forest Service did not want to close the area to climbing. With the help of the Access Fund, climbers and managers came together in a series of meetings and, by 2008, worked out a unique management approach. It allowed the climbers to install fixed protection, that is, to continue bolting. In turn, the climbers agreed to work with the Forest Service trail crews to construct rock steps to the base of the cliffs and harden the staging areas to concentrate their presence, minimizing their impacts on the surrounding vegetation.

These Rumney climbers wanted to keep their access to the cliffs open, and they were willing to help protect the land itself in order to do so. In fact, for safety as well as environmental and aesthetic impact, they have governed their own actions and striven to keep a reasonable distance between bolted routes. To some of the climbers who come to real rocks by way of indoor walls, the learning curve can be as steep as the cliffs, but it also has the power to change lives. Places like Rumney can serve as entry points to the outdoors—and inspire an ethic of stewardship that can help to grow a constituency of future conservationists.

When the Mount Washington Cog Railway revealed plans in 2016 to erect a thirty-five-room luxury hotel seven hundred feet below the summit of Mount Washington, this ill-considered proposal placed the building in the midst of the fragile alpine zone. A number of conservation groups banded together to fight it, among them the Appalachian Mountain Club, New Hampshire Audubon, the Nature Conservancy, the Society for the Protection of New Hampshire Forests, and Keep the Whites Wild, a newly formed group of climbers dedicated to halting this project. Traditional stories of the local Abenaki warn against commercial development on sacred sites such as this mountain. Paul Pouliot, who is Sag8mo (council chief) of the Cowasuck Band of the Pennacook-Abenaki peoples, said that if the project was approved by the county zoning board, the band would "speak out stronger against it."

Mount Washington has been topped by buildings of some sort since the first hotel was opened in 1852, but there are no overnight accommodations now, though a welter of infrastructure covers the summit, including a weather observatory, a restaurant, a museum, as well as an ample parking lot accessed by the Mount Washington Auto Road. Another building—especially one set off from the cluster on the summit—would fracture still further any sense of wildness and cause irreparable harm to already heavily impacted tundra.

Back in 1869, the little cog train, the first such in the world, must have captured public appeal as it chugged picturesquely up to the skyline, followed by businesslike puffs of black smoke. The Cog's management has responded to environmental cleanup efforts in recent years, principally (and importantly) by switching from coal power to cleaner-burning biodiesel fuel. Cog personnel engage in cleanup by removing debris from the sides of the tracks. Staff members have been supportive of the outdoor community by giving hikers free parking and access to trailheads near the railway's base station.

So it was a grave disappointment for the Cog to propose a luxury hotel so blatantly at odds with environmental values. The very act of construction would irretrievably damage many alpine plants. It would impact, as well, the habitat of such rare birds as the American pipit, and two butterfly species, the White Mountain arctic and the White Mountain fritillary, found here and nowhere else. But the Cog Railway owned the land and could, according to the law, do what it wanted with the plants and creatures on it. No snail darter swam to the rescue.

Indeed, the proposed site might seem an awe-inspiring place for a hotel. The alpine meadows nearby are rarely visited since no path currently goes there, though it is within one hundred yards of the Appalachian Trail, a national route set aside by Congress with its own protective requirements. Out of the orbit of the summit, and visited by few hikers, this alpine spot carries a real feeling of wildness. The view through the windows of the proposed hotel would center on the Great Gulf Wilderness—also designated by Congress as a protected area—renowned for steep and rugged glacier-carved ravines that fall away into the forests below. Tiny Spalding Lake, two thousand feet lower, gleams like the surface of a diamond. The Great Gulf headwall itself, bigger than either Tuckerman or Huntington Ravines and far more difficult to access, is favored by climbers and hikers alike for its remoteness and isolation.

In the tradition of adventure, on January 27, 1905, three men set out to climb the Great Gulf headwall, starting from the town of Gorham, six miles away from the trailhead. Each man, prominent in the Appalachian Mountain Club, had an instrumental role in building the precipitous trails out of the Great Gulf. It was well after the noon hour before they reached the base of the Great Gulf cirque, a bay in the mountains carved by glaciers. Above loomed the 1,800-foot headwall, draped in snow and ice. A storm had kicked up, but they exchanged snowshoes for ice creepers—an early form of crampons. The labor of chopping steps spun the time away, and chunky bits of ice and crust hissed down the slope around them. Long before they reached the rim, they overran the daylight, but, spirits high, they groped through the wind-driven swirl toward the Cog tracks and followed the rails to the summit. Taking refuge in one of the buildings, they consumed a dinner of crumbs from the lunch bag. Stopping only to remove their creepers, they pulled up the rug for a coverlet.

This spirit of climbing exhibited by these three winter warriors is alive in the hills today. Its practitioners continue to reflect that impulse of adventure by climbing steep thin ice in cold, high winds, glorying in the moment and training for alpine peaks around the world. There are already enough human shelters in these mountains for them. A luxury hotel perched on the very edge of the Great Gulf would be visible to anyone climbing up out of the ravine; by its very presence, it would banish much of the remaining sense of wildness, that quest for sanctuary, that here in the Northeast is precious beyond words because of the very scarcity of wild land available.

At the present time, no action has been taken to erect this building. But there is no assurance either that the Cog managers have given up. We can hope that a model of restraint for the Cog's owners would be the AMC's wise decision not to build a hut in Sphinx Col. They should consider the example of countless hikers and climbers who give up their treasured time for recreation to care for the trails and cliffs, and who, by this action, remind us that this landscape needs to be protected, not just for our enjoyment and for replenishment of our spirits, but for the living creatures that call this place home.

In 1980, when Guy and I became adopters of the Franconia Ridge Trail through the Appalachian Mountain Club's program, we made sure that not more than three weeks would go by without getting up there. Often we followed the circuit of heading up the Old Bridle Path, working as we crossed the ridge, and descending the steep and rocky Falling Waters Trail, a nine-mile loop, in a day. Just as often we stayed at Greenleaf Hut, located a mile below the summit of Mount Lafayette, and then we could spend several days up on the ridge. In the evenings we often had the opportunity, under the AMC's Naturalist Program, to talk to the hikers there about the alpine vegetation and the importance of its protection.

Our tasks on the ridge trail consisted of reconstructing cairns and building new ones, freshening paint blazes, cleaning water bars, and clipping a small amount of brush where the trail dipped into the scrub. With the Forest Service's permission, we dragged dead brush out of the krummholz. But our biggest and most constant job was a housekeeping task: replacing the small rocks dislodged from the low scree walls and that fell into the trail. These marked the edges of the path and were meant to separate hikers from the plants.

In fact, the object of all this maintenance was protecting the plants. And it didn't take long before we were, without being aware of it, turned into educators.

Picture this: a hiker sees two people bent double, tossing grapefruit-sized stones back onto a scree wall. He stops on a clump of mountain sandwort on the other side of the wall. "What are you doing?" he asks.

"If this is your first time above treeline," I offer, "you might be wondering how those plants adapt to living in this very harsh environment."

The hiker looks down, sees he's crunching plants under his boots, and steps to our side of the wall.

"Yes, the plants can take the savage weather we get up here," Guy says, "but they don't like to be stepped on." There is a brief flurry of mutual laughter. "That Labrador tea, for instance," he continues, reaching over to a shrub with white flowers near the wall. "This leaf, you see how its edges are slightly curled?" He turns it over. "Look at these orange-brown hairs on the underneath side. They allow this plant to capture and hold moisture. That's essential in a windy place."

"But isn't it wet enough up here?" the hiker asks.

"It rains a lot," I say, "but it's also extremely windy, and that desiccates the plants." The hiker grins. We're all wearing the necessary clothing. But since we've been working in the wind for hours, our rain jacket hoods are cinched around our eyebrows and our hands are well gloved. "Another useful survival strategy," I go on, "is to grow together, in mats or clumps. See how these plants are gaining shelter this way?"

"It's beautiful up here," the hiker says. He looks around as though seeing for the first time the wonderful visual impression of these plants in bloom, the crimsons and pinks and whites, the varying forms of the flower structures, the leaves in shades of dark green, some shiny, almost waxy in appearance. "It's like a garden," he adds.

"These plants are very old," Guy says. "Their life stories go back to the time we humans were first walking upright, but in a much warmer climate." The hiker laughs, as it's anything but warm on this July day on Franconia Ridge.

"So you're protecting the plants," he says. We enthusiastically nod. A raven swoops in and lands on a rocky crest above us. We all look up as the bird takes off in a great flap and a loud croak. "These plants are awesome," the hiker says. "I didn't know." He turns to continue on the path, staying inside of the scree wall border.

We resume our work, backs bent, tossing fist-sized rocks back on the low wall.

This scene is repeated in various scenarios all summer long in the alpine areas of the Northeast, from Maine's Katahdin to Acadia National Park on the Atlantic coast, across New Hampshire's White Mountains, on the alpine high points of Vermont's Green Mountains, across Lake Champlain to the Adirondacks where the Adirondack Mountain Club runs an exemplary

Summit Steward program that watches over 170 acres or .27 square miles of alpine terrain that covers twenty-one summits. Most of the mountain clubs and public agencies have summit steward programs that hire college-age men and women who are trained to spread the educational message of just how precious these plants are and how vital it is to take care of them.

I think back to my own path, my own journey of education to become the kind of person I wanted to *be* in the wild. As humans, we seem to have difficulty taking the mountains on *their* terms, and I realize new threats to wildness will always crop up. We ourselves will slip back, grow complacent about our own best behavior as campers, as hikers, as climbers. The path to safeguard wildness from ourselves is a constantly evolving process. With the passage of time, issues might change, but more often it seems the same issues return. The work is never done.

Yet we are all on the path to becoming mountain stewards once we've been intoxicated by the beauty, by the vital qualities, by the restoration of our spirits that can happen when we go to the mountains. We are arriving closer to enlightenment when we've reached the point at which we want to give back for the privilege of being amid all that alpine glory.

The ecstatic experience of being on a mountain top, in a storm above treeline, in the presence of the song of the white-throated sparrow—or in any of a thousand ways that we can feel carried out of ourselves in the mountains—can be just a momentary escape. Or it can affect an alchemy that transforms our whole existence. Once again, in such instances, we morph to become a part of the places we love. Again we promise ourselves to be vigilant to the imperative to maintain wildness.

12

Light in a Cabin

This chapter reads like an apologia for the homesteading life; it's certainly not a recipe for "how to run a successful homestead." Yet, who knows? There still must be the Natty Bumppos, the Henry David Thoreaus, the Ed Abbeys out there somewhere who would turn back the clock, even as we move, day by day, into the deeper waters of the twenty-first century.

Reading through this chapter I feel the zen in the work we did at Barra. I feel the meditative quality. Each of what concerned us most: wood, water, maple sap, garden—all labor-intensive jobs—delivered, when all was in synchronicity, a calming flow. We never discussed this. We were unaware of it. But I've come to see it was so, years later. It strikes me as remarkable that we could have missed this, but I think when you are immersed in the experience of your life, as we were then, it is just about impossible to draw yourself into the perspective you need to gain a full objective view. Children live like that. Especially children at play, which children do, in some form, until they cease to be children. It isn't until the game is over that you can stand back and say: "Well! So that's what it was all about." Meaning your life.

~

The beauty of the type of artificial light we used at Barra was that it was not bright enough to close out the night. We could be sitting at our table reading after dinner under the light of our kerosene lamp in the wintertime darkness, yet look out at the stars. We were aware of the moon's progress from dark to full, a subtle change. You can't do that in an electrified house. Electricity is an efficient banisher of darkness.

After I finally left Barra for good, I immediately became aware that I was no longer connected to the night sky, and felt the loss. I still feel the loss. I find myself walking out on my porch in the dark to learn what the night is up to. Are the stars out? Which ones? Has Orion come around again? I want to know. Is the moon rising? How full is it? I want that connection to the natural world that we had at Barra just by our daily living that was more suited to the nineteenth century than to the twentieth, let alone the twenty-first.

I can remember times when I would walk the mile and a half from our cabin to the village to find, upon entering the post office, that it was dim inside. The power had gone out. At Barra, of course, Guy and I had been completely unaware—our life was unaffected by power outages. Now, all of that has changed.

A young couple, who were living at Barra after Guy died and I had moved, once said to me that the cabin seemed dark to them. "Dark?" I said, surprised. "What do you mean?" It had never seemed dark to me. In a nonelectrified house, you don't keep lamps on or candles lit during the day. I had become completely used to the quality and quantity of light that had filtered its way through our windows.

In June 2000, when I moved from our homestead, a distance of two miles, to the house where I have lived in ever since, I was not expecting the reaction this relocation provoked in my friends, who were quite aware of the jump across centuries that it entailed.

At Barra we had built a small room for washing up, using a pitcher and basin. We located the outhouse a short walk uphill, perhaps fifty paces from the cabin. In the summer we took daily baths in the bath house we'd constructed by our stream. In winter we used a small cattle trough for a tub. This sounds primitive and inconvenient, but it worked very well for us.

I had moved to this home with its bathroom: a sink, shower, and indoor toilet that flushes. I moved, as well, from kerosene and candlelight to electricity. I moved from heat entirely generated by a woodstove to—still a woodstove, but also the option of propane. I moved from carrying water from our stream uphill to our house for drinking and cooking to turning on the hot or cold water taps: no need now to boil water for washing dishes or doing laundry. I moved from doing our laundry by hand to a washer-dryer in the basement. I moved from a root cellar to a refrigerator. (But a root cellar is so useful for storing winter crops that I had one built into the basement of my new house.) I moved from using no power tools for working up the eight cords of wood we needed each year for cooking, heating, and our maple syrup operation to having the two or three cords of wood I needed delivered, already cut and split. My job, now, was reduced to stacking. If a chunk was too big for my stove, I used the maul and wedges to trim the log.

I had moved from a sort of isolation that could have us walking up to a mile and a half to reach our house to a place that demanded no walk at all. We'd had a car at Barra (we never figured out a way to do without it), but we closed off our road—impossible to keep open in the winter anyway—and left the car in a variety of spots along the walk to our house, depending on the condition of the road itself. It was dirt, with several hills, including a long challenging one that needed a rolling start to get up. We had established water bars—drainage ditches—and kept them scraped out. We made a practice of not driving on the road if we might cause ruts, or damage the road surface after heavy rains. Most important was not to drive on the road until it had completely thawed out after the spring mud season. That's why we had the intermediate parking spots. We took a fair amount of satisfaction out of maintaining our road in a way that embraced the notion of restraint. Aside from this, our car—that hunk of metal—in our eyes offended the beauty of our clearing. The car did not fit in.

It didn't take us long to feel the benefit of walking from where we might park the car. It gave us a chance to wind down from a long drive. We often carried heavy packs if we were coming back from several days in the mountains and had added to their weight by picking up needed items at the hardware store or market.

Doing this walk in summer was one thing, but I'll not forget our first serious winter walk. The snow and cold had held off that fall of 1973, giving us the good weather we needed for completing last-minute jobs. To celebrate we decided to make a three-day backpacking trip to the Adirondacks. By then it was early December, and, when we left home, the ground was still bare. By the second day of that trip, it began to snow and it kept on snowing. We drove home in snow on barely plowed roads to find that the storm had been equally generous in Vermont. Our friends, the Williamses, who lived in our village, had offered us a spot in their three-car garage, anytime we needed it, they said, during the winter. We drove into their driveway, parked the car and turned it off, and put our hiking headlamps on to shuffle gear when John came out, inviting us in. We could see Freda's friendly, beckoning welcome from their kitchen. We entered and were offered tea but said a polite no-thanks, wanting to get home, with an added thanks for the space in their garage. John quickly responded by offering to drive us up the road from the village to the start of our road.

Both John and Freda must have seen that I was under some stress, and Guy did too because he accepted John's offer. I had been thinking about that mile-and-a-half walk now through close to a foot of unpacked snow with a monster heavy pack, and I was not looking forward to it. In fact I rather envied the Williamses' plowed driveway and their garage attached to the house. John's offer of a ride cut a good half mile off our walk. Once at our road, John left us buckling on our snowshoes. I was, needless to say, most grateful for this lift, but there was still a good mile to go. Our walk started with one of those generous uphills. Guy was in front, breaking trail. I mushed along in his tracks illuminated by my headlamp, still feeling somewhat sorry for myself. But the amazing thing was—we could not have been much past the top of that first rise—I soon stopped thinking about anything much at all. It was lightly snowing. No stars shone. It was cold, but that uphill warmed me. I was heading home—to this house we'd built together—and this walk was a part of the return journey. A ritual walk. By the time we reached our cabin I was unjangled from that winter drive and relaxed. My bad mood evaporated. I was tired, yes, but a good kind of tired that left me feeling ready to start the stove, warm up our cabin, light the kerosene lamps, and fix supper.

While our friends had moved into the world of emails, the Internet, and Google, at Barra Guy and I wrote letters by hand that were mailed in an addressed envelope, and we bought stamps at the post office. Stamps, in fact, were an important portion of our monthly budget.

We wrote our books on manual typewriters and sat facing each other across our table, where we ate and read before bedtime, in the darkness of winter with the kerosene lamp between us.

We did our research in libraries. By the 1980s libraries were transitioning from file drawers containing a card for every item of their holdings. We were not called upon to use a computer to access what we were looking for except once, in the New York State Library in Albany. There we spent a frustrating day, not even being sure that we were finding all we were looking for. I imagine the librarians were glad to see us leave. But, truth be told, their gray unsmiling faces seemed to say that they themselves were not entirely happy with this momentous change.

To us, our world was simple and understandable. Sure, it demanded hard work. It was labor intensive to a degree that had people shaking their heads. Projects like collecting our wood using hand tools probably quadrupled the time needed. But this slow, deliberate way of going about things added to our pleasure. As example, we forked up our vegetable garden, a fenced-in 200 ft. by 70 ft. piece of ground, twice a year, spring and fall. We devoted twenty minutes to this, after lunch, every day, figuring the numbers of days we would need to complete this job. This slow and steady daily progress turned a task that could become onerous and back-breaking to something that fit comfortably into the routine of the day and the season. In spring, as the woods surrounding our clearing were turning green again, we were aware of birdsong, new arrivals every day. We kept a list. In autumn the foliage changed from green to full-on yellows, oranges, and reds of the maples, ashes, and aspens, and by the time we had completed the garden digging we were left with the russet-browns of the oaks. As the last leaves fell, our work in the garden was finished for the year.

By then the mornings were frosty and we were wearing hats and gloves as we topped off our wood cords, ready for the next year's use. We were always a year ahead of ourselves. No one wants to burn green wood!

Hard, labor-intensive work. That's what had people shaking their heads. It really wasn't necessary to go to this extreme in the twentieth century, and our friends could not help suggesting how we could reduce our work by putting in labor-saving devices. Why not find a way to bring water to the garden instead of lugging it bucket by bucket? Well, we explained, our water source, a small stream, was below the garden, so a gravity-fed system wouldn't work. This was not strictly accurate, as one of the enterprising stewards who cared for our homestead after I left did indeed find a way to set up a series of hoses and directed the stream to the garden. The minimal grade from the water source—an underground spring—was virtually level, but sufficient in May and June when the pressure coming through the hose was at its strongest. Our stream was not robust, though, and as summer heated up, the water pressure decreased and the hoses proved ineffective.

When the steward proudly showed me his garden watering system, did I feel that Guy and I had missed an opportunity? No. I could see what effort it took to nurse the slow stream of water, adjusting the hoses as the flow slowly became a trickle. That kind of tinkering did not appeal to us. It was much more satisfying to water our seedlings by hand, with a watering can, with the clear cold water that we hand-carried from our brook. Embedded in this work was a devotion to the plants themselves, those small and fragile seedlings, that were going to grow into substantial healthy vegetables that would feed us throughout the year. This kind of hand-watering that required labor from us gave us a connection to the soil that we had built up from low quality to a rich fertility. Our plants flourished and watering each evening by hand—the effort that entailed—added to the pleasure, the satisfaction of our whole garden year.

Soon after we had moved to Vermont, we heard about young home-steaders—back-to-the-land folks—who had sought to cut down on the hard work with labor-saving tricks, *systems*, we heard them called. For the most part, these systems had not turned out well—too complex, too time-con-suming to maintain, too expensive, and they kept breaking down. Because of such repeated troubles, these folks became discouraged, pulled up stakes, and returned to the city.

Inventing devices that cut down on our labor did not work for us. We were not mechanical. Changing the oil in our car was just barely manageable. Besides, we discovered quickly that the physical work had its own appeal. Had its own rhythm. There was a meditative aspect to carrying water from the stream to our garden, or to be in our forest with axes and saws, cutting firewood then carrying long logs from the woods to our sawhorse behind our house. It was calming work, even relaxing in that you found yourself sinking into your own thoughts. Or, perhaps you had no thoughts at all. It was also very good exercise and kept us in shape for hiking or climbing. It was in the same order of our long walk back to our cabin in the clearing, especially in winter.

Though not everyone who visited us—and we hosted many visitors over the years—saw the point. One young man (I'll call him Bob), with whom I had worked at Camp and Trail Outfitters in New York, wanted to help us collect wood. He'd stay for three days, he enthusiastically assured us. That morning we carried wood that we had already felled and cut in lengths that could be sawed in four-foot intervals. We stacked our wood in four-foot lengths to be later sawed to stove length. The three of us began this task after breakfast at 8:00 a.m. We traded off hauling up wood with sawing, so there were always two people hauling and one sawing lengths. The round-trip walk with the wood, up the slight incline from the forest, through the garden—we left the gates open—to the back of the cabin, took between five and ten minutes, depending where the woodpiles were located. The right amount of time to fall into a meditative, easy pace. The trick was not to feel rushed. Like hiking, you wanted to be able to sustain this "walk" all day, or, in the case of hauling wood, all morning. We reserved such heavy work for the morning hours, with a midmorning break to munch a few crackers (homemade) and drink water. Quitting time was noon. Lunch! That was it for wood hauling; we'd do something less taxing in the afternoon.

Guy and I always took a nap after lunch that lasted ten minutes. The trick here was to fall asleep within seconds of lying down and to sink into an unconscious state. Ten minutes later we woke up feeling completely restored. This short nap provided such a complete break, it was as if we had two days in the twenty-four hours instead of one. For a while, we were dependent on an alarm clock to wake us up, but at some mysterious point our bodies began to wake up on their own. We didn't need the alarm. I can't explain it, and I continue this ritual of ten-minute naps.

I don't know if young Bob took a nap on that first day, but he had evidently put in the time making a decision. When we assembled for the afternoon, Bob let us know that he remembered an important appointment back in the city that had slipped his mind. He needed to leave. Now! We said we were sorry to lose his company, that we'd appreciated his work, but understood about forgotten appointments. So Bob walked over to the shelter we had built—a three-sided small building like a mountain lean-to—grabbed his backpack, which was already loaded, hoisted it, shook hands, wished us luck, and headed out, quickly fading into the greenery of our path.

Guy and I thought this incident amusing and frequently told this story of a young man, strong, healthy, and apparently willing—it *was* his idea to help us haul wood—who left after a morning, having promised us three days, but we knew why Bob had left. What we were doing seemed totally ridiculous to him. And, as I remember, he was kind enough not to say so.

We told ourselves that Bob's inability to join in the pleasures of wood collecting demonstrated some deep character flaw—in him. This young man gave up too easily. He didn't know how to push himself. He just quit when the going got tough. He would be a failure in life if he couldn't sustain something as simple as carrying a good-sized section of a tree uphill on his back. Then repeat the process until four hours had elapsed. It was obvious to us that young Bob just didn't "get" wood collecting. Or hard work, for that matter.

What hung in the air, his parting words: *What is the point?* he generously never spoke. And, to be frank, Guy and I never asked them of ourselves. We never questioned why we gave ourselves over to such toilsome work for nearly thirty years.

The simplest answer was that we enjoyed doing it. This kind of labor—hauling wood, cutting with a handsaw instead of a chainsaw, carrying water to the house and garden, moving manure by bucket a quarter mile from where we had it dumped to the garden, carrying sap during sugaring season by bucket instead of letting it run through more convenient tubing made us feel good, physically. And mentally. We felt tremendous satisfaction in watching our wood cords build up, or in knowing that the care we gave our garden would feed us for the year ahead. The way we had chosen to live at the homestead we called Barra was very real. This reality meant more to Guy than writing speeches for General Electric top executives—or for anyone else. It meant more to me than editing manuscripts. For some reason—well, because I had discovered climbing and had fallen in love with Guy Waterman—I was not interested in using my mind to edit manuscripts. Although the work I did with Bill Kemsley at *Backpacker* magazine, my last job in New York, came closer to having real meaning. This was because our vision for the magazine was to encourage campers, hikers, and climbers to be aware of their own impacts in the woods, in campsites, on trails, in alpine areas, and on summits.

Moving to Barra allowed us to continue this work, and not just for *Backpacker*. The Boston-based magazine *New England Outdoors* gave us a monthly column, and, by the end of the 1970s, we had published our first book, *Backwoods Ethics: Environmental Concerns for Hikers and Campers*.[1]

So, we were living this life of physical labor, outhouse, and candlelight, combined with the kind of writing that we hoped would change

1. This is in its third edition, under the title *The Green Guide to Low-Impact Hiking and Camping*.

thinking. We weren't the only ones, though we were an early voice. The backpacking boom, along with the back-to-the-landers, the hippies, and the general, all-purpose nature lovers were taking to the mountains as well as the rural countryside—looking for that reality that Guy and I had found on thirty-seven acres of Vermont woodland with a clearing giving room for a hand-built cabin and a large vegetable garden, an orchard, and sixteen highbush blueberry bushes.

Was young Bob reacting to what might have appeared as artificiality? Artificiality? Hmm.

To us, as I've said, Barra felt very real. More real than anything else Guy or I had done before. When we had left New York, we had said to ourselves that if this experiment didn't work out, we could always return. A year later we looked at each other and realized we couldn't go back. We were totally unfit to return to the commute, the meaningless work, the disjointed feeling of what we loved—mountains, hiking, climbing—being so separate from how we earned a living.

We had decided to live "simply" because that's what we could afford on what we knew would be a very reduced budget. Or it started out that way. Then we found that being unable to drive to our front door turned Barra into its own separate world, that the outhouse provided an excellent bird blind, that our kerosene lamps gave room for the stars and moon to shine in. Digging our garden with large-tined forks twice a year kept us in touch with our soil's health. We did not feel the lack of anything. And this transition happened quickly.

Artificial or not, it was a *chosen* life.

Guy picked up from his coworkers at GE that they expected he'd be back in the office after the first snowfall. They wanted to see him fail, he suspected. His decision to make this huge life change showed that they, too, who chafed under the daily grind, could change their lives, a change they perhaps preferred to think was just not possible. On the other hand, the change we made, I think, in some way spoke to others, especially our younger friends; what we had done gave them permission to *choose* their lives, too.

Yet my dear friend, Annie Barry, who had visited Barra many times over the years, said to me after Guy had died, "The way you lived at Barra, Laura, was 'weird.'" I was hurt by this and urged her to explain what she meant by "weird," but she never did. "Weird" was very far from my mind to describe our life, though perhaps "weird" was in young Bob's head when he walked down the path to his car. I cannot know, but I wouldn't be surprised. And what difference does it make now? Or even then? The life suited us. We believed we were playing for keeps. We'd jumped into the deep end; we weren't going to swim for the edge now. We depended on our garden, on our woodlot, on our skills to build our structures, on our strength, on our presence of mind, on our ability to make good decisions, on our good health, and on a certain amount of luck.

Guy, who struggled against depression, needed the life we made at Barra to keep his "demons," as he called his low moods, at arm's length. Certainly, all did not always run smoothly—life never does. For example, our stream was always problematic. Our best solution was to keep the waterhole dug out. In late summer the flow could occasionally dry up during the day, renewing itself at night. We always kept a bucket under the log we scooped out for a sluice and learned to live with our meager water flow. It's not a bad thing to be aware of one's use of water, which is not a resource to be wasted, to be used inappropriately, or to be taken for granted. (I think of the American Southwest and how the spread of housing developments and condominiums has drawn down its aquifer—talk about overtaxing a precious resource!)

But our meager water supply wasn't the sort of problem that could unduly upset Guy. It was just a practical ongoing concern we learned how to live with. It had no emotional component. Life bore down on Guy when the outside world barged in. Disagreements with the Appalachian Mountain Club, for instance, when we were the trail adopters on Franconia Ridge, Guy found especially stressful. Our thinking and theirs often collided. What saved the situation for Guy was that the US Forest Service, the managers of the White Mountain National Forest, saw eye to eye with us. We found ourselves turning to them when we had questions on how to cope with areas where hikers continued to cut through the alpine vegetation. With the Forest Service's permission, we were allowed to fill in those spots where the trail needed better definition with dead and down krummholz—the low-growing scrubby trees near treeline. The Forest Service also supported our efforts at reseeding, sowing nonnative grasses that provided a cover for the alpine vegetation to move in, a method that had been used, with success, for years in the Adirondack High Peaks. The nonnative plants, unable to adapt to the harsh conditions, died out in two or three years, leaving room for native plants to achieve a foothold and colonize.

However, Guy found the continual pushback from the Appalachian Mountain Club very hard to bear. Sometimes I would be aware that he was splitting wood with much more than his accustomed vigor, or I had the sense that he had been in the woods longer than the time the job he'd gone for should take. I could see, as well, when he returned, that he was in a better frame of mind for his communion with our maples, trees we tapped and had named.

Yes, I kept pretty close tabs on Guy's moods. Not so much in that first decade when all was new and fresh and our efforts gave us both joy in the accomplishment. But later, after losing two of his sons, the darkness closed in for Guy, and that had its effect on me as well. Monitoring his moods, I guess you'd say, became ingrained. Though I was careful not to let this show. Sometimes I felt anger that he couldn't just get over it—brush the mood away as one does a pesky fly. But that flash of anger would dissolve to a heart-wrenching sadness. Sadness for Guy, a mix of sadness and anger when Guy growled that "talking didn't help," moving both of us into our separate universes of despair, until it became clear to me that Guy's step was light again and his quick smile, when he looked my way, had returned.

I did not wish myself somewhere else. My commitment to the life we had made together was solid, founded on love for the work and Guy. My mother had found ways to keep her marriage together—our family together—by building a separate working life for herself. She had to fight for this. My dad was opposed. She, however, was determined. My situation was different but her strength must have been a model for me, though it took me years to see this.

In many ways we were not cut out to be homesteaders. We weren't skilled carpenters, we eschewed "systems" because we were unable to conceptualize the mechanics. We had no interest in chainsaws—too noisy, smelly, and costly. When they broke down you lost a day of work, whereas it took only a few minutes to replace a dull saw blade on our bucksaws. We kept extra blades on hand. We enjoyed the rhythm of our crosscut, its raspy sound as we pulled the saw back and forth between us, each stroke delivering a small pile of wood chips as the cut deepened.

Using the crosscut could challenge us. It can test two people of different strengths. The key to success is to keep the saw moving back and forth as smooth as silk. At the best of times it should feel like you're cutting through a well-made loaf of bread. If Guy was beset by his demons—I often wasn't aware when this was happening—he could take it out on the saw by jerking it back. This signaled to me that I wasn't sawing fast enough. I would try to keep up, but there came a point when I couldn't saw any faster. The rhythm was thrown off, we weren't working together, in fact we were fighting each other. Guy was only a few feet away, but in my concentrated effort to maintain my own cut, I couldn't see him. I sensed, however, a grim silence. What was troubling him? I didn't know. What was I doing wrong? I began to feel resentful and cross. He was ruining a beautiful day in our woods. It never occurred to me to ask him to slow down. Offering to talk about it would only make it worse. Yet, we would get through the cut. And each move on to other tasks, giving me—giving him, too—the needed space to regain balance. This was exceptional, though the impact on me was big. Mostly, when we were in the woods working together we enjoyed calling each other's attention to the bird life around us, the piliated woodpecker that had just let out his cackle and made us laugh, or the chickadee pair dancing above our heads. Using hand tools allowed us to tune into what was happening around us.

I remember once we had badly hung up a large ash, easily twenty inches in diameter, in a neighboring tree. We were working in the woods with our friend Ned Therrien, and he said, after we had determined that this tree was really good and hung up, "I've got my chainsaw in the truck, I'll run out and get it." We laughed, since Ned knew us very well. Surely he was kidding. But when he said, "I'll be right back," we shouted, "No!" "So how are you going to deal with this?" Ned asked. He knew the answer, but he needed to hear it from us. He said, "You'll be working on this ash for the next week." And he was right. For the next week, Guy and I devoted the time needed to saw four-foot lengths off this ash, working our way up the trunk until the tree was shortened to the point it finally came loose and fell. We sawed off six or seven lengths in as many days. Ned understood. He knew the sound of a chainsaw in our woods would have been most unwelcome. He knew how we broke jobs like this down into manageable, bite-sized chunks. We spent about twenty minutes a day for the next week, working the crosscut back and forth between us in easy strokes.

We needed to keep things simple. So we went back in time, found a suitable place and settled there. Take working on wood—the process: walking into our woodlot, tools in hand, selecting the trees to cut, each requiring a separate reason that fit in with the care, maintenance, and health of our entire woodlot. That was only the first step. Then comes the actual felling of the tree, a process that requires a raft of decisions to avoid hanging it up or injuring other trees when it falls. Next the limbing, sawing into lengths, and transporting logs to the woodshed where they will be sawed and split. Yes—there are many steps. Since we liked working with the trees themselves, each one of these steps was deeply satisfying.

Weird?

Artificial?

It was what Guy needed for his own peace of mind. He had landed on the idea, and I found meaning for my own life in becoming his willing partner.

What I find interesting is that when it came time for me to move from Barra into a house, and a way of life that I could sustain as I grew older . . . and older, the reaction of many was: Now you have electricity! Running water! Plumbing! All this spoken in a way that indicated I must be thrilled to have these conveniences back in my life. How had I put up with all those years without them!

My feelings on that subject were mixed. I deeply felt the separation from nature—the outside, outdoor world—yet, I knew that I had made the right decision. I had elected to enter a way of life I could carry on into the future.

I would be living without Guy. We had located a building site, a 6.5-acre field bordered by woods and the Tabor Valley Branch, a half-mile walk from the village. We had a chat with our friend John Nininger who agreed to build a house for me. Guy was clear that this was "Laura's house." He was consistent about this and if mildly questioned said the odds were, being nearly a decade older, he would likely predecease me. It made sense, in a way. Guy was expert at sidestepping difficult questions. The house plan we worked out with John made a space suitable for one person. It did not include room for Guy's Steinway grand. It was clear that this house would not include Guy.

It was "Laura's house."

It would have electricity. I came to see this as the most major change, on the level of soul.

That soft light at Barra: candles and kerosene, created its own world. It came into its own in winter when the hours of darkness overtook the hours of daylight. I would come in from outside work at dusk, and light the hanging lamp near the cookstove. I'd remove the iron rimmers, crumple up paper, add kindling, strike the match, build up the fire by adding wood graduating in size. It's an audible process: the clink of the rimmers, the hum of the fire as it catches hold. The whole process marks a transition to the end of day, darkness descending. Each action gives comfort. When I see the fire is burning well I descend the ladder into the root cellar for potatoes, onions, garlic, a quart of green beans put up last summer, or broccoli, some of the acorn squash left over from last night.

Guy was in the woodshed finishing up splitting the eighteen-inch logs we fed to the Ashley, our main heating wood burner. When I hear Guy's step on the porch the potatoes and onions in the cast iron frying pan are beginning to smell like dinner. The lamp is in action with its mellow glow, two candles illuminate my kitchen counter. Guy enters, bringing in a fresh breath of the cold air of January, sits on the ash log and unlaces his boots. He glances up and we smile at each other. I watch his hands as he loosens the laces, large, thick working hands. We might exchange a few words about the day, or plans for tomorrow as he crosses the pine floor to sit down on the piano bench. He hits the keys. I'm grinning to myself as Jelly Roll Morton reigns supreme and Guy rides the surf of those ten-note spans. He plays for the next quarter hour, fitting in with dinner prep, and as I'm lighting the candles on our small square table he pounds out the last rollicking chords of a rag he's played since his teenage years.

I stand at the window taking in the early evening darkness, the softness of the interior light letting me see out to the garden—the eight-foot fence posts—and up to a sky full of stars. The temperature will drop tonight. Guy joins me with a hug and we sit down to eat.

Now, in "Laura's house" the metaphor has changed. The electricity is responsible for that.

I can't say I mind leaving behind the finicky kerosene lamps, but I do miss their gentle light, which permitted darkness to enter our cabin slowly. I miss the ritual when the inside light had softened to the moment I would begin the deliberate process of lighting the lamps. Carefully, I'd turn up the wick, touch it with a match, and the delicate mantle brightened, filling the space with its own circle of light. Enough to write a letter by, enough to read by. But not so much that I couldn't tell, by looking out the window, whether the night were starry or cloudy, or the moon was showing signs of rising. It was that, the deep subtle connection with nature I took for granted, if I was thinking of it at all, that became the beautiful and unexpected gift of our thirty-year experiment.

13

Prospero's Options

This is Guy Waterman's take on his own life, expressed in ledger-like terms of credit and debit, success and failure. Portions of this unpublished memoir, formerly titled "Willed Oblivion," are in our papers and are published here courtesy of the Dartmouth College Library.

When I read these last three pages I was upset to realize how little I saw of Guy's dissatisfaction with his own life. Yet, whenever I picked up that he was in a low mood and asked him to talk, we got nowhere. I remember once at breakfast he seemed to be unusually downcast—Was it something I had done?—and asked him to talk. He remained stonily silent, not looking at me, wrapped in his own blackness. This time I could not hold back the tears and suddenly he was hugging me. Or was it I who reached out to him? I was sitting on his lap, but still no words came. I felt him draw away, and then I realized this conversation—if it could be called that—was over. Breakfast was over. He had work to do: wood to collect, gardens to plant, whatever was on the schedule, and he was losing time trying to comfort me. I felt hurt, and something close to anger, but mostly a great sorrow—for both of us. I thought about leaving. But I didn't want to leave our marriage. Strong in me was that if I hadn't married Guy I would not have married anyone. I knew he loved me—as much as he could. I came to learn that he realized I was good for him. Not from anything he said, just from the course of living our daily lives together. Who can explain love?

~

. . . the exhilaration of that most glorious of all pastimes, setting foot where no human being has ever trod before.

—Bob Marshall, *Arctic Wilderness*

Guy wrote a cross between a memoir and an autobiography that he titled "Prospero's Options." He pounded it out on his manual typewriter in the still-dark early morning hours. I was in bed. Occasionally I'd hear him at work, a comforting steady clacking of the keys, broken only by a pause to roll in a clean sheet of paper as he proceeded to commit his life to the page. He made no revisions, but then Guy rarely needed to revise. Certainly he never labored, as I did. The sentences and paragraphs accumulated— organized, organic, and orderly. (For a long time I thought of myself as an inordinately slow writer, always crossing out and rephrasing. While this is true, I have come to accept that it is just how I write—different from Guy.) Did Guy have in his mind as he worked the opening lines of *David Copperfield*? "Whether I shall turn out to be the hero of my own life, or whether that station will be held by anybody else, these pages must show."

When he completed a chapter, he gave it to me to read. It took about a year—the last of his life—to grind out, and it was clear to me he enjoyed this work that took "a backward glance," as Edith Wharton had titled her autobiography. His goal was to record the stories, highlight the turning points of a life that was in many ways remarkable. There was much of it I hadn't been around for. He was in his late thirties when I met him at the climbing cliff.

Rereading the pages again many years later, I see how determined he was not to spare himself—no whitewashing here, but a clear assessment of his strengths, and a steely, hard look at where he felt himself a failure.

He took his title, "Prospero's Options," from *The Tempest*, Shakespeare's story of Duke Prospero's exile on an island with his servants (slaves, really): the spirit Ariel, who embodies light, positive impulses, and the dark-spirited monster Caliban, intent on violating anything good. For Guy, that made him Prospero, and the homestead we called Barra the island. Guy's life, as he saw it, was a struggle between these two warring forces. He wrote this record, this assessment of his life—for himself, but also for his family, a few close friends, and, perhaps, most of all, for me.

For my purposes here, I will pick up the story with his discovery of climbing that led to more testing mountain adventures, all of which were life changing for him. The climbing was pivotal in opening up a pathway to sobriety. (He told me he was an alcoholic as soon as we began climbing together.) Climbing and mountains continued to be a centering influence of paramount importance to his mental health. Here's what Guy had to say about those earliest climbs.

In the fall of 1963 I made two moves toward becoming more seriously a climber.

First, in October I signed up for the New York AMC rock climbing instruction. That weekend—actually I went only one day, not wishing to spend too much time away from my family—I first saw the gleaming cliffs of the Shawangunks, just two hours' drive from Stamford, and destined to become my spiritual home for years. I went on my first two rock climbs (Beginners' Delight and Gelsa) and was absolutely transported at the excitement of climbing vertical rock.

(Guy had moved his family from Washington, DC, to Stamford, Connecticut, to write speeches for General Electric Company's chief executives.)

Second, in November, I took a four-day trip by myself to New Hampshire and headed for what the road map vaguely indicated as "White Mountains." I found the trailhead in Franconia Notch and pitched my old Army tent there. On two days, in my work boots and work clothes, and in absolutely awful weather—perpetually shrouded in dense cloud, soaked by rain (even borderline snow at upper elevations)—I hiked up the Franconia Ridge (also destined to be a later spiritual home) and the Kinsman Ridge to Cannon. The bad weather only added to my excitement in seeing this new world of real-life mountains.

In 1964 I slowly expanded these tentative efforts, but I did not rush headlong into becoming a climber. I passed up the spring climbing program at the Gunks, but returned in the fall and every season thereafter. I explored more hiking country nearby. In August I took John (and nephew Wayne Christian) on a four-day hike on the Appalachian Trail in Connecticut. In September (or the week before Labor Day) I took Bill (and nephew Tim Carney) on an eight-day traverse of the AMC Hut system in the White Mountains.

Thinking back on how slowly I moved toward climbing, I'm almost surprised to notice that a key consideration for me was my attachment to my family, notably my sons. I didn't go rock climbing more than once or twice a season until my two oldest sons became interested and began going with me.

I also took up winter climbing. In 1967 Bill and I made our first winter trip to the White Mountains, which turned out to be an epic adventure (the first of many smashing epics in the Whites in winter for me). It was on Lincoln's Birthday weekend in the Franconia Range. We encountered very severe weather without an inkling of what we were up against. Though we had no thermometer with us, we later found out it was 41 below on Mount Washington and 36 below on Cannon that weekend, so perhaps somewhere between on the Franconia Ridge. We spent two nights in the cold empty Greenleaf Hut (big buildings may actually be colder in winter than tents, as one's body heat is dissipated in the larger area). On the day between we struggled up in very high winds and extreme cold, but turned back from our original objective of crossing the range. We did reach the summit of Lafayette. With totally inadequate equipment, I succeeded in ripping my trousers with a crampon and developing an impressive bit of frost bite on one knee. Quite an experience, for a first winter venture in the Whites.

It is interesting to note that Guy and Bill made the decision to turn back. A common mistake that can end with death, or a very close call, is to press on. It's easy to have your better judgment swept away by your ambition to complete a goal. Right at the beginning of Guy's climbing career he demonstrated the trait that makes a successful climber, which means a smart climber: the willingness to turn around when you feel yourself close to getting in over your head. The crucial words here are "close to." Once you've crossed that line, it takes a rare set of circumstances to emerge from the woods alive. I always felt supremely safe with Guy, and know others did as well. More than that, I never worried about him when he was out on a solo trip. He took a greater chance driving to the mountains, especially on winter roads, than he did climbing them.

Climbing, for Guy, less so for me, led to a dissatisfaction with working life. Guy was looking for a way out by the time I met him. His goal was to line up his working life so that how he lived felt as pleasurable as climbing did.

Here's how he recalls that happening:

> In February 1971 I went on an ice climbing trip to Mount Washington's Huntington Ravine, and for some reason Laura did not accompany me; perhaps we felt she was not yet experienced enough on ice to cope with that serious locale. Anyway I went with a climber who had become a good friend, Brad Snyder, a 29-year-old teacher of German at Mount Holyoke college; and a 19-year-old friend of his, Dave Troe. (I was 38 that winter.) The three of us were all concerned about where to go in the future, and devoted long hours in the car, on the trail, and otherwise to discussing the dismaying prospects. (Brad was not happy as a college teacher, Dave unsure what to do in a fast-changing world of that time.) During that trip Brad and Dave told me of a book by Helen and Scott Nearing, about their taking up a simple country life during the 1930s, away from machines and pressures of traditional 20th century working life. This passing suggestion proved a momentous one for me. I read the book and began to think about the possibilities for myself and to discuss them with Laura.
>
> Gradually that spring Laura and I formed ideas about possibly quitting our jobs and moving to a primitive location and trying to live in something of the manner of the Nearings. . . .
>
> That summer we began contacting real estate people all over northern New England and New York, began looking at remote acres almost every weekend. Finally on July 17 we were

shown a piece of land in East Corinth, Vermont, which seemed to answer all our desires. On July 25 we made the decision to purchase 39 acres there. And on August 23 we closed the deal.

Now with our land in hand, we began seriously planning for the big break. We set a timetable: in the summer of 1972 we would spend a two-week vacation on the land and try to build our first building, a simple 8' x 12' open-front shelter, with floor; and if that worked out, we'd quit our jobs at the beginning of the following summer, June 1973, and move up for good. We wanted to make the break at the beginning of the summer, so as to be able to start a garden that first year, and have time to build a house before winter. So we had a 21-month plan laid out. We soon had fixed the date, June 9, 1973, as Barra Day. (We elected to call our land Barra, after the island in the Outer Hebrides where my family came from.)

During these 21 months, we did all we could to prepare ourselves for the big break. We started a garden in the backyard of the apartment where we were living, subscribed to *Organic Gardening & Farming* and began to keep extensive notes about growing vegetables and fruits. We also bought how-to books on house construction, and often examined houses under construction to understand the principles of building. We also began slowly weaning ourselves away from meat, since we figured lack of refrigeration (plus the Nearings' precedent) would mean we'd probably give up eating meat when we moved; so we cut out breakfast bacon in early 1972, stopped dinner meat in late 1972, all meats completely in early 1973. We figured that our regular winter weekend habit of camping out in the Adirondacks would stand us well for the lack of plumbing and other amenities when we made the big move.

In fact we held to the schedule we set ourselves. During that vacation in the summer of 1972, we did indeed build the shelter at Barra. It came out reasonably well, and we were of course immensely proud of it. We also dug up soil in the future garden area and planted a cover crop of winter rye. We also contracted with a local man to build a cement foundation for the cabin we would build the following summer; this was the only work we had done for us.

In August of that summer (1972), with my divorce finally official, Laura and I were married. The ceremony was at the Mohonk Mountain House, the guests mostly our climbing friends. We spent our wedding night on the cliffs, on a tiny ledge just big enough for a small tent. We considered the two weeks spent earlier in the summer on building our shelter as our honeymoon.

As the date for our move approached, we realized that we were cutting it very close financially, and that it would all go a lot more smoothly if we worked for one more year, putting away a lot more money. But by that time, we were spiritually committed to moving in June 1973. We found we just couldn't face another year of commuting to jobs in New York City. So we went ahead with the move on June 9, 1973.

Jim [Guy's youngest son] graduated from high school about that time. (That was another reason for the timing of the move, an important consideration.) We left the apartment we had to Jim. He was not planning to go to college right away, and would become financially on his own when we moved away. In fact, though I had put away a special account of money for his college education (and the completion of college for the other sons), I didn't even come close to allowing for the inflation in college costs. What it came down to is that I walked away from that responsibility, leaving my sons with a difficult time to finance their own college. My mind was on my own future, from which there was no turning back for me. On June 8 I bid goodbye to my colleagues at General Electric and to Manhattan Island. On June 9, 1973, Laura and I moved to Vermont.

What these paragraphs show was that Guy was good at planning. He was good at setting a schedule and sticking to it. Good at envisioning that end goal. Yet, he knew how to be flexible when cause demanded. You don't just stick to something for the sake of sticking. "To quote Winston Churchill," Guy would say, "'When it is not necessary to change, it is necessary *not* to change.'" And in the course of our homesteading years, plans were made, and changed when needed, again and again.

These few paragraphs show, as well, his commitment. I recall on our two-hour train ride into Grand Central Station, that while our fellow commuters were reading the *Times*, staring out the window, or napping, Guy was working on the plans for our house. He carried these in his briefcase where they took up a lot more room than his GE work. He ended up with a list of every stick of wood, from basement to loft space, with an estimate of the cost, all of which we took to the folks who sold us the lumber. He was possessed, in a positive, forward direction for this life change that had these GE coworkers shaking their heads, predicting he'd be back, begging for his old job, as soon as the snow flew. Guy felt they were hoping he'd fail. Many of them shared Guy's feeling of entrapment. But how to shake loose? Guy's bold move was making it hard for them to accept jobs they chafed against.

Yet, there was collateral damage, as Guy admits, with his inability to fulfill his financial obligations to his sons. He was well aware he was putting his own plan first. Did he know he would pay the price for this later? He was too caught up, too driven in engineering this momentous change to pay attention to the consequences.

Since our move to Vermont was in many ways an almost unqualified success, and we have lived this rather unusual "lifestyle" for almost 25 years now (to use a word which causes both and Laura and me to wince), we are often asked why we made this move. Neither of us are very good at articulating a response on the subject of why. But we understand that for many people it's an important question. While some others move to the country, few people give up so many elements of 20th century living and develop a systematic way of living without electricity or power tools of any kind, without plumbing or central heat, without communications such as telephone, radio, newspapers, and of course without computers, fax, and the other modern devices which we know next to nothing about, as they came into common usage long after we moved away from society. Why?

I usually disappoint listeners by stating flatly that we (or I—I shouldn't implicate Laura in what follows), that I am not a deep-thinker on these points, not a philosopher on these matters, and my ideas are full of inconsistencies and doubts. For me the reasons for the move were mainly quite simple. All my life I've been inept at fixing motors or dealing with things like electric wiring and plumbing, and poor at dealing with servicemen and others when needed. By abandoning all such matters and building our own, small and simple, house, fetching our water from the property's small stream, and cutting our own fuel wood from the abundant woods, we avoid dependence on complex modern systems or servicemen. Beyond these physical arrangements, one side of me has always had trouble dealing with people, especially when I'm in a bad mood. By living in relative isolation, the only person I ever really have to face is Laura, who is unfailingly pleasant and sensitive to my bad moods and indulgent of them (probably more indulgent than is good for me). (Or her.)

But these are mainly negative points. I think there are positive elements to this life as well. We have worked out an elegant blend of the physical and mental. By not overscheduling physical work—something we picked up from the Nearings' book—we reserve ample time for work of the mind—for us, primarily reading, music, and writing. But we also like the purely physical side. I get untold satisfaction from working in the woods, gardening, building with primitive methods, tending the land. I find this work absorbing and, with few exceptions, hugely enjoyable. The garden has become a gigantic mosaic we put together each year, a thing of beauty and enormous fruitfulness, slowly brought into being over slow cycles each year. Sugaring—the process of making syrup—is a thoroughly engrossing preoccupation for about one month each spring (early March to early April). Building our buildings, in our own peculiar fashion, from wood we cut and dry ourselves, has had its share of frustrations, but on the whole has also produced some results we take great pride in. For me the most satisfying work of all has been tending the woods: trying to work with the trees to produce a long-term firewood supply, better sugar production, healthier trees of all kinds, wildlife habitat, and all in all a woods of beauty and function. Meanwhile the almost daily work of splitting and sawing firewood has become an indescribably satisfying preoccupation of mine.

This is why. This life is the reason we made the move. I'm sorry I can't invest it with social significance of deep philosophical meaning, but I'm just not inclined to. (Nor, incidentally, do we preach that others should do as we have. The only message our life has for others, we believe, is that each person should think out what it is they want to make of their lives and not feel restricted by society's formulas or demands. Exactly what we've worked out is for us, not necessarily for anyone else.)

In short, we are doers, not philosophers. Homesteading is something we do, not verbalize about.

In reading back over the foregoing, it strikes me I've given an accurate but bloodless accounting of those first years in Vermont. In fact both Barra and climbing gave me great joy, pride, emotional riches.

• It was tremendously exciting to launch onto the uncharted terrain of homesteading and make it work. The risk was really there: had we failed, it would have been humiliating and depressing to crawl back to the world of "work" and ordinary living, whipped. But by hard work, meticulous planning, and deciding what was important to us, we succeeded, by gosh, we won. Wow, what a source of "joy, pride, and emotional riches."

• Climbing was equally fulfilling in those years. I improved my standard, doing so almost invariably on the lead, accepting full risk. Perhaps only climbers can fully appreciate the intensity of that challenge and how gratifying it is to respond successfully. And the fun of it all too. Again: joy, pride, emotional riches.

• I've also understated—well, not stated at all—what the relationship with Laura was. I'm an odd mix of Yankee reserve on such matters and an almost absurd heart-on-the-sleeve emotionalism. That is, I used to cry in movies, still do in books (especially dog stories!), love Wuthering Heights and Green Mansions, and easily get too choked up to finish speaking any time my emotions are primed. Yet I also dislike openly confessing personal matters. Maybe I could just say that Laura proved both the perfect homesteading mate—hard-working, perseverant, resourceful, steady (much steadier than me, which helped)—and the perfect companion for me—fun, compatible as to interests and tastes and priorities, unceasingly sympathetic, warmly affectionate, unbelievably patient through my bad moods. So great, after 19 years of a bad marriage, to be embarked on this great adventure together. Again: joy, pride, emotional riches.

All in all, these years, 1973–79, were the happiest of my life.

Guy addressed here how and why our move worked for him, for us. I'll only add that the sentence about our relationship—on why our life together, as a couple, worked—was news to me. He never articulated these feelings. What he thought, felt, and valued in me was plain through our daily interactions as we gardened together, collected wood, went off for a day of climbing, or sat facing each other at our table grinding out the next chapter for one of our books. I had never really thought about what I meant to Guy. Nor did I come close to saying what I loved in him. It was just a fact that needed no explaining. So, when he handed me this chapter and I read these words for the first time, it was eye-opening. Guy wrote what he could not speak. These words meant more to me than any spoken words he could have said. Words—writing them—was Guy's medium.

"All holy men dream, and by following holy men their disciples attain that power," Kipling wrote in *Kim*. Guy was a teacher, like my father who would put the book—one he felt I would both enjoy and learn from—in my hand. Guy operated this way: few words, but actions. I was the willing disciple/apprentice of first my father, then my husband. And my discipleship/apprenticeship gave me power. Much was carried out with few words, even nonverbally. I always felt listened to, even though we might disagree; even if I lost the argument.

I would have liked more words, more verbal exploration of emotions and feelings. Both Guy and my father, strong presences, remained guardedly sparing of words. I remember overhearing a heated discussion my parents were having over their ritual before dinner cocktails when I would be upstairs laboring over my homework: "I am who I am," my father pronounced in a voice that brooked no discussion. It comes to me, years later, that my father was saying: I'm not going to change. He was also saying: I am not going to explain myself. For most of my life I had seen my father and my husband as very different animals and I was proud to think I had not, as Dr. Freud says women can do, married my father. Their similarities ran deep, much deeper than the remark that if my father was asked to engage in physical exercise he opted to take a nap. To counterbalance, my mother stood up to her husband, and I absorbed that, too.

> During the 1980s life at Barra seemed to continue much as it had in the 1970s. We made no major changes in the way we lived, and we still climbed and hiked, read and wrote. But there were several new or changed elements; and underlying these few changes in what we did lurked some fundamental shifts in

my view of life, or at least a resurgence of calibanian darkness, shadowing the arielian light of those first magical years at Barra.

First as to some different activities. One major change was in the focus of our writing. During those first 6½ years in Vermont we wrote magazine pieces, especially that monthly column on camping and hiking for *New England Outdoors*. In the fall of 1978 a small publisher, Stone Wall Press, contacted the magazine about assembling the best of those columns into a book. We signed a contract, and devoted the period between Thanksgiving and Christmas to editing the columns, writing a few new ones to supply gaps, and producing the manuscript for this, our first book. It came out in 1979: *Backwoods Ethics*, the first edition.

The appearance of *Backwoods Ethics* changed the way we and others saw ourselves as outdoor writers. It cast us in the role of major advocates for a point of view about mountains and backcountry and wilderness. We began to have a role in backcountry policy; we and others began to take ourselves seriously, maybe at times too seriously.

One consequence was that AMC Books, the publishing wing of the big hiking club, approached us and asked if we'd like to do a book for them. We thought about it, and presented them with three alternative suggestions. The one they picked was for us to put together a comprehensive history of hiking and climbing in the northeastern United States. Had they selected either of the other two ideas, perhaps the job might not have been as large. Even with the comprehensive history, we thought we'd get it done in perhaps two or three years. Instead [*Forest and Crag*] turned out to be the exclusive focus of our writing for the next decade.

This was a big change. This move into the world of writing books was followed, in 1981, by the death of Guy's middle son, Johnny, well known as a brilliant climber, on Denali in Alaska. It looked like a suicide. John's death caused Guy to realize he might have lost his firstborn, Bill, as well. When last heard from, Bill was in the wilds of northern Canada. He could be alive but Bill hadn't been heard from in nearly a decade. If dead, his death was unconfirmed. The impact of these loses caused Guy to draw back—not from the mountains—but from roped climbing.

I should not leave the impression that I quit climbing, rock or ice, casually or out of boredom or preoccupation with more important things. Climbing had been central to my emotional life. My gradual alienation from it caused deep pain. I always yearned to get back up there, still do. To be unable hurts, bad.

My pattern of summer hiking changed too. In 1980 Laura and I took on the responsibility for tending the Franconia Ridge Trail, a high mountain traverse with the reputation, for many, of being the finest mountain walk in the east. For 16 summers, we gave a lot of time and effort and creative thought to the problems associated with heavy hiker traffic on that ridge. We tried not to let three weeks go by without getting up there to work on innovative solutions to the problems. This is not the place to explain all that was involved, especially as we have written extensively on the subject (e.g., Chapter 16 of *Backwoods Ethics*, 2nd edition). But our commitment was deep. Most of our other time in the mountains in summer was also geared to stewardship rather than self-indulgent hiking. Especially after *Forest and Crag* appeared, we became a well-known force in northeastern mountains, and leading exponents of the philosophy of stewardship for eastern wildness, of giving something back to the hills, of preserving the eastern mountains from the harsher impacts of hiking and climbing.

There was also a negative aspect of this involvement. Some issues were controversial, we were outspoken, and over the years of the 1980s we gradually found ourselves on the opposite side of many issues from the Appalachian Mountain Club, the dominant organization in northeastern backcountry. These disagreements often erupted into major disputes, and we—I, more than Laura—became overly emotional in championing what we believed was right for the Franconia Ridge and for the backcountry in general. While many vociferously applauded our stands and regarded us as the chief champions for the beleaguered cause of wildness in the east, I'm sure our opponents felt we were insufferable, self-righteous, a pain. We probably provoked fights unnecessarily at times: the influence of Caliban in places where Ariel might have made more progress. I won't catalogue details of these controversies—partly because it's painful to recall them and I'd rather let the sleeping dogs of those memories lie.

I could often tell when Guy was overcome with thoughts of disappointment and failure. If we were in our woodshed, me sawing the four-foot lengths to cookstove size and Guy splitting, I sometimes became aware of how forcefully he was attacking a log. I sensed a desperate energy, all his efforts concentrated in single-minded determination to *split that log!* He mentioned, more than once, that a lot of his aggression toward the current frustrating issue, and toward himself for his own reaction, got worked out with the maul, splitting wood.

On the day that Guy left to lose his life in the mountains, February 6, 2000, he handed me, at breakfast, the last three pages of his memoir.

"Don't read them now, Laura," he said, "wait until I've gone."

Reading them now, and I have read them many times, has helped me to see a little deeper into Guy's dark world, so different from my own. This was his clear choice. And because I loved him, I honored it.

> The transition away from deep involvement in the mountains and in the issues of preserving wildness in the northeastern backcountry has been painful, associated with a sense that we were retreating, defeated, from the field. A few people have said some very nice things about our books, but on the whole they and our ideas about eastern wildness seem to be sinking into oblivion unnoticed. All this is accompanied by a feeling that I could have done better.
>
> To be retreating from that arena is to remind myself that I retreated from others at other times in my life. I left jazz piano playing without ever finding out whether or not I might have had something important to contribute there. I walked away from an amazingly promising start in Washington politics. In many ways, thinking of the public service aspects of my work in Washington, I think the most useful thing I could have done with my life would have been to remain in the center of staff work there—I might have contributed in important ways to the nation's business. Of course there are people who would say that the example Laura and I have set in living as we have for 25 years is a shining beacon to others. But we are not cut out (as Helen and Scott Nearing were, for example) for a leadership role in this arena. For one thing, we really have shaped a life relevant only for the two of us, not a pattern for others to imitate. And

if you look closely at almost anything we have done, it doesn't stand up to scrutiny as a model for others.

Considerations like these have left me with a sense of dissatisfaction about what I've accomplished all my life. When this feeling first became uppermost, as we pulled away from our mountain involvements, it was very depressing. The year or so before and after my 60th birthday (May 1992) were particularly depressing. The years since have not really been much better, only more numbed. I play the role of genial host and wit, as best I can, so that few of even our closest friends are likely to be aware of how I feel. The opera *Pagliacci* seems to me particularly poignant as a result: that's what I seem to be walking through these days, trying to provide sparkling company for everyone but ready to give up otherwise. Laura is the only one subjected to the blackest of my moods—an intolerable burden for her, which she bears with inexhaustible patience and sympathy.

I could add that the physical process of aging appalls me. I have been uncommonly lucky physically, all my life, have sailed through with no major broken bones, no serious illness, not even significant pain. But now I find all kinds of minor aches and pains, and physical limitations I never knew before, harbingers of advancing age which are only bound to become much more evident, more limiting, more uncomfortable. As I look at people in their 70s and 80s, even those who are cheerful and uncomplaining, I see they put up with many things I hope I never have to. I'd not be cheerful and uncomplaining. So longevity has ceased to be an objective of mine.

I have used—probably to excess—the metaphor of Ariel and Caliban to describe the warring tendencies within me all my life, the constructive and positive versus the negative and destructive. Sometimes I think of my father and my son Johnny as embodying these two impulses.

My father—Hawee, as all the family called him—stood for everything positive, a deep sense of public service, and "Olympian calm" (my sister Anne's apt phrase), always in control, upright and strong, though always gentle and reserved. If this sounds like hero worship, let me add that he was never, for me, a warm father or able to be close to me, or to help me with my childhood, teenage, or young adult problems. I do not revere his memory. But I see in his dedication to public policy a side of me that has always struggled for expression.

Johnny, on the other hand, poor Johnny embodied those impulses in me which have been destructive, as they were so finally for Johnny. He was always at war with the world, never knew calm, always teetered on the verge of being out of control— and frequently was. As Hawee seemed to dwell in a world of sunshine, in the service of his fellow humanity, Johnny struggled always in a world of darkness and storm, alienated irretrievably from his fellows in this life.

Both in me. I know that the same high positive impulses of Hawee's have been prominent in me at times—wonderful tendencies. But the same demons which drove Johnny to destruction have always intervened—where, after all, did Johnny get them from? And though I've grown a protective covering of smiles and talk, I too am alienated from my fellow humanity and dwell in a private world of storm and darkness.

Ariel versus Caliban. Prospero's options—the world was all before him, where to choose his place of rest. As I look at where I have come to, after 67 years of struggling, I see that Caliban has won.

Lighting Out for the Territory

III

Lighting Out for the Territory

14

Two Sides of a Promise

This is my attempt, two decades later, to fathom out Guy's need to take his own life, and my own role in supporting his decision.

We walked with our naturalist friend Dan Smiley in the forest of the Mohonk Preserve after a May snowstorm of thirteen inches that brought down many hemlocks. We remarked on the devastation. That was the word we used to describe this sad sight of so many hemlocks knocked down. "Hemlock is a brittle wood," Dan explained. He smiled at us as he waved his hand through some slim, newly budding branches, "their loss creates an opportunity for this young beech." I have never forgotten Dan Smiley's words that contain the lessons of how to handle loss. For sure, that death of a tree, even, in this case, many fine trees, does not hit our lives the way the death of a close family member or friend does. Nonetheless the lesson remains. Will we take the opportunity? Will we branch and grow into a new life, like the beech?

⚮

An act like suicide is prepared within the silence of the heart, as a great work of art.

—Albert Camus, The Myth of Sisyphus

I am already about halfway through writing this book, and I realize that Guy's suicide cannot be left out. The logic of this is immediate and takes me over. He has been gone more than twenty years. I have the perspective, now, to make an open-minded, concentrated examination of my own role in Guy's decision to take his own life.

It is easy getting started. Immediately Guy is strongly living in my mind. I can feel the benefit of those twenty-plus years during which I have moved into another phase of my life. I can look back on our marriage and view my own actions with the refreshing clarity of a deeper introspection, and no—or little!—impulse to censor. I have entered a roomy space—windows wide open—that Guy feels a part of, too. His presence, as I move forward day by day, is solid, steady, cooperative, encouraging. I feel no resistance. We had been accustomed to working together on writing projects. In a sense, we still are.

So often when people kill themselves, we wonder whether they truly meant to, or if they were secretly hoping someone would save them. What made Guy's suicide different was that I *knew* he wanted to take his own life. I had known this for a year and a half before he did. That he was looking for a way out was something he'd been talking about. I was aware of Guy's low turns of mind—his "demons." I was familiar with them because they could cast a deep gloom over our life together. But if I suggested that he get help, the conversation came to an abrupt halt. Guy was not interested. End of discussion. I never connected Guy's demons with depression, and certainly not with mental illness, of which depression is a part. Demons became our code word. A nice nineteenth-century word, a century whose aesthetics, literature, morality, technology formed a mutually comfortable place, a place that had drawn us together in the beginning and on which we had built our homesteading life. There was the proper distance that this word "demons" gave to Guy's low moods that kept the more twentieth-century sounding word "depression" shut out. I never connected the two words because I never thought of Guy as depressed—that they described the same thing: the possibility of a mental illness. The word demons also shuts out the possibility of further discussion of the freight this word carried.

A depressed person, as I understood it, had trouble getting out of bed and accomplished little during the day. Guy arose at 4:15 a.m. and spent the day fully engaged with the activities of our homestead. He was productive and his life was disciplined and scheduled. He made daily use of those three-by-five index cards I was introduced to on our first backpacking trip over the July Fourth weekend of 1970. Now he was in his late sixties and, from what he'd told me, it seemed he'd been wrestling with these moods for most of his life.

He had read *Final Exit*, the book the Hemlock Society offers about ways to end it all. I took a look at this book, but not a close look. He spoke of physical problems that in his opinion would only grow worse. One of these he saw our doctor about. It turned out to be a vitamin deficiency, not uncommon with long-term vegetarians. His other issues seemed minor to me—sore muscles, possible knee problems. Certainly not life threatening. Though, for Guy, perhaps they were, if he was physically compromised. He was hiking with friends more than half his age who were hard-pressed to keep up with him on the rough White Mountain trails, and especially on bushwhacks of which he was a master.

We never discussed aging, though I discovered after I turned sixty that aging could become a conversational topic. But it must have been on Guy's mind, because he wrote in words he left for me to read, "I could add that the physical process of aging appalls me." Possibly, what "appalled" Guy was that we have no control over our aging, and for Guy, though I didn't see it at the time, maintaining control was top priority.

There was a lot I didn't see. Guy was such a strong force that what he didn't want discussed got conveyed to me without words. My words were silently resisted. And I, being the good daughter in my alcoholic family, had excellent skills in smoothing over the rough places.

When I was a child, and even as a young adult, I was called gullible, also biddable, meaning ready to entertain another viewpoint. The gullible quality made me easy to kid. The kidding was always friendly, good-natured, and fun. The biddable quality was more problematic and got me in trouble when I was spending a college year in Paris. It was a lonely time for me. My French was not particularly fluent. I chose not to pal around with my

American classmates. I was here to experience Parisian life, and I took this seriously. I took a lot of things seriously, as well as literally. And these qualities ended me up in an organization then called Moral Re-Armament (MRA). Here I met an engaging handful of young people from various countries, and my loneliness—a feeling hitherto unknown to me—was alleviated. The mission of MRA was to fight Communism. I never questioned how or why—this was near the end of the Cold War of the 1950s. Communism was a bad word, not compatible with democracy or capitalism. In essence, I was invited to MRA's home place, a former tubercular sanitorium in the Swiss Alps. This location—the Alps!—having grown up with *Heidi*, did its seductive work, and I abandoned the college program to join up. I tell this story in more detail in *Losing the Garden* but give an outline here to show how it is my nature—for better or worse—to follow my instinct, bypassing much rational thought. If someone I like and respect came up with what seems to me a good idea, I'm likely to jump on board. I'm not indiscriminating, but that's why I say there was a lot I didn't see in relation to Guy. I had fallen in love, and this had much the same effect as the brainwashing process that happened with Moral Re-Armament. In that case, my vigilant mother, who knew her daughter better than her daughter knew herself, flew over, and with the help of my college advisor and our family friend, Louis Rubin, who was teaching summer school in southern France, brought me to my senses, and transported me back across the Atlantic.

But this experience—what was at its roots—I feel, later fed into my marriage and relationship with Guy. I respond to ideals, and what Guy was proposing with the homesteading/climbing life was most agreeable to me at that intuitive level, especially as it expanded to writing about mountain stewardship and backwoods ethics in service of keeping our mountains wild. Then, Guy, with the behavior of his treacherous demons, was, in a sense, territory as familiar as my own alcoholic family and my role therein. Mostly, all I could do was stand by as Guy's low moods played themselves out. Urging psychiatric help only angered the demons and we both suffered for it. Perhaps Guy needed someone to do for him what my mother had done for me. But no. I could be worked around, I was pliable. Guy could not be talked around. I have no need to maintain control, whereas control was essential to Guy in keeping his mental balance. We were well matched this way. Though there was a cost and Guy was aware of this. But it was a cost I would willingly pay again—if life repeated itself.

In his early sixties, Guy took on a part-time winter job for the Randolph Mountain Club caretaking a cabin, Gray Knob—a destination for hikers—

located just below treeline on Mount Adams, the second highest White Mountain peak. He did this for three winters in the early 1990s. He shared weeklong stints with another, much younger caretaker and, always, he returned home in a good mood, relaxed and settled in his mind. He relished his role as host and his ability to advise people on their trips above treeline in winter.

The week-on, week-off pattern worked well for me, too. I had been writing short stories and Guy's mountain cabin opportunity gave me more writing time. I was comfortable at Barra by myself, my concerns on only the basics of bringing in wood for the stove and water from our stream. The mile-and-a-half walk to our post office in the village made a good afternoon snowshoe outing. I knew Guy, up at Gray Knob, had time alone, too, that he put to use cramponing up Mount Adams, by himself or with a visiting friend. By the end of the week I was looking forward to hearing his step on the porch, and over dinner he told me the stories of his week. I knew the terrain, so could visualize his excursions, and I knew the friends who had snowshoed up to visit him. Especially I was glad for the peace of mind these stints in the world above the trees gave him. The physical exercise, combined with the wildness to be found in the Northern Presidentials, could quell Guy's demons (depression), at least for a while. Guy's unspoken goal must have been to concede little or nothing to age.

These romps, though he never verbalized this, were his fix. There was so much I didn't see then. What I did see was the deep pleasure he took in covering ground, the joy he found in the harsh beauty, in the wild wind, the gelid temperatures, and the challenge of low visibility. He told me once of the confidence that filled him, of his awareness that few could equal him. It was not until much later that I came to equate how all this wildness must have matched his own mental hurricane, his own existential despair. This was his world that could put him right with himself. Caliban was beaten back. When Guy burst through our cabin door bringing in with him the tang of spruce and fir, I knew immediately, with relief, that Ariel was in ascendence.

Guy had told me about his demons when we had first met at the Shawangunks. It didn't set off any alarms for me. I wasn't sure what he meant. I appreciated his frankness, didn't ask for details, and saw little tangible evidence of his low moods for about a decade.

The year 1981 was a watershed that brought out in Guy those demons that had lain dormant. The death of his son Johnny in the Alaska Range forced him to accept that he was likely not to see his eldest son, Bill, again, either. Bill had disappeared somewhere in the Canadian wilderness a decade earlier. An unconfirmed death leaves the question of actual death open forever. Guy lived with the possibility of Bill's walking onto our land at any moment. Johnny's death, though his body was never found, was confirmed by the National Park Service, and it looked like suicide. Was Bill's suicide as well? Guy's youngest son, Jim, lived in the west. They saw each other rarely.

Because of these devastating losses, I became acutely attuned to Guy's dark moods. If he was having a bad day and we were working in our woodshed on the daily task of sawing and splitting wood, I became aware of the grim determination with which he wielded the maul, bent on working out what he felt but would not express. If I asked him what was troubling him, my question was not answered, or his reply was "talking doesn't help." Talking usually helped me, but Guy meant this, and I only seemed to make life harder when I persisted.

His moods could have been triggered by the loss of his sons, but there were other issues that had to do with our trail work on Franconia Ridge—disagreements with the Appalachian Mountain Club that affected Guy deeply. He was also troubled that the books we had written about keeping our mountains wild had little effect. If I tried to point out that our books had in fact captured the attention of the managers and agencies, he brushed this aside. It wasn't enough. I later read in what he had left for me that he felt he had failed with the most important parts of his life: being a good father and being a champion for wildness. I might know what bothered him, but by pressing him to talk it out I only seemed to make life harder for Guy. That was the one thing I didn't want to do, and I felt terrible when I saw I'd gone too far. Years later, a friend said that what had kept Guy silent must have been "badly scary stuff," so terrifying that it enabled his demons (aka depression) to skew his self-understanding. Perhaps so. All I knew at the time was that my pushing only made things worse for him and harder for both of us, just what I wanted to avoid.

Boris Pasternak, in *An Essay in Autobiography*, had this to say about taking one's own life: "A man who decides to commit suicide puts a full stop to his being, he turns his back on the past, he declares himself a bankrupt and his memories to be unreal." ("Unreal." Does Pasternak mean not to be trusted?) As irrational as this act might sound, this description of suicide seemed to fit what I could understand about my husband.

I have time, now, as I've made my own life, separate from my married life, to realize how strongly suicide figured in Guy's psyche.

During the early years of his first marriage, when he was working on Capitol Hill in Washington, he had walked out onto the Calvert Street Bridge crossing Rock Creek Park—DC's most famous jumping-off spot for suicides—with that intent, but then walked back again. He had told me about that not long after we began climbing together. "What made you walk back?" I asked him. He shoved my question away with the back of his hand, as if it were not worth answering. "I just worked through what steps I needed to take." Whatever this meant, he had found a way out. Yet his answer did nothing to help me envision the blackness he was fighting as he stood staring over the railing of that bridge. Or, how he pulled himself out of it. What is your existence like when you reach the level of despair where your life feels worthless, rotten? I had no idea, having plumbed nothing more than a bad day.

Suicide interested him as a subject. We talked about well-known individual cases like Arthur Koestler; I had read *Darkness at Noon* in college. Guy knew about William Styron's *Darkness Visible: A Memoir of Madness*, though he didn't read it; I picked it up several years after his suicide and found it a heart-wrenching, depressing book, though the darkness Styron wrote about remained invisible to me. That made me aware that while I might, to some extent, understand what triggered Guy's demons, what was going on in his head was largely a blank to me.

Guy would occasionally talk about a classmate at Sidwell Friends School in Washington, Warren Groome. Warren had seemed to have it all—a high-achieving academic and athletic record as well as leadership qualities that got him perennially elected class president. Guy was particularly impressed with Warren's character. He was genuinely nice to everyone, including outsiders, which Guy felt himself to be. But when Guy encountered Warren again a decade later, it turned out that he had not sustained his promise at Princeton. On top of that, he was an only child who had lost both parents. Guy, by this time, was working successfully on Capitol Hill, while Warren's self-esteem seemed shattered. Within the year, at age twenty-eight, Guy heard that Warren Groome had put a bullet into his brain. "It's a tragedy that has stayed with me for the rest of my life," Guy told me.

We didn't have conversations about suicide often, but neither can I say we had them rarely.

Quite regularly Guy soloed in the New Hampshire mountains. I came to see these hikes as restoratives for him. This alone time was a break for me, as well, from my on-the-job vigilance of Guy's moods. Aside from day trips, each winter Guy took backpacking trips of four or five days, combining trails and bushwhacks, often setting up his camp away from lean-tos or campsites. Most people regard solo trips in the winter as risky, the main issue being if something goes wrong you're on your own to solve it. This is also the point: you're on your own. Guy needed those confrontations with mountain wildness. We never talked about it, but I was sure, as I came to understand how these trips were important for Guy's mental health, that he knew I understood. A lot was unsaid between us. I would have been glad for more talking, yet had to settle for being mutually understood. Perhaps little was understood by me, since words like depression or mental illness were never used by Guy, and not a part of my vocabulary either.

One morning he left at first light for Franconia Notch, and I could tell from his goodbye hug—a kind of desperation—that he seemed more down than usual. He was in my mind much of that day, July 3, 1998, as I went about my work in the garden.

Late that afternoon, I welcomed an unexpected visitor, Mike Young, a climbing friend we hadn't seen in months whom I knew Guy would be glad to see. Mike and I were on the porch, talking, when Guy came down the path through the trees and passed through the gate at the bottom of the garden. I could see in his slow and deliberate pace that he was taking his time reaching us, and that the day in the mountains had failed to restore him to himself. This concerned me. But he was back, and, always the welcoming host, Guy greeted Mike warmly. His mental turmoil, which must have been considerable, was visible to neither of us. Guy was especially careful around guests to be the genial host. Only once, during our last sugaring season—always a time of many visitors—did Guy articulate to me the strain this took. I had seen this, but this time I saw it with new eyes—the effort, the constant smile, yet a haunted, hunted look infusing his determination to entertain—as he always had.

We all had supper together and at ten o'clock Mike went out to sleep in our guest house, which we called Twin Firs Camp. I began writing in my journal, as I did every night before going to bed, and then sensed Guy pacing the floor behind me. He stopped and said my name. I turned around to his voice telling me that he had tried to jump off Cannon Cliff, and failed.

Those words sliced deep, yet like the knife cut before the blood wells up, before the shock and pain, I felt a kind of paralysis, as if I'd been stunned. It was hard to make what I heard real—Guy was standing right there, fully alive, in front of me.

"I've heard that after an unsuccessful suicide attempt," he continued, "you can feel glad to be back in the land of the living. I don't feel that way. I feel utterly defeated. I don't want to be here, Laura, and I don't see any way out." He paused, but before I could gather my thoughts he went on, "In a few days I want to try again."

My immediate impulse was a quiet determination that I was not going to let this happen.

"But I don't know if I can do it," Guy said. "I'm terrified of making that big step."

My instinctive reaction was, as I always had, to want to help him do what he wanted to do. But he was saying he was going to leave me, to kill himself! Yet, I instinctively knew that Guy had already made up his mind. I would get nowhere trying to talk him out of this. He would only draw deeper into himself and close me out. At that moment, I felt the jolt a small animal must feel, desperately searching for a safe place to save its own life from a hawk or fox.

"Guy," I said finally, "if this is what you want to do, I have to be in a better position." He nodded.

I wrote in my journal before going to bed, "If he really feels this way, we should plan for it. This is awful. Guy feels totally uninterested in life."

~

As for suicide: the sociologists and psychologists who talk of it as a disease puzzle me now as much as the Catholics and Muslims who call it the most deadly of mortal sins. It seems to me to be somehow as much beyond social and psychic prophylaxis as it is beyond morality, a terrible but utterly natural reaction to the strained, narrow, unnatural necessities we sometimes create for ourselves.

—A. Alvarez, *The Savage God: A Study in Suicide*

I think Guy looked at suicide this way, though I don't believe he knew the Alvarez quote. Alvarez is writing about the human condition. And what Guy had just demonstrated was that he was sick of dealing with it. How do you not despair? You go above treeline in a raging tempest. But at past sixty your days on the heights are running through the hourglass.

What is unusual was that Guy chose to tell me. He could have kept this suicide attempt a secret. He could have not said a word and gone back over to Franconia Notch a few days later. Thinking about this now, I see that even at the time I was not surprised he told me. We did a good job of being honest with each other, even if Guy could not—would not—articulate his demons, that is, bring that word depression or even mental illness into the conversation. Perhaps it was these words that contained the "badly scary stuff" my friend had mentioned. In a sense it was his business, what he wanted to do with his life. But Guy believed in acting responsibly.

Suicide is an act conceived and conducted in secrecy. The one left behind can be in the ghastly position of finding the body—hanging from a rafter, in a bloody pool on the bedroom floor, or dead by some other self-inflicted means that leaves him, or her, alive yet an eternal prisoner to that moment of *finding*, condemned to a lifetime of that nightmarish moment of discovery.

If Guy had managed to jump off Cannon Cliff and his body was found at the base, as it would have been, perhaps by someone who recognized him, or if I had contacted New Hampshire Fish and Game, which handles rescues, as I would have if Guy had not returned, my life now would be very different. I would have had to suddenly face what our life together had meant: what, if anything, our love had meant—questions that would have plagued me and would have been impossible to answer.

During the next few days after his return from that unsuccessful attempt, we talked, and the talking drew us together. This felt healing, but at the same time it felt like I was living in the eye of the hurricane. Guy was very clear that he wanted to make an exit out of life. He was not interested in medical help of any sort. If that were the case, I was equally clear, I needed to be in a better position if I was going to go on living without him. Barra was a two-person operation, meaning Guy and me. I was not interested in continuing without him. Setting me up to transition away from Barra would take time. Guy understood that he would not be driving over to Cannon Cliff any time soon. As it turned out, it took eighteen months.

Near the end of the summer, my friend Carolyn Hanson invited me to be her traveling companion on a trip to Australia. I'd love it, I told her, but I'd have to check it out with Guy. A trip to Australia was not going to fit in with his plan, which now had him, as soon as winter arrived, walking up above treeline in the White Mountains and letting himself freeze to death. Guns, hanging, drowning, jumping—he'd discussed all of them with me— were not agreeable to him. Extreme January cold was his choice. January was the time Carolyn suggested for Australia—summertime Down Under.

So I was surprised when Guy said, "Go, Laura, go to Australia with Carolyn."

"But I don't want to take away from our time together."

"I can wait," he said. This meant he would put off his suicide for more than a year.

I knew he would wait. It was something Guy could do. Later, I came to see he was making me a two-sided promise: he *would* commit suicide, but he would put it off for me to make this trip. I knew he could do this because all I was asking for was a postponement. He could postpone, because Guy was a man who lived a scheduled, planned, intentional life, with daily tasks—and long-term projects—recorded on index cards he kept in his shirt pocket. I was comfortable with this. Later, friends asked me if I wasn't nervous to leave Guy? Wasn't I concerned that he might not be around when I returned? Not at all. I had always taken him at his word. I never doubted he would be there when I got home again. It was a simple matter of trust. Of course, if Guy said he could reschedule his suicide to accommodate my trip, that's what he would do. Later, I came to see that this was so crazy it was almost funny. Yet, on another level it was completely sane. It was pure Guy! He had accomplished much in life by being organized and setting timetables. His desire to take his own life, and in his opinion that time had arrived, was the last item to be crossed off. He had, in a sense, by telling me his plan, asked for my help. Together we were on a last expedition that would part to reach separate summits in eighteen months. While I had not abandoned conversations asking him to get psychiatric help, when I brought up the subject, he continued to make it clear what he wouldn't do by refusing to talk. He just shut down, shut off. This was hard on me. I was better off if I didn't keep pushing. Meanwhile, together we had found a resting spot, a kind of concord; we were working together as we always had.

In a recent conversation with my friend Doug Mayer, who knew and loved Guy and with whom I've had countless conversations as we both attempted to make some kind of sense of Guy's suicide, Doug said that when Guy withdrew into silence, he, and others, just let the conversation go. "This was Guy's way of keeping his life in control," Doug said. "We knew about his sons, his past, we were respectful—too much so." Doug added that he could usually push uncomfortable conversations with a peer, even joke a bit, but not with Guy. He went on to describe the magnetism Guy exerted, his charisma, when he was winter caretaking at Gray Knob. Hikers who only knew him by name snowshoed up the steep Lowe's Path for

3.2 miles. "People were in awe," Doug told me, "they hung on his words."

I could imagine this. Guy was in his kingdom at Gray Knob. There was very little about that much-loved cabin, at 4,400 ft., that spoke of comfort; because of the limited supply of dry wood, caretakers were not to light the stove until evening, and then, only if the inside temperature was below thirty-two degrees. It was a dark and ill-lit place, its floors wet from climbers' boots. Clothing, hung to thaw, never thawed on a January day at Gray Knob. Yet spirits were always high. It was an exciting, even fabled mountain cabin, where stories were told and retold of bold ascents and close calls, legendary searches and rescues, famously high winds and mammoth snowfalls. Mount Adams's summit, a desirable and challenging goal for winter hikers, could be attained if they spent the night at Gray Knob.

Guy told me not long before he ended his life that he had felt best about himself—most confident—when he was above treeline, alone, in marginal conditions: raging winds, blowing snow, visibility poor. (If he had succeeded in banishing Caliban, with the therapy of wind and storm, I've wondered since, could he have given up his desire to take his own life?)

The pared-down, elemental world of Gray Knob—its only contact with the valley a daily radio call with Bill Arnold of the Randolph Mountain Club, reporting the weather forecast from the summit of Mount Washington that Guy posted for the guests—suited Guy. His duties varied from working up wood for the evening fire, hauling water from the nearby stream, making sure the path to the outhouse was snowshoed out, and keeping an eye, at dinnertime, on the guests as they cooked over their small backpacking stoves. Perhaps Bill Arnold would call in to report a missing hiker, and Guy, in the position of first responder, would head out into the night—perhaps with one or two others who were capable—to see if they might intercept a lost party or come across an injured hiker.

When he came home for his days off I was always, always relieved to see him upbeat, cheerful, Ariel in ascendance. I wanted to hear all the stories. Guy made a point of saving them up, listing on one of his much-employed three-by-five cards the birds he'd encountered or the animals—snowshoe hare, ermine, red squirrel—whose track he had crossed or that he perhaps caught a glimpse of, or visitors to Gray Knob (often friends who had hiked up to see him). And I filled him in on everything that had happened at home: visits from the chickadees, or the evidence of a porcupine by the deep trough of his track near the woodshed.

Gray Knob gave Guy, at sixty, not just a vigorous outdoor life, but a responsibility. Guy took responsibility seriously, as he wrote in a speech for the president of the General Electric Company thirty years earlier: "We are each inevitably and terribly and forever personally responsible for everything we do."

I now see that life at Gray Knob was also something he could control. When he came back from Cannon Cliff and told me he had failed to jump, and then announced that his plan was to return, he was essentially asking for my help, but not my help in stopping him, or helping him to find a therapist. This was another kind of help. He wanted my support in carrying out his plan. It was the rare instance of Guy ceding control. He did not have to bring me into his plan, but by doing so he showed me his love and trust. (Looked at another way, I suppose, this could be seen as enabling, which goes along with the role I played in my own alcoholic family.)

At the end of Guy's third winter at Gray Knob, the Randolph Mountain Club folk gathered to thank him after he had descended the mountain for the last time. This gathering celebrated, as well, Guy's eligibility for Social Security. Sitting beside him I felt his intense discomfort; he was, for Guy, close to inarticulate in speaking his thanks, his voice constrained and formal. I didn't really know what to think. Why couldn't he just be relaxed and enjoy this honoring? Years later, a friend wrote, "In reading your book [*Losing the Garden*] the one thing which saddens me is the anger which Guy felt towards himself. It's a very hard feeling to explain yet an easy one to justify." For a man who had, as my friend Rebecca Oreskes expressed it, such "personal power," Guy lacked self-confidence to an equal degree. At Gray Knob that personal power elevated him to the status of cult figure.

"We all wanted Guy's approval," Doug later told me.

Carolyn's invitation gave us both a year-and-a-half reprieve. Together, we began to look for a place for me off our homestead that would be within walking distance of the post office and the library in our village. My friends were here. I had no desire to return to New York or to live anywhere else. I didn't want to carry on Barra with anyone other than Guy. So much of both of us was in everything we did. I began to see that we were on two different trains, and though we were moving in divergent directions, we were connected by mutual, but separate, goals.

The same friend who had said that what kept Guy silent must be "badly scary stuff" also pointed out that it all seemed highly unusual: we had created a contract, a mutually agreed-upon pledge. But why, he asked, hadn't I pushed it further? In other words, why hadn't I talked Guy into changing his mind? He felt I hadn't made use of the opportunity those eighteen months gave me. Though, I felt, I had made good use of them.

I was unable to redirect Guy, but that year and a half set me up for a future of my own choosing, one to which Guy gave his blessing, as I, ultimately, gave mine to him. Always, during that time, my deep hope was that he would decide to live. I never stopped attempting to renew the discussion about getting help, though it continued to be received in silence.

"Why don't you talk with Mike or John?" both of whom were climber friends, advancing through medical school. I had repeatedly made this request. I believe he had once attempted the subject, but so tentatively that nothing came of it.

Silence.

"Well, why not?" I could hear the frustration in my own voice as Guy spun away from me to stare out the window. I felt his resistance like a shove.

When I tried to push, it pulled us apart. He never wavered. Guy was not going to change his mind, though I hoped right up to the moment he walked out the door on that cold morning of February 6, 2000, that he would.

I hoped he would, but on the other hand I was so well launched aboard that moving train, so well prepared psychologically as well as committed to the material plans we had made for me, that jumping off it onto a different platform would have caused a major adjustment. For so long I had been living in two worlds, mentally preparing for one without Guy while at the same time not wanting him to leave this one. Yet, that was what he wanted. He had, by bringing me into his plan, asked me to take his words—his intention—seriously. Initially, I had found a way to keep him from returning to Cannon Cliff. He agreed to wait until I would be able to settle into a life without him. This was our "creative contract," in my friend's words. Adding amendments to the contract after the fact never occurred to me. In my mind was the conviction that Guy had entrusted me with a last wish that I could perform as his wife, as someone who loved him. Enabling? Supportive? I think we have a teetering balance of both here.

None of our friends or relatives were aware of Guy's plan, though those who knew him best and had a rough understanding of his dark moods—only the top of the iceberg—probably would have described them with the word "depression." Doug, in the weeks after Guy's death, told me he had thought that Guy might commit suicide, but not for at least ten years. Physicians say depression is a mental illness that can kill. George Howe Colt aptly titled his authoritative book on suicide *November of the Soul: The Enigma of Suicide*; in it he claims suicide remains poorly understood. In the opening words to *Moby-Dick*, a book Guy was drawn to read multiple times, and that we read together, Melville's Ishmael calls his depression a "damp, drizzly November in my soul."

We had told no one, which was one of those silent agreements that seemed to punctuate our marriage. Guy never asked me to remain silent, but I never thought to talk to anyone about his plan either. Thinking about it now, I suppose this sounds odd, but I was so aware Guy didn't want help that saying to anyone that my husband was planning to commit suicide would have felt like betrayal. The ask for help had to come from him. If I spoke up, he would have seen this as interference.

Even so, I did tell someone. For many years, I had taken an annual trip to New York to visit Annie Barry, my dear friend from my days as a New Yorker, and on a visit early in January 2000 I told her what Guy intended. I did this because I wanted her to know in advance, from me, and not hear about it after it happened. I wanted her to know this was what Guy wanted, he wasn't going to be talked out of it, and that it was going to happen soon. He was waiting for the deep, arctic cold of late January and early February. His plan was to climb Mount Adams, an intimate from his Gray Knob days, and sit in the cold and wind for as long as it took. I was torn about telling Annie. It felt like betrayal to Guy even though he had never asked me to remain silent. Annie was shocked by this news, and I felt from her that I should have steered Guy into the psychiatrist's office. She seemed unable to accept that he could not be brought around. I knew she was concerned for me, but we left it that I had told her because I wanted her to know I was prepared, that she shouldn't worry about me. (And it turned out, within a few weeks she read Guy's obituary in the *New York Times*. So, yes, I was glad I told her.)

I mentioned nothing to Guy about my conversation with Annie after I returned. Less than a week later, Annie wrote me, urging me to get help—if not for Guy, then for myself. Since we read all our mail together, I was not surprised that Guy became upset with me for telling Annie. Yes, I had interfered. I felt bad that Guy was upset. But I did not regret telling Annie. I was surprised, however, when Guy stood, legs apart, in the middle of our cabin floor and pointed to our front door, spun, and thrust his arm toward the window at the far end. His gray eyes were wild. "If Annie and her husband walk in the door, I'm out the window!" he ground out between his teeth. He would do that. No question. It was a dark, cold night. The snow was deep. He would not have paused for coat or hat or boots. He made this clear to me in a way that only actions can underline how intent he was on taking his own life.

While I was not apologetic, I hated doing anything that upset Guy. It was the strength of his reaction that made me most sorry, and I saw then that my telling Annie could have felt like betrayal to him. I had broken our unarticulated promise.

Guy's fear of being hauled off by men in white coats to a mental institution was not so far-fetched. At seventeen, his parents had become so concerned about his drinking and defiant behavior toward his teachers that they insisted he be placed under the care of a psychiatrist. Those weekly sessions were, Guy felt, totally unproductive, a waste of his time. He disliked the doctor, felt from him a lack of sympathy and the lash of caustic criticism. Guy was told he was a deeply disturbed young man. An evening session, attended by his parents, ended with Guy being placed in the psych ward in George Washington Hospital *that night.*

"It felt very much like jail to me," Guy told me, describing how the stairway doors and elevators were locked. "I was very unhappy. I deeply resented the loss of freedom." The ensuing fifty years had done nothing to soften his view of psychiatry.

He had decided, he told me, only a few days before he left, to revise his plan and take his life near the summit of Mount Lafayette, on Franconia Ridge, a place that had seen his best work and some of his happiest days. This resonated with me. Here, I knew, he felt an intimacy with the rocks and the tundra plants, with the homelike mountain landscape of deep forests and steep trails leading to a rare alpine glory of open spaces filled with sunlight and birdsong, with wind and wild storms.

The morning he left and was putting on his boots, he looked up at me as I was washing the breakfast things. "I'll always be with you, Laura," he said. He said other words that let me feel his love. In the note he gave me to read after he was gone, he assured me he was leaving me to carry on with my life, that he knew I would do it well. In those eighteen months we said goodbye together to the homesteading tasks that made up our typical year: sugaring, wood collecting, planting, harvesting, and so much more hard and useful work that made our life such a great joy. Over the years since, I have come to believe that keeping alive was not that important to Guy, especially after the loss of his sons, the disappointment (as he saw it) about our books, and the terrors—loss of control—he would confront as he aged. Guy's decision to bring me into his intention to take his own life gave us both a last gift of working toward an end together. He had always lived his life with goals; this was no different. For him it was the last goal.

For me, though it has taken a long time to see this, it has been a beginning.

15

A Vision of Wildness

My thanks to Mike Jones and Liz Willey who invited me to write the foreword for their Eastern Mountain Guide: Natural History and Conservation of Mountain Tundra East of the Rockies *(2012). Their work opens our eyes to a vision of wildness that knows no borders and is not impeded by boundaries, if, that is, we keep in mind that once such roadless areas are roadless no more their wildness is crowded out, banished, and lost forever.*

Guy and I came to Aldo Leopold late, long after we'd written those columns in New England Outdoors *that turned into our first book,* Backwoods Ethics. *Then* Forest and Crag *took up the decade of the 1980s. It was our forester friend, Ned Therrien, who expressed amazement to find out we hadn't read* A Sand County Almanac. *We hastened to amend this omission in our wilderness reading and Leopold's prophetic and mostly unheeded words informed and gave a mission-like focus to our* Wilderness Ethics. *We wanted to speak to wildness, so easy to disregard if you have in mind to make an "improvement" like a hut, or even a trail or a bridge. Can we make wildness more accessible? That, to me, is a contradiction in terms. What I like about wildness is that we can experience it in our own back yards, or a scrubby nearby patch of forest, or a lake or pond. In my childhood summers lived in the woods at our camp in Vermont I was in "wildness" without any conscious thought except to know that I was content. I was happy! Guy spent his young years around the large roots of tall trees, creating paths for his toy cars or trucks. He felt that close experience with trees informed his relationship to the care he took of not just his own woodlot, but of the alpine zone on Franconia Ridge. I believe it's these early experiences that lie deep within that can emerge later in our lives and, if we are lucky, take us to our true work.*

∼

Conservation is a state of harmony between men and land.

—Aldo Leopold, *A Sand County Almanac*

Wildness can be found in the forests of the eastern mountains of North America, but, to my mind, it is most readily tracked in the alpine tundra, perhaps because tundra is old. This tundra is a landscape that has survived, possibly because much of it is relatively inaccessible, subject to little human impact. Looked at this way, tundra connects us to land that is wild. But wildness is intangible—more a perception than anything else—and it can be compromised, even erased by unbridled human contact.

In the northeastern United States, this remnant of ice age vegetation graces minimally scattered high points. But tundra, and therefore the possibility of wildness, becomes more prolific if we tramp due north, up through Maine, and cross the international border into eastern Canada. Here, in the provinces of Quebec, and Newfoundland and Labrador, authors Michael Jones and Lisabeth Willey and the other contributors to *Eastern Alpine Guide* identified more than forty alpine ranges, many of which are little known and support thousands of hectares of tundra. It was my great pleasure to write a foreword to their book, because the value to the human mind and heart of keeping a few blank spots on the map—wild places, difficult to access, terrain that can terrify us with its indifference to humans—is all too often pushed aside for economic advancement, tourism, or even science. It is easy to rationalize, to bow to so-called progress. But we do so at our peril.

To those of us whose grandest encounters with alpine in eastern North America have occurred on the eight square miles of New Hampshire's Presidential Range (and to whom the 110 acres on Vermont's Mount Mansfield are precious beyond price), or on Quebec's Mont Jacques-Carter, or Newfoundland's Gros Morne, this expansion of our vision is nearly ungraspable. The very names have a ring that can fill us with longing to shoulder our packs and set off: the Lewis Hills, home to the arctic hare and the rock ptarmigan; Labrador's Mealy Mountains; and the nearly unknown Otish Range of Quebec, which by the authors' estimate contains thousands of hectares of alpine terrain; the Monts Groulx in Quebec, where wolves roam, the very symbol of wildness, having never been extirpated as they have from Newfoundland, Gaspésie, or New England.

Many of these mountains in eastern Canada are barely half the height of Mount Washington (1,916 m/6,288 ft.), the top of the world where I live. But loftiness counts for little there. These peaks on either side of the fiftieth parallel benefit from a lower treeline with every degree that they dance north. Many rise swiftly and steeply in a curve of cirques, their massive shoulders rounding up to a windswept tableland.

Here is found beauty. Here are alpine plants familiar from the Presidentials, Katahdin, Mont Jacques-Cartier, and Gros Morne: the cushions and mats of mountain cranberry, three-toothed cinquefoil, bog-bilberry, Labrador tea, and diapensia. Their roots interlock as the individual plants compete for moisture and nutrients. For shelter, too, since summers are short and damp and cold, and winters long and icy. But there are dozens of other plants not seen on these mountains unique to the uplifts farther north with their own particular geology. Caribou can be common on the tablelands. From where the authors of the *Eastern Alpine Guide* stand, they can see no roads, no buildings, no powerline corridors. Except for the caribou, they are alone. Remoteness is an attribute of wildness. They have walked few trails. Difficulty of access is an attribute of wildness. There is no safety net in the event of an accident. Uncertainty, too, is an attribute of wildness.

The far northeastern mountains are unique in their combination of geology, climate, weather, animals, and plants. Yet looming threats (climate change, highways, logging to the extent of deforestation, iron mining, wind turbines, and dams—one 213 m [700 ft.] high and nearly 1.6 km [1 mi.] across) lie just beyond, threatening the wildness, this seemingly endless expanse of eastern alpine—the total extent of which, in the *Guide*'s words, "has never really been articulated."

It is a landscape where those familiar with the Northeast's alpine zones would recognize some of the plants. The *Guide*'s authors have called the Mealy Mountains and Monts Otish "frightening untamed ranges." Mystery is an attribute of wildness, and in size, this eastern Canadian alpine could overwhelm those of us whose main experience with above-treeline tramping is the Presidential Range, or the more often frequented peaks of Quebec and Newfoundland. Because of its size, the alpine tundra of eastern Canada possesses wildness to a degree not present in the northeastern New England mountains. That is why it matters. This eastern alpine, with its remnant of ice age plants, is relatively undeveloped and intact. Since wolves still live here, the predator-prey cycles remain intact. It is landscape worth preserving.

Every incursion into wildness diminishes us as humans. We can ensure its preservation. But first we must come to value and love wildness for its own sake, and, as we do, ourselves.

New Hampshire's White Mountains saw early visitors, the botanists and the artists, at the turn of the nineteenth century. By the 1850s, Mount Washington boasted two hotels on its windy summit, taking tourists who arrived by foot up the trails, or, more significantly, by the 1860s were transported by the Cog Railway up a western flank or by the Carriage Road to the east. Mountain hotels sprang up on other New Hampshire summits. Hikers can see remnants of their foundations on Mounts Moosilauke and Lafayette. Great hotels filled the White Mountain notches from Pinkham to Crawford to Franconia for those who arrived by rail from Boston and Providence, Philadelphia and New York. Most did not come to rough it or to experience its wildness, though by the 1870s Moses Sweetser's guidebooks detailed the trails and described the summit views.

This pattern of recreational development can be traced across the northeastern United States and southeastern Canada. It spread to the Green Mountains and the Adirondacks, south to the Berkshires in Massachusetts and further south into Connecticut, and north to the mountains of Gaspésie. Of the more prominent peaks of the northeastern United States, only Katahdin escaped some sort of summit building. Its trail system, too, lagged behind the ranges more easily reached by rail or road.

No sooner was the trail system firmly in place in the White Mountains than logging began. By the 1880s, hundreds of miles of railway tracks penetrated the deep wild heart of the mountains. Logging roads, laid out like contour lines on a map, switchbacked up the steep-sided mountains so as to get at more trees to be hauled to mills by teams of horses. Men and horses lived in the logging camps, rarely coming out of the woods. Sparks, spewing from the trains' smokestacks, set fire to the forests, burning thousands of acres. Those in the mountain villages, where summer colonies devoted to tramping had taken root, complained of "the smokes." The air, even on the highest peaks, grew thick and acrid, views obscured. Hikers had no sooner cleared trails from loggers' slash than they would be covered again. By 1911, the Weeks Act, leading to the establishment of the White Mountain National Forest, ended this excessive despoliation. The forests grew slowly back.

"We abuse land because we regard it as a commodity belonging to us," wrote Aldo Leopold in *A Sand County Almanac*. "When we see land as a community in which we belong, we may begin to see it with love and respect." Once machines are turned loose upon the tundra, its recovery becomes unlikely. While our eastern forests can begin recovery from extensive logging in a generation or two, it takes centuries to grow tundra plants. But there is precedent. It has been set by those who fought to save New Hampshire's White Mountain forests with the passage of the Weeks Act. Before that, in the Adirondacks, in 1892, a conservation effort established the Adirondack Park that today contains a unique landscape of towns and forest industries, yet remains as wild as any comparable mountain landscape in the northeastern United States.

Wildness, as I see it, is perhaps the most threatened "commodity" on our planet today. Yet there's no denying the pull it has on us: being in a wild spot can lift us out of ourselves. Captain Alden Partridge, on the summit of Camel's Hump in 1818, a Vermont mountain whose alpine expanse, even then, was measured in square feet, wrote in a letter to *American Monthly Magazine and Critical Review* (November 1818), that he found the view "grand and sublime. . . . The whole appeared to me so strangely illustrative of the original state of chaos."

It *can* be frightening. Thoreau found it so on Katahdin in 1848. "Nature was here something savage and awful," he wrote in *The Maine Woods*, "Here was no man's garden. . . . It was the fresh and natural surface of the planet earth." Reaching the tableland, he wrote that a man found himself "deep within the hostile ranks of clouds," trapped in the "cloud factory. . . . Vast, Titanic, inhuman Nature has got him at disadvantage." Thoreau turned back, and did not reach the summit of Katahdin. He desired only to regain his companions, whom he found on the lower slopes, picking cranberries. Thoreau had been overwhelmed by mountain wildness, an entirely different degree of wildness from that found along the shores of his beloved and familiar Walden Pond: "[W]ind on our cheeks!" Thoreau wrote with exuberance, about his experience on Katahdin. "[T]he *solid* earth! the *actual* world! the *common sense*! *Contact*! *Contact*! *Who* are we? *Where* are we?"

We can feel, as well, his fear.

Some will visit eastern alpine wildness with books like the *Guide* in hand. Others will choose to stay beside their own Waldens in New York,

New England, southern Quebec, and the Maritimes. For them, it will be enough to know that farther north, enduring because of great size and isolation, abides a landscape of opportunities for remoteness, uncertainty, and mystery.

Aldo Leopold wrote in *A Sand County Almanac*, "Many of the diverse wildernesses out of which we have hammered America are already gone; hence in any practical program the unit areas to be preserved must vary greatly in size and in degree of wildness." Wilderness, as a resource, *can* shrink. It cannot grow. The same can be said of wildness. Our time here is short; our impact large. We must be mindful of what we leave.

16

At Home Above the Great Gulf

This unexpected, unlooked for day on Mount Washington demanded to be writ-ten. And the writing of it brought into even clearer focus what these mountains have to teach, even as my time ascending them moves into the past. I hoped Christine Woodside would publish this piece in Appalachia, *and she did, in the Summer/Fall 2020 issue.*

Great mountain days! We write them up in our journals. We mount our photographs; we draw our sketches. We reminisce with the friends we made the climb with, calling up that stream crossing where a misstep cost you a wet sock. How the thunder chased you all off that alpine ridgeline. Remembering sitting on the summit rocks passing around the gorp bag, the chunks of chocolate. Not thinking about anything. Letting the view fill you, the mountain air, the sun warm on your back. Someone points to a faraway peak, saying, "Let's climb that one next." And it goes on. Your whole life is defined by what you've climbed and what you're going to climb next. There will always be a "next." It could

*be something new, or a mountain you know better than your own backyard.
There will always be a summit, and from that summit you'll look outward, as
far as you can see, clear to the last blue mountain on the outermost ridge. It's
waiting for you, calling your name.*

~

"Perfect Weather for the job," George Leigh Mallory wrote in the note he left
before departing his high camp for the summit of Mount Everest on June
7, 1924. He never returned. Those words go through my head ninety-five
years later, as Dave Govatski drives Ryan Harvey and me up the narrow,
twisty Auto Road to the summit of Mount Washington in late June.

Below, where we set out, temperatures were in the sixties. In the
parking lot when we arrive the car thermometer reads forty-one degrees.
We were aware of the wind on the drive up, though it was hard to tell just
how strong it was after we'd left the trees behind, but as we get out, Dave
advises, "Hold on to the car doors when you open them." He'd once very
nearly had a door ripped off when he was remiss in offering this cautionary
advice to a passenger. We step out into gusty winds that rattle our pants
and shirts, and scurry around to open the trunk, quickly pulling out wind
gear and putting on extra layers, hats, and gloves. Climate-wise, Mount
Washington is equivalent to Labrador.

We are here to walk a mile-long section of the Gulfside Trail that
Dave, a retired forester with the US Forest Service and an amateur botanist,
has identified as needing major repair. Ryan and I have come representing
my small foundation, which works to protect the alpine habitat here. The
problem Dave has identified aligns with the heart of what the Waterman
Fund supports. Ryan, a forester and former trail crew and alpine steward,
can aid in assessing the damage and how to repair it. As for me, I remain
familiar with techniques Guy and I worked out with the Forest Service
and the Appalachian Mountain Club years earlier to protect the footpath
on Franconia Ridge, and I have tried ever since to communicate to hikers
the fragility of the alpine tundra landscape. We are here to observe where
hikers are walking and assess the current damage. And because our hearts
are here, in the wild beauty of this alpine world.

As we begin to walk, I see that our botanist has his eye on the plants.
Dave frequently stops to raise his camera and snap a picture, most frequently
photographing diapensia. It's a revered inhabitant of the alpine zone and is
usually past its peak, flowering by mid-June, but perhaps because we've had

such a cold, wet spring it still blooms vigorously up here: a five-petaled, waxy white flower on a short stem that emerges from a thick mat, or cushion, of small, dark green leaves. Though resilient when faced with subzero temperatures and hurricane-force winds, these cushions cannot withstand hikers' boots. We pass places where the soil has broken away, damaged areas caused by a combination of foot traffic and heavy rains. Diapensia lives in high mountains around the world, the circumpolar Arctic, but not the Rockies or the Alps. It needs year-round humid conditions without strong summer sun and desiccating drought. As the winds buffet us, I look down on these mats of plants, one of the most beautiful of the June flowers, flourishing in the thin soils, and I marvel at the ability of these communities to make a home in the windiest, most exposed sites, where they've grown since the glaciers melted away ten thousand years ago. Their leafy cushion has the ability to flatten when encountering winds that could kill humans. Many concerned about the health of our alpine world feel the imperative to communicate this story of alpine vegetation to every hiker who journeys above treeline. I stop walking to look around, my heart pounding, grateful once again to be up here and among these plants.

As we proceed, the background noise and commotion of the busy Mount Washington summit is left behind, and what we see, mountain ridges rolling out before our eyes, takes over. Looking down from the great height of Washington's shoulder, a vast wilderness stretches far out below us. There are no houses, no buildings, no highways, not even trees. At our feet lie rocks and the unique vegetation of alpine tundra. The farther summits of the Presidentials swell in the foreground, and beyond them mountains stretch to the skyline, a wild and inspiring (if you are a hiker) horizon of opportunities for a lifetime of exploring. And, if you don't hike, perhaps it is sufficient to know such wildness exists.

I am not the regular visitor I once was up here: I hike lower mountains now. One issue is speed. I cannot hike fast enough to manage, say, a ten-mile round trip that gains three or four thousand feet on steep, rocky, rooty White Mountain trails. That's why I seized on this opportunity to drive up with Dave and Ryan by means of the Auto Road. Even so, I have concerns. Can I keep up? Of course not, but they adopt a pace that I can manage. How about staying upright in these famous winds? I have my hiking poles. My balance is not what it used to be, but, again, I will manage.

My reading, by coincidence, over the last couple of days, has done nothing to quash my apprehensions—apprehensions that never crossed my mind when Guy and I were regularly running up and down from the Franconia Ridge. *Appalachia* arrived in my mailbox and I have been reading the Accidents report. Rather obsessively this time. There is something mesmerizing about accident reports, and I read them with an extra-heightened feeling of—*this could be me.* The winds in the Presidentials always have the final say about what one can manage. Today, the wind I am experiencing, if I were trying to weed my garden at home, would cause me to quit, retreat inside, and make a cup of tea, but it is certainly not a strong wind by Mount Washington standards. The three of us can talk without yelling in each other's ear. Our clothing is not rattling excessively. Even so, the wind is strong enough, now and then, to set me off balance, and I am grateful for my poles. Dave and Ryan don't seem affected by it, but they are bigger and younger. It has been many years since I was in a wind this strong. Then I realize that all my apprehension is gone. I am loving this exciting wind! I can sense my physical and mental adjustment as I relearn to navigate a rubbly, stony trail, even a trail in disrepair. Whenever Dave stops to photograph a plant, I catch up.

We descend steeply along the precipitous edge of the Great Gulf, which is still a remarkably wild place. It was never logged. The forests rising out of the gulf give no hint of the trails that lead up this steep-walled glacial cirque, most of them built between 1908 and 1910 in a breathtaking spree inspired by Warren Hart. As the Appalachian Mountain Club's councilor of improvements, Hart believed trails should offer adventure in precipitous and rugged ascents. Under his leadership emerged such challenges for today's hiker as the Madison Gulf Trail, Adams Slide (no longer on the map—too steep, too much loose rock, but climbable nonetheless), the Buttress Trail, Wamsutta Trail, Six Husbands Trail, and the Great Gulf Trail that shoots straight up the wildly steep headwall itself. (Guy and I had climbed up Hart's Great Gulf Trail from Spaulding Lake, whose waters are shimmering in the sunlight two thousand feet below us now; we had climbed the gullies on nearby Mount Clay, both thrillingly steep winter ascents, with ice axes and crampons.)

To our left we see the tracks of the Cog Railway, which form a trestle five or six feet above the tundra. In some spots we are close enough to be walking on coal. Only a few years ago the Cog changed to cleaner-burning biodiesel fuel. But chunks of coal and cinder that spewed out as the locomotive's boiler was fed over the years still remain ground into the alpine vegetation. This is not pleasant to see; for the benefit of tourists the Cog continues to operate one coal-burning engine. We discuss what coal is doing to the soil these plants receive their nourishment from. Dave tells a story of how a flying spark from the Cog burned a hole through his brand-new Gore-Tex jacket. In our view ahead are Mounts Clay, Jefferson, and Adams, arcing away in a curve to our right. Mount Washington is at our backs, its summit buildings dominating the skyline. We head for a spot a mile from the summit, at the junction of the Gulfside and Westside Trails, not far above the col that separates Clay from Washington.

We are not in wilderness. People pass us on their way up Washington's summit cone and go around us on their way down. We are here to observe. Most of them are not even walking on the trail, but on either side, on the tundra, doing this because the footing is so much easier. Many of these hikers wear sneakers or running shoes; perhaps they prefer less jagged footing. Some have on traditional hiking boots.

Ryan, Dave, and I exchange glances at the sight: this trampling is very hard to watch. It hurts. We feel it deep inside, like watching someone get slapped across the face. You clench your teeth, you wince. This trampling on the plants produces that same kind of visceral reaction. Guy and I experienced this when we saw it on Franconia Ridge. I hope every alpine trail worker reacts this way when witnessing such casual damage. Here, where we are standing, the tundra on either side of the trail has been worn down to the soil, with hardly a plant left. It's hard to fault the hikers for walking there, since the damage has already been done. But we can see some skirting farther out because there are enough people up here, going in both directions, that it is easier to leave the trail entirely than dodge around to let people pass.

While we're observing these hikers, Ryan asks Dave a question about climate change. Is the treeline creeping higher as the planet warms, thus adding to the pressures on the alpine vegetation? Dave notes that Mount Washington's summit temperatures, kept by the Observatory since the 1930s, though trending toward warming, do not exhibit a statistically significant change. He explains that thermal inversions and a high incidence of cloud fog may explain the summit's resistance to climate warming. It's a reply that could seem reassuring if the changes in our climate weren't such a real threat. He hastens to add that the same does not hold true for Pinkham Notch at the mountain's foot, or the nearby valleys. They are warming noticeably.

All too frequently the Cog rumbles by. It sounds like a full-sized train, and it has a whistle that sounds like a regular train's whistle, too. I surprise myself by waving to whoever might be looking out of the windows. Ryan and Dave wave too. The windows appear shut, the tourists cut off from chill air and this alpine world we are standing in. The train certainly has its charm. What's not to love about something that's so much a part of the mountain's history? It consists of one car for tourists and an engine that appears too small—too toylike—to be doing the heavy work up such a steep incline. But the Cog has been toting people up and down for 150 years. Mount Washington's summit is accessible to anyone by the Cog Railroad to the west and the Auto Road to the east. I'm glad this toy train has cleaned up its act. (Although with the trade-off from coal to diesel, hikers on the mountain have been left with more engine noise.)

Many hikers and climbers turn their noses up at the tourists who choose to ride and not walk, a silly, snobby attitude that I bought into for many years. It gives a meaningless feeling of superiority. When Guy and I began maintaining the Franconia Ridge Trail and had the opportunity to interact with our fellow hikers—often newcomers, many with questions when they saw us building a cairn or scraping out a water bar—that interaction often opened up a pathway to a conversation about our alpine world that could help it become their world to care for too. The same could be true of a tourist in the train's car.

What is going on in the small space of Mount Washington's summit is, in part, an effort to show people something beautiful and worth protecting. In the summit buildings are signs about being good mountain stewards—not littering, not picking or treading on alpine plants. There is a museum with displays on geology, botany, meteorological data on the lowest and highest temperatures, great storms of snow or rain, how frost feathers form, and how many people have died since the first death in the Presidentials in 1851. It's all in an attempt to stir wonder and arouse appreciation—even awe—for the natural world just outside the plate-glass windows. If Mount Washington and the Presidential Range can generate awe among those standing in a comfort zone, that could well be the first step to expanding their horizons.

Yet while Ryan, Dave, and I are not in wilderness, we are in the wild. We stop for a moment to savor it. We talk about wilderness, and how we would define it: a place with few to no people, difficult to access, with no human-made structures. When you enter it, you're on your own; you must be self-reliant and well prepared. We talk about what *wild* means to us. Right now we are surrounded by it, the Great Gulf spreading out before us, emanating wildness, as do the summits that ring the gulf, summits of pure rock, with no soil, or very little. Guy and I once marveled over a diminutive birch that clung to a toehold just below the tip top of Mount

Adams. Is it still there? Could it have survived the trampling of recent years?

These summits are hard to walk on—just great stone heaps. Mount Washington is referred to as "the Rock Pile." Footing can be tricky, dangerous to ankles and knees: mountains are indifferent to humans. And beautiful beyond belief. Washington's summit—a sacrificed wilderness—is accessible to everyone so that, it is my hope, those who visit can come to see beyond the buildings into the heart of wild.

Now, as the three of us stand at the edge above the Great Gulf, I feel as if I'm really seeing this monstrous glacial carving for the first time. Its size, at least by the standards of our eastern mountains, is enormous; it's a gaping, forested, green hole that dwarfs all other features on Washington, even the ravines to the east, Tuckerman and Huntington. The gulf is deeper, larger, and certainly more isolated. Because of this, it demands much more commitment to climb out of, to reach its rim. I look into the gulf with fresh eyes. During all those years I was actively climbing, I took such a scene for granted—just a part of my climbing life. I had no ledge on which to stand to see it otherwise. Today, perhaps because I haven't stood on this spot in a long time, I bring with me an overlay, or perhaps a foundation, of history. I appreciate not only the magnificent trail building that opened the Great Gulf to people, but also my own history of climbs here, mostly in winter and mostly with Guy.

The path we are on, the Gulfside Trail, was constructed by J. Rayner Edmands from 1890 to 1891. It extends throughout the Northern Presidentials, connecting the cols of Madison, Adams, Jefferson, Clay, and Washington, entirely above treeline. It does not go over the actual peaks but rather involves long, slanting, gradual grades, most suited to Edmands's conception of path-making. It is now part of the Appalachian Trail, and consequently among the most heavily traveled routes in the White Mountains, and therefore in the East.

An astronomer with the Harvard Observatory, Edmands possessed an intense, tightly wound nature and was called by some "a high-strung organism." His characteristic brand of trail construction differed from that of Hart and his sort, who made trails that went straight up, steepness and rocks be damned. Edmands made paths that slid along the contours to avoid steepness. He constructed graded, smooth, well-manicured footways suitable for ladies in their long skirts. His wife was partially disabled, and he applied the principles that he'd seen in Colorado, where graded trails were used for pack animals, to make the Presidentials more accessible to his wife. At least, that was one reason given for the kinds of paths he built. Perhaps what really drove this painstaking and conscientious man was imposing order in the chaos of the boulder fields above treeline, discarding angular and sharp pointed rocks, selecting large, flat specimens like paving stones, to form a stable and level treadway. To me, Edmands's deliberate care speaks to a deep love of his home mountains and a strong desire to share them with others in hopes that they would come to value them too. At the time, the White Mountains were being heavily logged and there were no laws in place to control this threat. Now his Gulfside Trail, built 130 years ago, is under another kind of threat, this time from heavy use.

Dave, Ryan, and I are conscious that we and the other hikers are walking on an historic trail. Not so unusual in the White Mountains, where most footpaths were in place before the Second World War, but all the more reason to pay attention to conditions that cause hikers to abandon it for the easier footing of tundra. To put what we are witnessing in the language of trail workers, this is a *badly eroded trail* in need of *rehabilitation, definition,* and *stabilization,* a trail that exhibits *excessive widening, braiding,* and *downslope creep.* The footpath has spilled out of its original bed. Dave and Ryan use a tape measure and find that the impacted area ranges from twenty-five to thirty-three feet wide. Most trails are constructed to a standard of four feet. *Braiding* occurs when hikers bypass the official way to create parallel trails. *Downslope creep* refers to the trail treadway gradually migrating downhill over time. This is common on steep sidehill slopes where footing is difficult, forcing hikers downslope to bypass obstacles. Some of the braiding is recent, which we can tell because organic soil is still present and compaction appears moderate. But other areas have lost most or all of the organic soil and the alpine vegetation has been damaged or lost. Remedies for this are the kind of work the Waterman Fund supports; not only do we help fund reconstruction, but we request with all our grants that ethical and educational components be incorporated into the plans. It's a way of making sure the word gets spread about human impacts on the mountain landscape we love.

Our small group arrives at the junction where the Gulfside meets the Westside Trail, our end point, a mile below the summit. It is midday now, and the lines of hikers coming up and going down have lengthened. Most are not walking on the trail, but when they do, we find ourselves stepping aside to let them pass. We want them to stay on it, this barely discernable treadway that has often caused us to stop, confused as to the location of Edmands's footpath, and not cause them to walk around us. Edmands's flat paving rocks are still here, but no longer continuously connected. Years of boot traffic and heavy rains have upheaved both rocks and soil. I think of ancient Troy, buried under the ruins of other civilizations. Even Edmands's carefully placed cairns are either missing or no longer in line with the historic pathway, perhaps because of the changes in the treadway itself due to human use. Whatever the reason, a misplaced cairn can take hikers farther off the trail, causing them to trample alpine vegetation. (All along, Dave has pointed out the occasional rare species.) In whiteout conditions, poorly aligned cairns also contribute to a dangerous situation, a scenario where hikers get lost. Yet, it is heartening to the three of us that the foundation of Edmands's work, in places, remains. We assure ourselves that it will be possible to restore this great piece of path-making.

We turn around now and retrace our route toward the summit. I am last in line, Dave leading, Ryan between us. We move along at a comfortable pace, close together.

A middle-aged man with a girl who looks to be not more than seven or eight is coming down toward us. There is room here for them to pass, so we don't step aside. But the man does stop—a sudden stop, right in front of me. I stop, too, in surprise. He is no one I recognize.

He fixes me with his brown eyes, claps his hands twice, and shouts, "Good for you!"

This feels friendly and positive, but I have no idea what he means, and my face must show this because he says, again in a loud voice that conveys his excitement, "You are keeping right on the heels of your two sons!"

I'm so startled by this outburst that I just resume walking. This whole interchange takes seconds; I barely break stride. I hope, out of my innate tendency to be polite, that I have smiled at him. Mostly I try to process what he just said. Ryan, who can't have missed that loud voice, peers around and gives me a slow smile. Which I return. Then I smile to myself. I could be the oldest person on Washington today. Kind of silly, but there's no doubt my reaction to being so singled out was definitely mixed: an interesting reality check—how I appear to others, compared to how I feel.

Dave, Ryan, and I eventually resume talking as we pass the Cog Railway tracks again on our way toward the summit. The Cog itself is part of the most recent threat to Mount Washington's alpine zone, the thirty-five-room lodge planned above the steep slopes of the Great Gulf headwall at 5,600 feet. The building, square in the alpine zone, would dominate this landscape on the west side of Mount Washington, looming to greet anyone climbing up Warren Hart's great headwall trail, irreparably harming the alpine tundra here, and the rare plants, insect species, and birds such as the American pipit that the tundra harbors.

Countless hikers, climbers, and lovers of mountain scenery have been active for decades to protect the range from excessive development, despoliation, or being loved to destruction by an overflow of trampling hikers. This ecology is too vital to lose. Too precious. There is a butterfly, the White Mountain fritillary, whose entire worldwide range is limited solely to the Presidentials' alpine zone. When the hiking and climbing community learned of the hotel plan, they moved into immediate action, forming a Protect Mount Washington campaign, raising money and collecting signatures in an online petition. For young climbers, many with international reputations, the Presidentials are sacred ground. They cut their teeth on these precipitous slopes and in this wild mountain weather, excellent training for loftier mountains. They are fiercely loyal. Alpine zones like this make up less than 1 percent of New Hampshire's land base,[1] and for the very reason of its rarity, they are willing to go all out to save it from development of any kind.

We approach the parking lot again, still talking about the hotel, the outrage of it, the harm to alpine vegetation, and the false sense of safety such a building would cause by its very presence. Where we have walked today, we would scarcely have been out of sight of the 25,000-square-foot building, all too aware of the Cog bringing hotel guests to it—guests who would doubtless start walking around on the tundra.

Money speaks loudly, but even so, as I situate myself in the car again, I feel confident that Mount Washington and its satellite mountains will weather this storm, too. Stewardship of our mountain landscape is in the blood of those who love it and climb in it. They are home here. It's easy to become fiercely protective of one's home. A good thing, because such threats will never go away.

So, the torch is passed along. We must continue to safeguard mountain glory like this, wildness just beyond our back doors.

---

1. New Hampshire's alpine is generally defined as being above 4,400 feet in elevation. The three figures often quoted to describe alpine are that it includes eight square miles, four thousand acres, and less than 1 percent of the state's land base. If the stunted trees known as krummholz, considered subalpine, are included, the figure is still a fraction of 1 percent.

17

Seeking an Ethic of Restraint

While newcomers can become future conservationists, there is a learning curve. We must become aware of our impacts that result in eroded trails, trashed campsites, and, especially, the irrevocable damage to the rare and precious alpine plants that can be crushed to pulp by footsteps.

After I wrote this op-ed for the Concord Monitor, *published on November 3, 2016, overcrowding got a lot worse. Stimulated to new heights (pun intended!) by the onset of the pandemic, the hiking season of 2020 saw an outpouring to the Northeast's mountains, accessible by one quarter of the North American population in a day's drive. (Only ten hours from Washington, DC.) Many of these visitors had little to no knowledge or experience of steep, rugged trails and changing-for-the-worst-fast weather.*

Much has continued to change on Franconia Ridge. The poor condition of the trail outlined in Sam Kilburne's report stirred action. The Appalachian

Mountain Club, US Forest Service, and other concerned groups and individuals have addressed problems not only with innovative trail repair, but with increasing coverage by summit stewards as educators. This work has been achieved by volunteers as well as those in paid positions. What's important to keep in mind going into the future is that newcomers will continue to seek this alpine ridge, meaning there will always be a need for stewards. Trails, by their very nature, especially on heavily trafficked trails where scree walls and even cairns can be broken down, can cause trails to lose definition and send hikers onto the tundra. Maintaining trails is essential. The point of the work on above-treeline trails is to safeguard these amazing plants whose ancestry began when the glaciers receded.

∾

The crisp air and nip of frost in the mountains of the Northeast make hiking and climbing the famous peaks there one of those ritually cathartic autumn pleasures. But on recent drives to New Hampshire's White Mountains I've found myself unable to locate a space in the overfilled trailhead parking lots.

My opportunities to be above treeline have dwindled for a number of reasons, not the least of which is the accumulation of my own years, but somehow, perhaps because of this aging, my perceptions and the wash of my emotions have become more sharply focused during these recent drives. I've become more aware of a deeply felt privilege to be in this terrain, so familiar, and I now see slopes and trails I have often climbed against a lifetime of past mountain days.

A frequent destination over the years has been Franconia Ridge, where Guy and I maintained a stretch of trail for eighteen years. On most weekends, I found cars parked along Interstate 93 a good half-mile before I reached the trailhead that gives access to the ridge's alpine footpath. You might think this to be a good thing, people getting out into the woods, up on the heights. But why, I would ask myself, haven't the state police cracked down? Where are the "No Parking" signs along this busy interstate? But it wasn't just too many vehicles I was concerned about. It was too many hikers. How could we regulate the crowds? How could we keep wild lands such as Franconia Ridge wild? What would it take to achieve a balance between recreational use and recreational abuse?

To better understand this situation, the Waterman Fund, whose interest lies in the alpine areas of Northeastern North America, commissioned in 2017 a young professional trail worker, Sam Kilburne, incoming Appalachian Mountain Club trail master that year, to assess hiker impacts there.

"Franconia Ridge was full of erosion as well as informal trails," Sam's report reads. "It is almost as if there is a second trail that runs the length of the ridge parallel to Franconia Ridge Trail. Countless informal trails lead out to rocks, presumably for views and lunch spots."

This 1.7-mile stretch of trail passes over some of the Northeast's highest—and therefore most sought after—mountains. From the summit of Mount Lafayette (5,260 ft.), it follows the backbone of the ridge over Mount Lincoln to Little Haystack, where the hiker can descend to a parking lot, closing a nearly ten-mile trail loop.

Sam continues: when he reaches the summit of Little Haystack, on a "busy Saturday, people are spread out to the ridge edge in all directions. Depleted scree walls are stepped on and over without a second thought. Major takeaways for me were, one, Little Haystack summit needs serious help and, two, informal trails all over the ridge need addressing."

The trail along Franconia Ridge is part of the multistate Appalachian National Scenic Trail, and over the last few years more than two thousand hikers have completed that route annually, an unprecedented number. The parallel trail Sam Kilburne reported is caused by such a high level of traffic that hikers cannot easily pass each other and so are pushed out of the defined treadway and onto the tundra and the delicate plants.

Obviously, Franconia Ridge's trail has, as far as the ecosystem is concerned, passed what managers call its "carrying capacity," its maximum level of sustainability. And for those seeking the spirit of wildness, well, forget that on Saturday when the weather is fine. Hikers who seek solitude and wildness would be better advised to make the crossing at midnight, or in a driving sleet storm.

What kind of trail rehabilitation and education would it take to stop the damage to the ecosystem on Franconia Ridge? How can such wild land be managed to withstand our recreational invasion? Land managers of the Northeast see defining and achieving this sort of sustainable recreation as the major topic of the years ahead.

While preserving the resource and allowing recreation at the same time is the mandate of public agencies, I worry more about the fundamental ethics of denying wild lands human-free breathing room, a state of nature that is the reason why we go out into nature in the first place.

One suggestion to control hiking traffic has been to curtail parking. When the lot is full, that means Franconia Ridge is full, too. Hopefully, as enlightened hikers, we'll hike elsewhere. But many wilderness hikers are independent sorts, who chafe at restraint: will they take the hint?

I have a sign, given to me by a fellow trail worker, that reads (in black letters against an orange background): "STAY ON TRAIL OR STAY HOME." It's not a friendly sign. No "please." No "thank you." Quite frankly, managers are not eager to control environmental damage like that—by slapping on regulations that limit capacity. Such an action runs counter to the sense of freedom we seek in the hills.

There are no simple solutions here. But that doesn't mean we should stop trying. Education is a key to making us aware of our own impacts on tundra plants that are so easily ground out of existence by boot traffic. Beyond learning about how our very presence affects flora, fauna, and geology, we need to come up with effective slogans that convey basic principles of conservation, such as the well-known "Leave No Trace." Perhaps better messaging could help hikers on their own bring a little restraint to the mountains (if the parking lot is full, go somewhere else), or responsibility (join a trail club and give back to the mountains by learning how to care for a trail), or respect (we exhibit our best behavior toward what we respect and love).

Some kind of major effort will certainly be put into rehabilitating Franconia Ridge and other popular alpine footpaths. After that, it will be up to all of us who love these wild places, as informed stewards of the land, to conduct ourselves in accordance with the privilege of being in that wildness.

Restraint. Responsibility. Respect.

18

A Wildness of the Imagination

When I was working on Starvation Shore, *published in 2019, I was often asked how I could write a novel about a landscape I had never lived in, or even visited. My answer came readily. For decades I had climbed in the mountains of the Northeast, especially the White Mountains of New Hampshire, in winter. I was familiar with brutal cold and mind-numbing wind, with snow and ice, with fog that shut down visibility, with freezing rain and sleet, sometimes all on the same trip. The dangers I faced were not on the same level as the men on my Arctic expedition, but they were enough to approximate, enough to put myself in the frame of mind to express the tactility to write this novel. People die in our northeastern mountains. Their dangers are easy to underestimate.*

It's the emotions—what we feel, sculpted in words—that can bring books to life. When I was writing Starvation Shore, *about the Lt. A. W. Greely Arctic Expedition of the 1880s, I turned to polar and mountaineering literature for inspiration to tell a story that I saw being as much about the inner lives—emotions and feelings—of twenty-five men as about danger and hardship, often extreme and prolonged, spent in the company of others in an attempt to reach a goal. I learned a lot from that. But, as important as articulating the tactility, I needed to consider the fact that these men had been abandoned by their own government who had sent them up to the Arctic. What did abandonment feel like? What did it take to draw on hope? Hope in the form of their own ability to rescue themselves, or even the seeming futility of clinging to the hope of a ship sailing into view? These men, in their day-to-day living, exhibited a wide spectrum of reactions to what appeared to them—what actually was—a hopeless situation. This was exciting to me. I saw that my job was to live with these men and find out what it took, when all the Fates are shrieking evil tidings, to build and maintain an edifice of hope.*

∾

We think we believe what we know, but we only truly believe what we feel.

—Laurence Gonzales, *Deep Survival:*
Who Lives, Who Dies, and Why

I loved writing *Starvation Shore*! It was the perfect project for several reasons, an outstanding one was the research gave me free rein to indulge in the genre that equates with comfort food for me: books of true-life adventure. Speaking broadly, adventure to me means anything that tests us physically and mentally. These books cause my world to fall away; I'm absorbed into the universe of the story. I wanted this to happen to my readers.

I had set myself the task of taking an historical expedition and casting it in novel form. I would be dealing with twenty-five men, most of whom were strangers to one another. Their Arctic setting at the eighty-first parallel placed them in one of the harshest environments on the planet. My research was revealing how ill equipped this expedition was to be not merely successful, but harmonious at an interpersonal level. To inspire and give me background to tell this story, I looked for nonfiction accounts that laid bare expedition members' truest selves—that placed them in situations that called for selflessness and responsibility, and challenged them to overcome their own crippling weaknesses and staggering flaws.

My expedition, the Lady Franklin Bay Expedition of the 1880s, was sent north by the US government to establish a meteorological station, to launch exploring trips throughout the northern portion of Ellesmere Island, and to smash the British hold on the Farthest North, held by them for three hundred years. These were all attractive goals for US Army soldiers to sign up for. Since these men were volunteers, I could work from the assumption that they were there for personal reasons as well. After all, self-discovery is at the bottom of most adventures, and, to my mind, it's the best reason of all. Without doubt, it's the hardest to define or defend, especially to ourselves. Perhaps it's the only reason that can keep us alive when we are in grave danger.

There can be no adventure without risk, and success comes from controlling, minimizing, understanding, and growing comfortable with the risk. We only court risk because the goal we hope to reach seems worthwhile. So, risk is an essential part of any adventure, as is the human need to aspire, to strive for something larger than what our everyday lives offer. Given the chance, we are capable of surprising ourselves by what we can, if not overcome, at least learn to live with.

Or can we? Were I a member of an exploring party, I found myself thinking as I dug deeper into the research, how would I hold up to the hardships? Would I crumple when it seemed too much was demanded of me? Would I find myself hating a fellow member just because she scratched her head in a certain way? I quickly saw, well, I had known all along, that this book was becoming something of a personal quest.

When I began my novel by turning to books on climbing and mountaineering, some I had already read, others had been on my list, still others were new to me. Often, I knew how the story would end. But this made little difference. I was reading to study how we react under stress of physical hardships, discomforts, and challenges, or the emotional pressures of cheek-by-jowl expedition life. I became voracious as I read about current cutting-edge twenty-first-century climbs, or turned back to the nineteenth, the Victorian age, when the rope was hemp and the summits were virgin.

I had long known that Edward Whymper's groundbreaking first ascent of the Matterhorn in 1865 had ended in tragedy. All seven, as they left the summit, were tied together on one rope. It took only one man to misjudge his footing, pitch forward, and tumble off the others like ninepins. The rope broke behind the fourth man, saving the other three from a headlong dive down that forbidding face. Whymper lived the rest of his life with this tragedy, in which was embedded the ironic stroke of luck that blew up the whole affair to mythic status. Years later, he soberly captured the incident in these understated closing words to his iconic book, *Scrambles Amongst the Alps*: "Climb if you will, but remember that courage and strength are nought without prudence, and that a momentary negligence may destroy the happiness of a lifetime. Do nothing in haste; look well to each step, and from the beginning think what may be the end."

When, at the age of twelve, I read Sir John Hunt's *The Ascent of Everest*, I knew that Hillary and Tenzing would reach the summit. It was recent news that coincided with the coronation of Queen Elizabeth in 1953. The whole world was tuned into this great achievement: the first human footprints on the loftiest spot on Earth. To read Sir John's book, this climb seemed like a happy expedition, no particular interpersonal squabbles. Yet, who is to say? The British are famous for maintaining a stiff upper lip and downplaying difficulties. Additionally, expeditions backed by governments, as this one was, were tightly controlled, as was what was written about them. But mountaineering books back then were not inclined to display much of what was going on beneath the surface anyway: the personal stuff, the emotions and feeling, especially if it involved discord. With Everest, the British had achieved a very great success that would reverberate positively throughout the lives of everyone on the expedition.

Writing about Robert Falcon Scott's 1911–1913 attempt to reach the South Pole, Apsley Cherry-Gerrard, in *The Worst Journey in the World*, wrote in 1922: "You forget how the loss of a biscuit crumb left a sense of injury which lasted for a week; how the greatest of friends were so much on each other's nerves that they did not speak for days for fear of quarreling; how angry we felt when the cooks ran short on the weekly bag."

There is plenty of raw feeling in Cherry-Gerrard's words, but it is presented in such a neutral evenhanded manner. Names are withheld. Who were the "cooks"? Who were the "greatest of friends"? We will never know. That's not what is important. Cherry is conveying feelings here, but without judgment, statements of fact, yet as readers we clearly feel the injury and the outrage.

But most expedition books gloss over feelings and sometimes the facts. On the first ascent of K2, by an Italian team, Walter Bonatti's effort to bring up oxygen was sabotaged, apparently to prevent Bonatti from joining the summit pair. This forced Bonatti and the Pakistani porter, Amir Mahdi, to face a freezing bivouac at 8,100 meters, during which Mahdi suffered severe frostbite. The summit duo used the oxygen and achieved success, but the leader, Ardito Desio, attempted to claim K2 was climbed without the artificial gas.

There is plenty that goes on behind the scenes on expeditions, but little disclosure until well into the second half of the twentieth century. I'm thinking of David Roberts's books on his early climbs in the 1960s in Alaska that tellingly revealed the strain of climbing and living for weeks with only one or two companions. Eventually you begin to get seriously on each other's nerves! More revealing, Galen Rowell's *In the Throne Room of the Mountain Gods*, published in 1977, is a tell-all book, but Rick Ridgeway's *The Last Step*—a K2 ascent—lifts the curtain on who was sleeping with whom and whose marriages were disintegrating at a time when women were beginning to break into what was hitherto largely a males-only game.

I read about Chris Bonington's expeditions to the Himalaya of the 1970s and 1980s as the books came out. Bonington, like Sir John Hunt, ran large, siege-style expeditions. But there is no assurance of safety in numbers, as recent assaults on Mount Everest have proved, and during Bonington's attack on the southwest face of Everest in 1975, Mick Burke died. He was seen last by Peter Boardman and Sherpa Pertemba as they were descending from the summit. Nick asked them to wait at the col below the South Summit while he went up to tag the top. Peter and Pertemba descended and waited, and in that short space of time the weather dissolved into high winds and driving snow. Still, they waited. For nearly an hour. Until, darkness descending, their extremities freezing, they were forced into the agonizing yet inevitable decision to retreat.

Another fascination for me are near misses: the hair's-breadth close calls. I want to know, at a primitive level, the guts it takes, the strength of mind, the exertion of will needed to pull through an accident that leaves you, say, with two broken legs—as happened to Doug Scott on his first rappel from the summit of the Karakoram peak, one of the world's hardest, called the Orge (23,901 ft). All went well for his self-rescue—the mountain was steep enough that Doug could slide down the fixed ropes on his backside—until the steepness lessened. Or, how about an accident that puts you in the bottom of a crevasse—alive, but can you climb out? Read Joe Simpson's *Touching the Void* for that. (Spoiler: he did.)

Then read Ralph Barker's *The Last Blue Mountain* in which such a fall turns blindingly, senselessly tragic. Four young men are on a mountain called Haramosh (24,270 ft.) in the Karakoram in 1957. High on the slopes, two are avalanched into a deep, steep-sided snow basin in a 1,000-foot fall.

Cushioned by the snow, they survive this, but they have lost their ice axes and mittens. The other two attempt to save them but are handicapped by the loss of a crampon. All four end up in the snow basin, and their two attempts to climb out fail. They have lost strength and are forced to spend the night at the bottom. The reader is plugging for them: these are likeable young men, their love of mountains is evident, and this climb is a dream come true. Most important, all four get along and work well together. It's a harmonious climb! The next day, with a stroke of luck, they recover one of the ice axes. It looks like they are going to make it—in fact, the two who had originally fallen in are out—when the one missing the crampon loses his footing and pulls off his rope partner. Two are now back in the snow basin—*the other two*—and the riveted reader feels she is in that numbingly cold, heartless crevasse with them.

The Last Blue Mountain is a harrowing tale of an accident that ends with young lives forfeited. What moved me most, as I watched this catastrophe unfold, is the way emotions are displayed, not through words, but through the men's actions—their care of each other—despite failing strength, debilitating frostbite, and desiccating dehydration. In the end, one man is forced to make an impossibly heartrending moral choice, at the price of his comrade's life. I've read this book several times, and I know how this story ends, but I say to myself, as I pick up the book again, maybe *this* time the words will stack themselves some other way.

Why this hope against hope? What does it mean about our human nature? Why do I put myself through this? In my own *Starvation Shore*, why did Private Elison, who had lived to welcome the expedition's rescuers, have to die on the voyage home? I wanted to create a happy ending for Elison, who had lived for months with frostbite that ruined his hands and feet. He was uncomplaining and brave, appreciative of the care his companions took of him, and his extreme helplessness drew the best out of some self-centered men. But Elison died; being a slave to truth, that was a change I could not make.

Now I had the opportunity to read much-admired books by Peter Boardman and Joe Tasker. They gave me exactly what I wanted. These two young Brits were breaking new paths in the Garhwal Himalaya in India, their theater of operation the West Wall of Changabang (22,507 ft.). This was in 1976. They'd moved beyond the big assaults, the cumbersome army of climbers and porters lumbering toward base camp, the way most of the 8,000-meter peaks had been climbed. Changabang was Joe Tasker's idea. He'd lived with a close-up view of the mountain the year before while climbing

Dunagiri, and he asked Boardman if he was interested in joining him. It would be just the two of them on the route. Both men were looking for something "totally committing," as climbers phrase it. Pete, in particular, sought to get right with himself for having recently stood on the summit of Everest with the backing of such an enormous force. He'd had enough of the siege approach. What Pete and Joe achieved on Changabang was regarded by their peers as the most outstanding lightweight Himalayan climb to date, a bold and magnificent feat of mountaineering.

Times were changing, and Pete and Joe *were* the vanguard: two climbers on one of the world's biggest, hardest, steepest faces, a rock face that's been described as appearing to be sliced vertically, as if with the blade of a well-honed knife. Wild! Each was reliant on the other. Total trust was called for. Everything was at stake. Both had close family ties; both had girlfriends. There was no room for error, not even small miscalculations. What was driving them? Whatever it was, they were held in its thrall. They were strung out, knew it, welcomed it. It was what they had come for: to find out what each was capable of, to be conscious, always, of that thin edge. How razor thin could they hone that edge and still walk away alive?

So when I read what Pete writes in the midst of their own extremity—"As we picked up our sacks and sorted our gear at the bivouac site, spindrift was pouring everywhere, into our sacks, into our gloves and down our necks. We were retreating under bombardment. The hardware was so cold it stuck to our gloves. 'Let's get the hell outa here,' echoed a thought in a voice like a John Wayne movie, and with it came the return of the strange realisation that I was actually enjoying myself"—I was caught by surprise. Yet, at the same time, I laughed. I recognized that it was exactly this moment of elation, of revelation, they'd come to experience. Again, Pete: "It was a bitter ordeal—feet frozen, legs shaking with cold, bodies screaming 'no more!' Yet we were completely in control, treading the fine line that separates the difficult from the dangerous. It was impossible for us to feel tired whilst we still had one more obstacle to overcome."

Both of these experiences that Pete recounts are open to anyone: essentially, in the midst of doing some hard physical thing, your mind becomes clear, you're relaxed, you're at your best—your best self—you're at home where you are, your life has meaning, a meaning perhaps unavailable in a city's streets. It's for *this* we hike or climb, or run marathons, or set up other goals for ourselves that might have us leaving those we love.

Or perhaps not. Maybe it's just a promise to ourselves that we make sure to go on a walk today. Or write a novel.

I think of George Rice, the photographer who was with Greely. George would have fit right in with Pete and Joe. His nature demanded he tread pretty damn close to that edge. He volunteered repeatedly for the riskiest assignments, ones that took him away from the camp, out into the Arctic winter wastes, in search of food when they were starving. He liked to use his strength and his smarts, and he possessed a strong humanitarian drive to keep the men alive. But there was something else in him that, like magnetic attraction, drew him ever closer to that razor edge. Something akin to what Joe Tasker writes in *Savage Arena*: "I knew then that I could not pretend to myself that I should have chosen some other way of life because I had had doubts before and had returned again and again to the mountains. Dreadful as our situation was, we had chosen to be in it."

How does it feel when you are close to the summit of Kangchenjunga, the third-highest mountain in the world, having made the commitment to climb without oxygen? Joe Tasker writes;

> There were no stages, each of us led the way for as far as he felt able. Every few steps we stopped to gasp and pant for breath. We went at the pace of whoever was slowest, but the slowest was not slow enough. Every stop was welcome, something indefinable had taken over to keep us moving upwards when all stimulus was swamped by the distress of muscles and lungs starved of oxygen. An urge beyond description got us to our feet after every halt and made us go a few more steps.

How does it feel to nearly die? Here is Joe, again, describing his own experience after he and Pete and Dick Renshaw became overrun, asleep in their tent, by an enormous avalanche, not far below the summit of K2. It has been snowing for the last eighteen hours:

> This second avalanche brought home to me how helpless we were, how tiny and insignificant our lives were on this mountain. There was no harmony with these forces of nature; we were specks in this colossal and uncaring universe. In my icy tomb I was terrified, fearing another death by suffocation, but I did not dare try to move from my position, embedded in the bank of snow over which the avalanche was pouring. . . . I waited, unafraid, for an outcome which I could do no more to

influence; unafraid of what death would mean but horrified by the suffocation by which it was arriving.

Then, after their perilous descent, which lasted three days: "I felt cauterized by the experience of being so close to instant death and then the strain of living for three days in the knowledge of how close we still were at every step. The experience had rendered unimportant the other anxieties of life. Having been given back my life I felt no urgency anymore, as if I had all the time in the world. Every moment was to be savored, every sensation treasured and valued more than ever before."

They were met by two of their porters, Gohar and Ali, at the bottom of the glacier, where Joe was wrapped in their arms: "They held me for a long while and I wept with relief, surrendering myself unashamedly to the care of these strong, capable men whom we had hired to work but whose concern and affection for us was beyond what money could buy."

Then, in this summation, Joe articulates as well as anyone the answer to the question so often posed to climbers: Why do you climb? "We had not reached the top of K2 but I saw more clearly than on any other climb that it was not reaching the summit that was most important but the journey to it, and though I would never have chosen such a trial as we experienced on that particular journey, having been through it I valued every minute."

All my self-indulgent reading had a purpose. I had an expedition of twenty-five men to think about. I wanted to get close to them, to reach, if possible, the emotional human core of each man. I wanted to understand what it was like for them, as individuals, to survive in a land of extremes: subzero temperatures, punishing winds, a superabundance of light or of blind darkness. What was it like to live in an unvarying landscape of black and white—rocks, ice, and snow, and no trees? No growing plants above ankle height? Even George Rice lost interest in photographing such a monotonous landscape. What was it like to be staring at the same faces every day and to know this would go on for the next year, and perhaps another, or longer if the ship coming to their relief never reached them? Then what? How do you live with this kind of uncertainty knowing your life is at stake? What does abandonment feel like?

Feelings and emotion was what I was after. The externals as well: a code of ethics, or a sense of morality. David Brainard was Greely's store sergeant in charge of dividing up their rations, a job he was made for by temperament. His sense of fairness, his determination to keep precise track of all food items, his willingness to fish, to rake kelp and seaweed, and to scrape lichen for the crew beyond the ordinary, a devotion to keeping these men alive. There was petty thievery, but one man, Pvt. Charles Henry, habitually stole food. He stole without remorse and he was hated for it. Brainard's raw emotions prompted him to call Henry in his diary "a born thief—a man without conscience, principle or heart—in short a perfect fiend." Since Brainard saw so clearly that to survive took fortitude, patience, courtesy, and a willingness to do one's best, he was stunned by Henry's utter lack of caring, his complete disregard that his thieving took food from them all.

And, always, from the beginning, driving me was a question: How would I react were I in one of those sleeping bags, not getting enough to eat, my teeth loosening from scurvy, hating my bagmate for no good reason other than his proximity?

So, it was for making contact with our inner cores that I read Laurence Gonzales's *Deep Survival: Who Lives, Who Dies, and Why; True Stories of Miraculous Endurance and Sudden Death*. Who could resist that title? Or, *Surviving the Extremes: What Happens to the Body and Mind at the Limits of Human Endurance*, by Kenneth Kamler MD.

I learned that we are already predisposed to act as we will act long before we are in a situation of survival. As these books point out, we already have our tool kit—our hearts and brains that make up our characters, our sense of morality, our very natures, composed of attributes like a sense of altruism, an ability to forgive, or perhaps their very opposites—a hard heart, a grasping nature.

With my twenty-five men, I had material from diaries to work with—not all of them—but as many as I needed. I had the facts of their situation, too. I saw that aside from the rigors of the Arctic environment, they would be placed in situations completely foreign to their experiences. Here, for instance, were army men confronted with a sea voyage in open boats. Ultimately, as they ate down their food, they found themselves face to face with their own starvation, a slow starvation that left them perpetually hungry as well as dehydrated, scurvy-ridden, and short-tempered. It was hard to think about others when you were so sorely pressed yourself. Yet, that is the very thing you must be doing for your own survival.

Ancel Keys, in *The Biology of Human Starvation*, reveals what happens to us physiologically and mentally as we slowly starve. His subjects were US Army volunteers and his study was conducted to understand what the long-term effects of semistarvation were on those who had been confined to the concentration camps in Germany during World War II. Keys's research fitted perfectly into the situation of Greely's men, and my interest in showing what perpetual hunger did to our bodies, brains, attitude, outlook, our sense of ethics and morality, our fears, and our ability to find humor in the worst situations, or to find hope and purpose, to retain our ability to think about others and be kind—all those aspects that make us human.

I read Scott and Shackleton, Stefansson, and Nansen and other great leaders of polar travel. I read their own books and I read about them. I studied their leadership and the reactions to them by the men they led. I read a great deal of Arctic history, about the reasons why expeditions failed, to learn how Greely's expedition fit in. So often expeditions that began with hope ended in disaster. For instance, the British of the nineteenth century shut their eyes to survival techniques of the Inuit, persisting in wearing heavy, close-fitting woolen army uniforms; when forced to retreat, as the Franklin party was, they loaded their sledges with the weight of the silver plate, since that is what a British gentleman ate his meals on, no matter where on the surface of the globe he stood. Then there was scurvy, which could wipe out an entire expedition if antiscorbutants ran out. In Greely's time, the 1880s, it was understood how to keep the disease at bay with fresh meat, and with lemons and limes (hence the reason British sailors were termed "limeys"). But it was not understood that scurvy was caused by a vitamin deficiency.

The books I read—more than one hundred—were a great pleasure, and each served to put me in deeper contact with those twenty-five men I had fallen in love with, and with whom, in my imagination, I, too, was sharing a half-frozen buffalo-hide sleeping bag in a hostile land.

What about the cannibalism? That figured in my story, and I was going to have to deal with this off-putting subject that makes even the least squeamish feel some degree of repugnance. The cannibalism on the Greely expedition was confined to the men who had died—no one was killed to be eaten. I had read *Alive: The Story of the Andes Survivors*, by Piers Paul Read, years ago, long before the Greely expedition came into my life. Now I picked up *Miracle in the Andes: 72 Days on the Mountain and My Long Trek Home* by Nanda Parrado, who writes thirty years later about this same well-known plane wreck of soccer players in the heart of the Andes, the hopelessness of rescue, and the recourse of some, not all, to eating the flesh of those who had died. I needed to understand what could drive a human being to commit this taboo act. I needed to examine what would drive *me* to partake of human flesh: a bold thought, but not an uncommon one. Everyone, at some point in their lives, I bet, has explored existential questions in their own minds.

From the beginning of writing *Starvation Shore*, that question was always with me. On a road trip with two hiking friends, the driver politely inquired how my Greely project was progressing. "Well," I answered, from the backseat, "I've been thinking a lot about cannibalism." Two heads spun around. "Maybe we should stop the car and let her out," came the reply, and a flurry of nervous laughter.

On the Greely expedition, the cannibalism didn't occur until near the end, that is, maybe a month or so before rescue arrived. When the men began to die, there could not have been much meat left on their bones. In the end, only six of the bodies were cut. They buried their dead in ground they had consecrated to that purpose. Or, when the few survivors left were too weak to trudge up to their Cemetery Ridge, the dead were dropped into the tidal crack—a downhill walk.

I could not refer to journals about this time: no one included cannibalism in their daily writings. By then, very few were writing at all, anyway. So I turned to other sources.

It is well known that there was cannibalism on the Franklin expedition in search of the Northwest Passage in the 1840s. *Fatal Passage: The Story of John Rae, the Arctic Hero Time Forgot*, by Ken McGoogan, details how devastating it was to Victorian England when Rae revealed the fate of the Franklin party: the evidence of cut bodies, and bones in the soup pots. He was severely criticized for claiming that members of the British Navy could have stooped to such bestiality. Sir John's wife, among many others, claimed that it must have been the Eskimos who committed the heinous act.

David Roberts, in *A Newer World: Kit Carson, John C. Frémont, and the Claiming of the American West*, makes clear that when the mountain men of the first half of the nineteenth century pushed the season for trapping, got caught in the western mountain winter, and began to starve, cannibalism was to be expected, a consequence of the risky life they led. One of the most famous episodes of cannibalism is the story of the Donner party. In 1846, eighty-nine pioneers left Illinois, headed for California, and were stopped by heavy winter snows in the Sierra Nevada mountains. Cannibalism kept the few who survived alive.

And then historical novelist Kenneth Roberts tells the horrifying true tale of a shipwreck near Boon Island, right off the coast of Maine, that features mutiny and cannibalism—in sight of Maine coastal towns. Like

Greely's story, *Boon Island* is an example of the ways that crisis can bring out the best—and worst—in human nature.

So I read and thought, thought and read, and worked my way inside the skins of Greely and his men. That was the only way I could imagine creating the scenes I needed to show cannibalism on this expedition. It happened! There were the six cut bodies brought home to prove it. As a writer of historical fiction, I was obliged to tell the facts. That I was going to have to show this scene hung over me all the years I was writing this book, but, when it came time to dig in (so to speak), to live it mentally, to commit it to paper, I was ready. I knew the men so well by this time that what I wrote—their actions, their conversations, their innermost thoughts—felt inevitable. I was living it with them, and I was loving it. In the end, I felt that what I had imagined was probably pretty close to how it had all played out.

The great thing for me working on this project was reading the men's diaries, which brought me as close to them as I could get. Lieutenant Greely kept one, as did Lieutenant Lockwood. We have parts of the diaries of two of the enlisted men, Private Henry and Private Schneider, and there are bits of others in the National Archives. But mainly I relied on David Brainard's Camp Clay diary. Jay Satterfield, head of Special Collections at the Dartmouth College Library, generously made me a copy. I learned to read Brainard's handwriting by starting my morning's work reading a diary entry and transcribing it. Brainard's diaries were in print, but had been reworked, with words left out or sentences smoothed, by him and by various editors. I wanted what he had originally written to be available, and I wrote an introduction that sets the scene, which is available on the Dartmouth College Library website.[1]

The following is an excerpt from that essay:

> David Brainard's Camp Clay diary is a meticulously kept account of the daily happenings at Cape Sabine on the Ellesmere Island coast, where the men of the Lady Franklin Bay Expedition lived

1. Laura Waterman, "Introduction to the Brainard Camp Clay Diary," Digital by Dartmouth, Dartmouth College Library, November 28, 2017, https://www.dartmouth.edu/library/digital/collections/manuscripts/brainard-diary/introduction-camp-clay-diary.html.

as castaways through the long and desperate winter of 1883–1884. In this spot, Lt. Adolphus W. Greely and his twenty-five men were faced with surviving subzero Arctic temperatures, months of darkness, battering storms of gale-force winds, and starvation rations that left them on the verge of madness.

Brainard starts his diary entries with the multiple temperature readings over the course of the day, perhaps supplied to him by Edward (Ned) Israel, their astronomer and youngest member. He notes the temperature inside their hut: twenty to thirty degrees higher than the outside air, but nonetheless below freezing. He notes precisely the weather changes of the day. He must have written his entries in the evening, perhaps after their meager meal. He could have been half reclining in the buffalo hide sleeping bag that held two other men, straining to see in the flickering light of the blubber lamp, a dirty fuel that left a greasy grainy film on hands, faces, and clothing.

He writes about their daily routine: the diligent hunting of Pvt. Long and the Greenland native Jens Edwards; his own success or lack thereof at the shore, netting the tiny crustaceans that composed much of their diet. He enumerates who is ill, who has recovered, and who, in the end, dies. His entries show a great concern for the men; one senses the responsibility he feels for their well being, especially for his commander's health. David Brainard was more aware than anyone of the importance of keeping Lt. Greely alive. He writes on May 5, 1884, "If the C.O. does not pull through the Expedition will have lost its best friend + the full benefit of our three years work lost." Brainard knows that without Greely's leadership the men would splinter; with him alive they have the possibility to operate as a unified group, helping each other. This was very much on Brainard's mind.

He writes about food. Talk of food dominates their conversations. . . . [Lieutenant Lockwood was the champion when it came to describing meals he had eaten, meals he was going to eat when he got home, and how much his mother's cooking meant to him.]

We learn from the Camp Clay diary who were the workers and who were the slackers and who were the men who seemed only to care about themselves. The whole spectrum of human nature is here. Brainard wants to think well of these men and is eager to compliment those who step to the fore. But he does not refrain from giving his opinion of the thoroughly rotten apples. "Whisler," he writes on May 3rd, "was caught in commissary store house by Bender. He had forced the lock + was eating bacon + had a large piece (about 2 lbs) in the breast of his blouse. He is the most abject cowardly + craven that ever disgraced mankind by his presence." . . .

[Sergeant Brainard did not always agree with Lieutenant Greely's decisions, specifically, Greely's choice to leave Fort Conger in late summer of 1883. On the open boat voyage, the evening after the attempted mutiny, Brainard wrote in his diary, "What a fine spring retreat could be made from Ft. Conger with sledges & how much less our sufferings would be compared with what they are now and will be one or two weeks from now."

What makes his diary so compelling is his ability to articulate his own moments of despair, even of hopelessness, in a way that objectifies his wretchedness by merely giving us the facts. In the entry for Saturday, May 31st, when, after a blizzard that left them wet through from the spindrift blown into their bags, he writes: "as we had no solid food consequently (we) had nothing to eat during the day—not even a swallow of water. Of all the days of misery of my life this caps the climax. If I knew that I had a month more of this sort of existence before me I would stop the engine this moment as I do not consider 50 years of pleasure a sufficient reward for another months (*sic*) suffering misery equal to the one just passed." There is no self-pity here. There is no blame. Like Apsley Cherry-Gerrard, writing about their semi-starving state, Brainard's lines abound with feeling by merely sticking to their actual situation.]

All the men of the Lady Franklin Bay Expedition had been requested to keep journals by the U.S. government which had sent them up to the Arctic, and all knew they were to turn them over to the War Department upon return.

David Brainard, however, kept in his possession the notebook containing entries made from March 1st to June 21st, 1884. These entries concern the final months spent at their starvation camp. By March 1st they had lost only one man, . . . but between April 5th and the arrival of their rescue on June 22nd, seventeen men had died. [Brainard's diary that contains the harrowing story of those fatal last months at Camp Clay was generously given to the Dartmouth College Library by Brainard's stepdaughter, Elinor McVickar.]

The journal measures 7¾ inches by 3 inches. It opens from the 3-inch spine, like a ledger. Brainard would have found it easy to slip into a deep pocket, perhaps of his uniform coat. There is a worn red leather strip wrapping around the top and a triangle of red leather on the left bottom corner of the front and the right bottom corner of the back. The cover itself is a thick cardboard in shades of brown. The binding is broken and the journal shows rough use on the edges, the cover, and at the corners, though less where the leather is. The pages are lined in blue and go the full 7¾ inches. Brainard, however, chose to write across those thin lines, using the three-inch space. Often just two or three words fill up a line. Some clerk in some government office stamped a number on each page. These are rendered in blue ink and end on page 240. Brainard's last entry, on June 21, 1884, is seventeen pages later. The diary, to me, still smelled of too many men living in a confined, cold, damp, space.

David Brainard wrote in pencil. The temperature in their hut moved from the teens into the twenties when their stove was lit for meals, but was always too cold to keep his ink thawed. He kept his lines very close. His penmanship is, when one becomes accustomed to it, readable, though he had written on May 3rd, still seven weeks before their rescue, "Will anyone ever be able to decipher this writing. It is in great part illegible, the sentences incoherent, and all written in a hurry and with great rapidity and under the most trying circumstances that our miserable conditions would admit of." [David Brainard was twenty-seven years old by the time of their rescue.] . . .

I made no plans to visit the Arctic. I would count on my experience with winter in the northeast mountains' alpine zones to connect me with what Greely's men had endured. I realized that their experience was unduplicatable, even if I had sought to visit the site of Camp Clay in winter. Reenacting what those twenty-five men went through was not possible, especially since by the time they had reached Cape Sabine, and erected the camp they named Camp Clay, they were already weakened from the sea voyage. Their clothing and equipment had been repeatedly soaked and battered from the many moves made between ice floes and their boats. They were beginning to starve.

I had been tramping around in the winter mountains from 1970 into the 1990s. This was before the full effects of climate change brought milder temperatures, and often more rain than snow. Guy and I spent around a quarter of our winter nights camped out, giving us more continuous time in the mountains themselves on our three-to-five-day trips.

Many of these excursions were above treeline, in New Hampshire's Presidential Range or along Franconia Ridge. Or, we could drive west across our state of Vermont and climb Mount Mansfield, with its mile-long traverse above treeline. Or, continuing on, farther west across Lake Champlain to New York State's mountains: Marcy, Algonquin, Skylight, Haystack, and the Gothics, noble eminences that yield their wild glories only to the persistent winter traveler. Maine's Katahdin is in a class by itself, with its treeline at a lower elevation due to its higher latitude. Katahdin's cirques are gullied and treeless, steep-sided cliffs. The mountain itself sits like a monadnock, rising above the Maine woods in isolated grandeur. It's hard to reach, but all the more prized for its solitude. And when you are in its alpine world, you see no habitations, no roads, or dwelling, only forests and lakes.

All these mountains Guy and I returned to, some many times, but our focus for above-treeline romping was the Presidential Range with its roughly eight square miles of tundra. This is diminutive compared to the great ranges of the world, but the Presidentials can prepare climbers well for larger mountains. There we can encounter not only below-zero temperatures but terrific, even terrifying winds. (The fastest land-surface wind speed of 231 mph was clocked at the Observatory on Mount Washington's summit in 1934.) Climbers who go above treeline on a winter's day can routinely encounter winds of 40 mph or higher. Coupled with single-digit temperatures, that can make for some brisk tramping. It's a great way to gain experience for the world-class ranges, as many climbers do.

Along with wind and cold comes the possibility of low visibility. Clouds can descend, fog can creep in with amazing rapidity and become so dense as to hide the well-placed cairns marking the path. A pea-soup fog—whiteout conditions—combined with cold and wind can be a deadly combination.

Then, of course, there are the mild winter days that give the lie to the Presidentials' fearsome winter reputation with clear blue skies, temperatures in the twenties, and light zephyrs. But mistaking it for the norm up there only lures hikers to calamity.

Most of the time as you tramp up the trail, but are still in the shelter of the trees, you'll begin to hear a roaring sound—the wind. As you gain height and the trees grow shorter, inexorably shorter, this roaring persists, deepening and shrieking, achieving the sound of an out-of-control freight train at reckless and terminal velocity. You become aware of the spruce and fir boughs waving about, and you know, with the increased thumping of your heart, that this wind is going to hit you like an avalanche right around that next bend, which you can see up ahead.

So you stop.

You've stopped right next to the sign that warns you are about to encounter the "world's worst weather." Perhaps you scoff. The summit you're aiming for is not above a mile away. What can stop you? You take off your snowshoes and put on your crampons. You add another layer under your jacket, and you draw down the toggles on your hood. If it is around zero, you might add a face mask. All the while you've been crunching granola bars or gorp—food not available to Greely—drinking water, and joking with your companions, perhaps the kind of chatter that's fueled by nervous excitement and adrenalin.

Now you are ready.

You have put yourself in a very testing situation. But you know how to play it smart. You know that if you begin to lose feeling in your toes and fingers, or are in danger of exhausting yourself fighting the punishing wind, or the cloud layer descends, cutting visibility to twenty feet (especially if all this is happening at once), you can turn around and head for treeline. As soon as you are in the trees you'll be out of the wind. But, don't forget, many have died above treeline from misestimating the margin.

One of the men with Greely, Winfield Jewell, was an observer in the 1870s when the US Signal Corps maintained a year-round weather station on the summit of Mount Washington. Jewell probably had more experience with cold and wind and poor visibility than any of the others with Greely. Sadly, he did not survive the expedition. The Jewell Trail that bears his name is one of the most scenically situated on the mountain—a ridge that gives sweeping views and an airy walk high above the trees.

I was counting on my own experience with cold and wind and fog to make the experience of these twenty-five men become real for me. I was relying on those frigid days above treeline, when the wind blew hard enough to knock me down and I felt, despite the layers of fleece and wind gear, that I had nothing on at all, when even a short stop for water and a quick snack numbed my fingers in seconds, to put me among Greely and his men.

As I wrote *Starvation Shore*, I knew that if I could truly experience again those tactile elements, if I could in memory be once more enveloped in that bone-chilling cold, in the relentless wind driving ice crystals in my face, and fighting off the disorienting panic of landmarks obliterated by fog, the words to describe them would come. Yet I wanted, as well, to capture the breathtaking, often frightening, beauty. That, too, was reason enough for climbing above the trees, into the inhuman wildness of winter above treeline.

As the writing of *Starvation Shore* grew, and I began to gain confidence, I took an especially deep pleasure from crafting what I saw in my mind's eye of the landscape and the reactions of Greely's men as they moved through it:

> Brainard remembered when they had traversed from Eskimo Point to Sabine how the landscape appeared without features, how he couldn't be sure of what he saw. Partly because the light was dim, not quite black dark, but gray. Bergs, hills, and hillocks, individual rocks and outcroppings showed themselves in tones of gray. These objects didn't appear solid. It had to do with the light—the lack of it—and the immensity of the space. Pulling the sledge, leaning into the harness, he was looking down so that when he looked up he was in a different spot and the object he was passing showed a different aspect. Was it the same object? It was easy to become confused. He had found himself fighting down panic.

I had the material—an assemblage of the memories of my own early reading, which had ignited my urge to climb, the tactility of all those climbs and mountains, my research of the exploration stories of others, the history of classic Arctic expeditions, and the immediate personal recounting in the diary entries of Greely's men—to write a novel. I had stockpiled a chaos of fragments—an immense accretion of detail, like a 5,000-piece jigsaw puzzle spread out on a table, awaiting the act of assembly. All this required, I desperately assured myself, was a certain demented application to the daily practice of writing, and an insane hope that I could breathe life into a long-ago adventure, now largely forgotten, when some ordinary men rose above themselves while others sank into abysmal self-absorption—the never-ending story of what it means to be human.

19

Advancing Technologies and Wild Places

I wrote an introduction for the third edition of Backwoods Ethics, *retitled* The Green Guide to Low-Impact Hiking and Camping *(2016). When the book was first published in 1979, Guy and I saw two concerns: protecting the physical environment, the land itself, and preserving what we go out there for, the psychological feeling of being in the wild. For this chapter, I've excerpted the section that focuses on those handheld digital devices, now ubiquitous in the mountains, that have revolutionized how we conduct ourselves. My objective is to give these portable game-changers close scrutiny: here's what we gain and here's what we have lost when we enter the backcountry digitally equipped.*

In the spirit of full disclosure, I've never carried a cell phone in the woods and I do a lot of solo local tramping around. If I'm in the mountains, the friends I'm with have phones. When I first realized that my hiking companion was carrying a cell phone, I experienced a psychological jolt—a shock even—that said you are not on your own. This was not pleasant. It changed in a flash my relationship to where I was. I didn't like that my vigilance could erode because here was this digital device that could take over in a pinch. I became aware of this thin edge between trust in your phone and yet the possibility you're in a dead spot, making the device useless. Years since experiencing that first shocking encounter with my friend's phone, I still react negatively to its presence. And sometimes it can do neat things with amazing apps, like plant and flower identification or mountain ID too. We talk about this, my hiking friends and I, we joke about how it makes our brains lazy, and sometimes we bring our plant guides with us, too. So, it's a mixed bag. The digital stuff is here to stay, and what you'll read here are a few stories about what to hold in mind when you bring these devices that have changed our lives to the mountains.

~

When I look out on such a night as this, I feel as if there could be neither wickedness nor sorrow in the world: and there certainly would be less of both if the sublimity of Nature were more attended to, and people were carried more out of themselves by contemplating such a scene.

—Jane Austen, *Mansfield Park*

So what about this communication technology we've brought along? Now we can carry our everyday lives with us when we're out in the wild. We can keep in touch with the office, our friends, and family. We can follow the news, check the gyrations of the stock market, work our brains with Sudoku or crossword puzzles, until it might cross our minds that we haven't really left home at all! We may sleep in sleeping bags and have sore feet from the miles we've walked, but our mind is on the message our boss texted that has us checking up on a lot more of our work obligations than we've expected. That call from a friend was nice, but kind of an interruption. The video drone our companion is flying to film above a scenic overlook has scared away the birds. These devices have changed our lives, revolutionized the way we communicate, how we learn, and possibly how we think. Instant communication has its place in our world, but there are two side to these devices as you'll soon see.

Take that global positioning system (GPS). It's a very useful device for trail workers. They can log all the data about trail repairs (water bars, stone steps, other trail erosion problems) right there in the field, saving hours of work back in the office. For hikers, the GPS can tell us where we are. It can help us orient ourselves if we get lost.

But GPS is not infallible. It's still pretty handy to be familiar with map and compass, as the how-to guides advise. Safety reasons aside, being familiar with map and compass does something for us the GPS can't duplicate: it puts us in touch with the terrain itself. We look at the map showing us the ridges and summits, streams and cols. The contour lines show us how steep the terrain we want to ascend or descend actually is. In this way we learn something about this physical place, actual on-the-ground information. Before any off-trail bushwhack, Guy and I would measure the compass angles of our intended route on the map, then write them on an index card that we carried in a convenient shirt pocket. Often we found ourselves walking through the dense woods, compass in hand, to make sure we stayed on course. Not that we can't do this with the GPS—all we have to do is keep our eyes on the screen. But by letting it do the figuring, two things can happen: First, our skill level with map and compass drops, and second, we change the relationship we have to the land itself. We've interposed a digital device between ourselves and the wild.

These days, accidents reported in newspapers or by the hiking clubs might start off like this: "At 9:45 p.m., New Hampshire Fish and Game received a call from the county sheriff's office notifying them of a cell phone call from a hiker who had broken his leg" (or become lost, or was overtaken by darkness, or was caught in a storm). Sometimes the party can be talked down and back out to the highway, but often the local search and rescue group is alerted and heads out to help. Calling for a rescue on cell phones has saved lives. But they can give us a false sense of security, and maybe cost lives (ours, or a search team's), if the phone we've relied on is stuck with us in a dead spot and can't receive a signal. Having these wonderful tools in our packs can work in contradictory ways. We're safer with them, or we think we are, and because we know that we may overextend ourselves. We might go for that extra summit or that shelter that will have us walking into the dark on a trail we've not been on before. The security of technology can turn out to be a false lifeline.

A very sad incident happened in February 2015 in the Presidential Range of New Hampshire's White Mountains when a talented and fit mountaineer named Kate Matrosova, carrying both a GPS and a personal locator beacon (PLB), set off to traverse the range on a day when the forecast called for below-zero temperatures, with winds from the north starting at 45 mph, rising by midmorning to 80 mph, and then reaching 100 mph. Russian-born Kate, thirty-two, had already climbed a number of the world's highest mountains. She'd driven up with her husband from New York City to celebrate her impending citizenship by hiking across the Presidential summits of Madison, Adams, Jefferson, Clay, and Washington. Kate was aware of the forecast on that particular Valentine's Day weekend. She knew such an undertaking would make for a challenging winter trek even in the best of conditions. She knew the Northeast had been experiencing a harsh winter, with the snow piling up to great depths in the woods, and she knew that when she gained the treeline she would be exposed to winds of hurricane force for the greater part of the day.

At 3:30 p.m., Kate's husband received a call from Tyndall Air Force Base near Panama City, Florida, where a signal from Kate's PLB had been picked up. He called 9-1-1, starting the search and rescue. Several location points were identified, and the search parties chose the ones they felt they could most easily reach, given the wind, the ferocity of the cold, and the darkness. Authorities speculated that the frozen air could have affected the beacon, but perhaps nothing could have saved Kate, given the belligerence of the weather, even if the coordinates had led the rescuers right to her. She was found the next morning, her feet tangled in the stunted scrub, her pack blown downslope. In Kate Matrosova's death lies a cautionary tale about nature's power, even over sophisticated technology.

Recently my friend, novelist Jonathan Strong, told me of a trip he'd taken with three other teenagers and their teacher in 1960. They were on a trek along the then-unmapped Inca Trail in the Andes. On their last day they found themselves stopped by the edge of a cliff—no way down. No way home! My friend's feeling, as he contemplated the enormous drop, was that they'd reached the edge of the earth. With no map or written directions, only their eyes and brains to figure out how to reach the valley below, they realized they'd followed the wrong ridge. After a frosty night on the ledge, with no food or water, the next morning they gained the correct ridge that took them out. In fact, their mishap turned out to be a great adventure, a story my friend enjoyed telling, partly because it is unduplicatable today. Their only point of contact, he said, was the American Express office in

Lima. That's where the parents would have called if, after a specified amount of time, they hadn't heard that all were out and safe.

That party—in fact all trips in the not-very-distant past of the late twentieth century—was best prepared by considering themselves *on their own*. Radios were available, but they were heavy and unreliable. Those words have a meaning hard to imagine now with digital technology at our fingertips. It's impossible to duplicate that "on our own" experience with a cell phone in our pocket.

The image I always carry in my mind is Rob Hall on the south summit of Everest, patched through to his wife in New Zealand by satellite phone. In that 1996 expedition, Rob had successfully guided his clients to the top of the world only to encounter on the descent an unforeseen storm of staggering fury. Rob fought his way down to the south summit but was too cold and hypoxic to go on. Nor could his teammates reach him. He was stuck. Yet that call connected two voices. Rob was isolated, cut off from his fellow climbers whose rescue attempt had failed, yet he could hear his wife say, "Don't feel that you are alone." He, in turn, could tell her to "sleep well" and that he loved her. Those were his dying words. No technological wizardry could withstand the natural forces that overcame Rob Hall, but technology did make it possible for two people to say goodbye.

Is something lost? Well, yes, and there is a sadness to that. The clock only runs forward. But I'd like to think we can gain something as well. For one thing, just because these digital devices can insert themselves between us and the wild doesn't mean we aren't given the opportunity to be more mindful of where we are when we're out there. We go into the woods and up on the heights for our souls. Who has time to think about their souls these days, or what those souls need? We must work harder to find that wildness now, and so it becomes more precious. And that which is precious we must safeguard. If our handheld devices can give us the opportunity to experience a more profound understanding of the fragility of wildness, that seems to me a good thing. Or, perhaps I'm being too optimistic here?

20

The Ascent at Eighty

It may be that when we no longer know what to do
we have come to our real work,

and that when we no longer know which way to go
we have come to our real journey.

—Wendell Berry, "The Real Work"

*Aging . . . like death and taxes, it's unavoidable. I had a college roommate
who dreaded turning twenty. Twenty seemed so old she said. I remember the
struggle I had with thirteen. I wasn't ready to become a teenager. It's the decade
markers that make us pause and cause us to reflect. Then, bravely, or kicking*

and screaming, we celebrate, or at least observe this passing of time. The way I coped with and confronted eighty was to write about it.

I think about our years of turning maple sap into syrup and how that process brought us closer to the natural world than any of the seasonal work we did at Barra, or I have done since. Every year was different. Every year was unpredictable. Every year fulfilled us and had us looking forward to next year. We became so attached to our trees, individually, the ones we had named. Year by year, we learned from them, and what we learned could not be found in books, nor were we aware of what it was that we were learning. It might have had something to do with patience. Slowing down, also. Giving up control was a part of it. Certainly not knowing all the answers. Or any answers. Tapping our maples the way we did—by hand, with buckets—put the season itself in charge. And by the time the snow had melted away and we were collecting sap in our shirtsleeves and the maple buds, when we looked up into the canopy, were faintly colored red, we knew that another season of sugaring was ending. Winter had turned the corner into spring and there was no looking back. And we ourselves had been changed by the passing of another sugaring season.

~

No woman should ever be quite accurate about her age. It looks so calculating.

—Oscar Wilde, *The Importance of Being Earnest*

Who expects to turn eighty? That's so old!

As seventy-five slid away, and the numbers kept mounting, it was beginning to look, when I achieved seventy-nine, that I had a reasonable shot at reaching eighty. I was in good health. My parents had both lived past eighty, my mother into her early nineties. Genetically, then, I was good to go for perhaps another decade; but did I want this? I had already discovered that aging has its drawbacks. I really was not hiking in the White Mountains the way I had been when I was in my forties and fifties. This was particularly apparent when I hiked with friends who were in their forties and fifties. I was slow and it bothered me. So, mostly I hiked with friends my age, which leveled the playing field.

But since eighty was on the horizon, it seemed that the best thing I could do, for my own acceptance of the fact, was mentally to prepare for it. I remembered how, when a friend of my father's turned eighty, he snapped his fingers, implying there was nothing to it. He didn't feel any different, he said, when he woke up the morning of his birthday than he had when he'd gone to sleep the night before. Well, of course not, I thought. I was half his age. I hadn't a clue, then, what eighty felt like, or the thoughts that filled his mind—as they now were beginning to fill mine as that birthday loomed. All I knew then was that eighty was old. Yet my father's friend didn't seem old at all. What did it mean to be eighty? For one thing, it meant that body parts start aging out, but I planned nonetheless to snap my fingers at eighty as well.

A few years ago, my good friend Nat Scrimshaw had offered me the opportunity to hike across Franconia Ridge and see the trail work he and his college-age crew had completed during the summer. This sounded like a great idea! Truthfully, it was I who suggested it.

Nat was engaged with the work my husband Guy and I had carried out for close to twenty years, above treeline on that flashing jewel in the setting of New Hampshire's White Mountains. I'll quickly add that its above-treeline counterpart, the Presidential Range, while equally jewellike, is opposite in character. Franconia Ridge is narrow, a spine, a knife-edge, a trail for dancing on. The curve formed by the Presidential Range, in contrast, is broad shouldered, massive, gouged with ravines and gulfs, and riven by slides shaped by avalanches or rockfall. Franconia Ridge shines with lightness, an exquisite airy delicacy, a froth of cream whipped into sharp peaks. Hikers prance along this ridge, their balletic movements outlined against the sky, arms and legs in graceful patterns, the breeze catching their clothing. A beguiling dream.

The feeling in the Presidentials is more one of grandeur; all is solid, unforgivingly stony—the range a stern taskmaster. The vision ahead and behind is of rocks in blacks and grays, lichen-covered, occasionally interrupted by a sudden shine of mica. There can be found an expanse of tundra, home to the Northeast's largest display of alpine vegetation. Called *lawns*, or *meadows* by the botanists, alpine plants there flourish between the rocks in a breathtaking variety of golds and whites and blues and crimsons and pinks, set off by dark green foliage during their brief summer flowering. The Presidentials' summits are masculine and muscular. They dominate and demand obedience. They are the ponderous double basses in the orchestra, the elephants and rhinoceroses in the animal world, commanding and confident of their place.

Franconia Ridge accompanies the hiker with piccolo and flute, with lute and snare drum. A white-throated sparrow trills close by, and in summer there is the easily recognized Eastern swallowtail butterfly drawing sweetness from a yellow mountain avens, a bumblebee milking a dwarf goldenrod. Crags abound and the hikers scramble among the spirelike turrets of stone that characterize this narrow pathway among the stars.

On both of these ridge crests hikers can be exposed to the full force of the weather, which is a big part of the draw. Both ranges can deliver staggering, bone-crushing, heart-stopping winds. While the highest velocities occur in the Presidentials, the sharpness and narrowness of Franconia Ridge can become a high-danger zone during a misjudged crossing in an electrical storm.

Our hearts, that is, Guy's and mine, were on Franconia Ridge. It took us one hour and twenty minutes to drive over from Vermont, and for those years of trail tending we were on the ridge every three weeks from early June to October, often taking three-day trips. This was in the early days, when the mountain clubs across the Northeast were first learning how to take care of above treeline trails. Hiking traffic had increased to the point where the paths needed to be better defined and stabilized to keep hikers on a single treadway and off the plants. The very narrowness of Franconia Ridge, making it easy for hikers to walk anywhere, had produced a seeming warren of trails through the tundra. Plant communities that handle winds we can't stand up in, gelid temperatures, upheaving thaws, and pounding lightning storms are easily crushed by hikers' boots. The hiking clubs and public agencies recognized that this precious habitat needed protection.

We signed up as trail adopters for Franconia Ridge and began working out—as all of us across the region were doing then—a variety of techniques to keep hikers on the path. Some of these, like blazing and cairns, had long been in use as a means of defining direction of travel. Now it was necessary to step up the game. For instance, where a slope had been eroded by many footfalls, trail crews began constructing rock steps and experimenting with how steep those steps could be: backpackers will go around rock stairs that take too much effort to step up, so trail crews began lowering the step-ups.

In the late 1970s, the AMC trail crew began building scree walls— low-level walls of small rocks built on either side of the footpath to better define the treadway. When we began working on the ridge, we felt a great aversion to those walls. We understood the need, but the walls, some knee height, felt too confining; a wall seems anathema to the glorious freedom of being above treeline.

So we began experimenting with them. We tried lowering those that felt needlessly high, and widened or even eliminated some that were on bedrock and so close to the edge of the drop-off that there was no danger of hikers stepping on the plants. Our most constant work—our most essential housekeeping chore—was to keep the treadway clear of the small rocks and stones constantly knocked off the wall and into the trail, placing them back on the scree wall again. Above all, we wanted to remove any obstacle that would send a hiker beyond the footpath and onto the plants.

Our hiking friends got so interested in what we were doing on Franconia Ridge that they wanted their own above-treeline trails to tend as adopters under the Appalachian Mountain Club's program. We—six or seven regulars—evolved into the West End Trail Tenders (WETT), meaning our sphere of action was on the western edge of the Whites (the acronym also described the weather we often found ourselves working in). Our reach, at our high point, extended from Mount Flume to Mount Garfield. Since not all of this was above treeline, we eventually cut back to focus on alpine trails only.

The Appalachian Mountain Club, back then, generously provided bunk space gratis for volunteers at Greenleaf Hut, located a mile below the summit of Lafayette, which allowed us to maximize our time on the ridge. AMC runs its hut system by employing college-age men and women whose job it is to physically haul up the supplies for the meals they serve to the guests. These hut crews also are the first responders in case of accidents or the need for rescues.

But to my way of looking at it, their most important job is their role as frontline educators. The "after-dinner talks" the crews gave at Greenleaf provided the opportunity to inform guests about the fragility of the tundra plants they would encounter the next morning when they crossed the ridge.

The huts attract first-timers, and often families new to the mountains, a captive audience excited to be there. If Guy or I were asked to put in a word, we would let people know that the good news was the plants could recover if hikers stayed off them. We were seeing this on the ridge, as were our counterparts in the Adirondacks and Vermont. In the Adirondacks, we said, plant scientist Dr. Ed Ketchledge had pioneered sowing a mix of grass seeds in harsh alpine environments that lasted only a few seasons, but long enough to provide a seedbed for the native alpine colonizers, particularly Mountain sandwort, to catch hold. We had applied to the White Mountain National Forest (WMNF), and they permitted us to sow Ed's mix on the Ridge in certain selected spots. We were also allowed to go into the stunted subalpine trees known as krummholz and drag up dead wood to lay over bare spots. (*Krummholz* translates as "crooked wood," and it forms a formidable barrier at treeline.) The krummholz served to give shelter to the young plants, as well as keep hikers off, and in only one or two seasons the Mountain sandwort moved into these disturbed areas. Be on the lookout, we told the hut guests, for this pioneer plant with five-petaled white flowers and a faintly green center.

This introduction of common grass seed in the alpine zone was not viewed favorably by the botanists, who predicted its full-scale conquest of native plants. But with the help of the WMNF, we kept up the seeding for several years, long enough for the Mountain sandwort to make a brave showing at covering some of the hardest hit areas. It's easy, above treeline, to make the mistake of thinking that stepping on a bare spot is okay. In reality that footstep blots out small, hard-to-see seedlings of native plants.

Over the course of our years caring for Franconia Ridge, Greenleaf Hut felt like a second home to us. Its sleeping space was bunkrooms, beds three tiers high, and at its long tables meals were served "family style," delicious, and all you could eat. We got to know those Greenleaf *croos* (so-called in hut lingo) well. If they had time in their own busy schedules, one or two would come up on the ridge with us to help in the work. Some became solid and lasting friends; we went to their weddings and welcomed their young children at our homestead. Our work on Franconia Ridge reflected the kind of work we did at home—hands-on labor, requiring thought and care. As we tended our large vegetable garden and our woodlot we had health, productivity, and certain fostering of beauty always in mind. Our work on the ridge was an extension of this, an easy step into a wild, above-treeline backyard.

My work on Franconia Ridge had ended several years before Guy's death in 2000. I was sidelined by failing knees, a common complaint among hikers, backpackers, and trail workers who often carry heavy loads up and down steep and rugged trails. Our descent path off the ridge, the Falling Waters Trail, was renowned for being a knee-destroyer.

After I had double knee replacements in 2004, I returned to the ridge a few times with my over-sixty-year-old hiking friends. We were slow. I was aware of just how slow when I remembered how rapidly Guy and I could traverse the ridge while putting in a full day of trail work. When I thought about Nat's recent invitation, or rather my too-eager expression of a wish to see his work and that of his young crew, I pictured myself at the end of a line, puffing hard to keep up. They would stop and wait for me and be polite about it. But did I want that? The effort to push uphill had always been a pleasure for me. It takes a mental tweak to get into that space of enjoying a certain amount of sucking air, and I could still do it, but now only at the pace of someone well past seventy. With Nat and his college-age crew—golly!—I realized I'd feel a certain embarrassment. I just wasn't the hiker I had been, and I didn't feel like placing myself at that disadvantage.

The best way, of course, to take the time needed on the ridge to see their work would have been to stay overnight at Greenleaf Hut. Nat offered to arrange this. Then it struck me that I didn't want to. Returning to Greenleaf was too much like returning to your childhood home, not visited in the intervening years, as a grown-up adult. I remembered being with my mother when that happened to her. She had taken my brother and me to visit her side of the family. When she walked into the house where she had grown up, she gave a throaty gasp, and put her hand on her chest. I looked up at her face with concerned alarm. She pulled herself together. But I've never forgotten her words: "It's all changed . . . where is . . . what happened to . . . ?" So, as much as I would have loved to have seen Nat's work—he had often described to me his own ever-evolving process of care for the ridge, more heavily tramped than ever—I said *no* to a return to the ridge and Greenleaf Hut. I felt, in consequence, a good deal of relief. At this stage of the game, I was just glad to be hiking at all. If you can't recreate the past, let it go and concentrate on what's happening next. As Piglet said to Pooh, "I say, I wonder what's going to happen exciting *today*?"

My birthday month is October. I've always felt that October, in my case early October, was a wonderful time to celebrate a birthday. Where I live, in Vermont, the days in October grow comfortably cool, the foliage is at its touristy best, the sky can be radiantly sapphire blue, and the sun is often shining.

Acorns are falling, the friendly squirrels and chipmunks are hoarding them away, the deer are not yet harassed by hunters tramping around with guns, and that means I am still going on my usual walks through the woodland paths I'm familiar with. I can walk up my dirt road, turn off onto a narrower dirt road, the terrain rising but never steeply, and pretty soon I enter the deep woods on an old woods road shaded by maples, birches, beeches, a smattering of evergreens. I'm immersed in the northern hardwood forest. Ancient stone walls border either side. They could mark property boundaries or signify that this woods road was once a thruway between two rural villages. I find this section profoundly comforting. It speaks to me of the stability of a place.

This sense of settlement carries on as I leave the woods and climb uphill through a hayfield—a high mowing—that tops out in a sweeping (nearly) 360-degree view. I always stop to take it in. It's a modest high point in the landscape, and reaching it never feels the same way twice to me, always different, atmospherically speaking. The light, the cloud shadows, the open sky, the wind (if there is a wind): it's not a feeling of wildness like reaching the rocky summit of a mountain above treeline, it's more an extension of the feeling of comfort, of home, that I had in the woods. All is familiar. I can pick out far-off fields and farmhouses. I know who lives in them. To the west I locate Vermont's Groton Range. When I turn to the east I'm facing the mountains in New Hampshire, peaks that Guy and I climbed many times. They feel like home, too—a past home that I've moved out of now. Aside from our work on Franconia Ridge, Guy and I just plain loved to hike. The White Mountains themselves became home ground to us. We climbed the four-thousand footers not just by the trails, but also seeking out the slides and streambeds, or bushwhacking up interesting ridges that took us to less-explored territory that could generate a real feeling of remoteness, of wildness. It was exciting to set a goal that led us to challenging terrain, perhaps in weather that could demand all our wits, nerve, and skill. We found ourselves doing much of this exploring in the winter months, when the deep snow cover made bushwhacking easier and the slides and gullies—there are so many of these, largely unexplored—turned into ice climbs. Franconia Ridge and our trail work was for summer.

This is all in the past now. What I do in the present is more like meandering, sometimes with wildflower guide in hand. A meditation: a rooted connection with the familiar that, through repetition, reveals something new, something finely private, like looking into the flowering parts of a lady slipper with a magnifying glass. I can piece together walks that take an hour or most of a day. I use no maps. There are no maps. In my mind are George Eliot's beautiful words from *The Mill on the Floss*: "The wood I walk on this mild May day, with the young yellow-brown foliage of the oaks between me and the blue sky, the white star-flowers and the blue-eyed speedwell and the ground ivy at my feet—what grove of tropic palms, what strange ferns or splendid broad-petaled blossoms, could ever thrill such deep and delicate fibers within me as this home-scene?"

That's the happy place where I am now. *This* hiking, this exploring, is new, and brought about by change. And on these walks I tell myself that I am fortunate to have no health issues that would cause me to keep from doing what I am doing right now.

So, it was not surprising that the fact that I was going to turn eighty in a few short months began to flood my mind. I was damn lucky to be turning eighty, I assured myself. While that might be true, I seemed unable to make peace with the fact that it was *I* who was turning eighty, and eighty was old! Eighty meant that I'd be smack up against the next decade: ninety. I correspond—or had corresponded—with a slim handful of ninety-year-olds who had reached that age with grace. Two of them had been hikers, one an active gardener, and one a cousin of my mother's. Would I be joining their ranks? Who knew? That was not a question I needed to tackle. Eighty was enough.

Aging and the significance of decades began to occupy my mind on my walks. Eighty was twenty years older than sixty, and when I had turned sixty, *that* had felt old. *I* didn't feel old, but sixty, by society at large, is regarded as old. Reflecting back to when I was forty, sixty was beyond a doubt old.

Now, from my vantage point of the hilltop I was standing on, eighty was just over the next rise, while sixty seemed, if not young, certainly not old. I wouldn't have minded turning the clock back to sixty. If I could, I would not be thinking about decluttering my house—a looming task I showed no signs of getting around to. Or having conversations with my friends about retirement homes versus "aging in place," which is what I seemed to be doing. We wouldn't be talking about our contemporaries who were on oxygen, or had undergone valve replacements and other heart-related episodes, or chemo treatment, or even the ubiquitous cataract surgery. At sixty it was likely that, other than one's parents, most of those whom one loved were actively living their lives.

Those knee replacements, without a doubt, had brought back my ability to hike again and made a number of other things possible that required mobility. They had restored mountains to my life. I became extremely aware of how fortunate I was that modern medicine had advanced to the point of joint replacements that—to a certain extent—can restore youth. I was not scampering over the ridges the way I had with Guy, but I had indeed tasted of the fountain of youth in my midsixties.

~

There seems to be something in the human soul that wants to make a garden.

—John Hanson Mitchell, *The Wildest Place on Earth*

I was sixty when Guy died and I moved off our homestead to my house near town, one we'd had built a half-mile walk from the village. I resolved to continue raising most of what I ate and began getting the soil ready for a vegetable garden. At Barra, our homestead garden, 70 ft. by 200 ft., had grown behind an eight-foot fence and was home as well to one hundred feet of raspberries, about the same of strawberries, an ample asparagus patch, and a dozen rhubarb plants; we canned, and stored food for winter in a root cellar. My new vegetable patch was fenced to a height of four feet and measured 30 ft. by 40 ft. It, too, contained asparagus (30 ft.) and one hefty rhubarb plant. I reduced the canning but had another root cellar built.

My intent was to minimize grass cutting by growing flowers between my front porch and the fenced-in vegetables, an area about three times larger than the vegetable garden. Guy and I had grown flowers as companion plants for the vegetables, in an attempt to protect them from harmful insects. We had grown daylilies in profusion and nourished a few small flower beds, but I knew little about growing flowers.

Gardening had always been a great pleasure. Now it became more so. Partly, I had more time to give to it since I wasn't climbing mountains with the intensity I had with Guy. The garden, always a happy, restorative place for me, felt even more restorative. My first love had been growing vegetables, and that had not changed, but the flowers and shrubs and the six blueberry bushes I added gave the garden shape and color and form, a whole new dimension.

I think the creativity involved in gardening is a hidden secret—unsuspected by those who don't get to do it daily. Perhaps hard to explain, but like writing it can be completely absorbing, filled with the same highs and lows, successes and failures—even frustrations and uncertainties. You have a vision; you make a plan, like writing or any other creative process. Claude Monet wrote, "Gardening was something that I learned in my youth. I perhaps owe having become a painter to flowers": gardening becomes something entirely one's own. It's you who are responsible for meeting the challenges, and for basking in and admiring your triumphs.

But gardens give us more. According to London poet and gardener Minnie Aumônier, "When the world wearies and society ceases to satisfy, there is always the garden." Whatever my worries, when I stride into my garden with trowel, clippers, bucket, hoe, and rake, and get down to the business of thinning the carrots or planting fifty more bulbs that will surprise and delight me next spring, my cares slough off like a heavy winter coat.

My garden—all gardens—give their gardeners a place of refuge, a retreat, a place to be with one's private thoughts. Or, better yet, no thoughts at all, just all-absorbing work. (I know that gardening was restorative for Guy.) And when the task is completed—hands dirty, gardener hot and no doubt sweaty—chances are that all will be right in the gardener's world again.

I think of a lady I knew, a devoted gardener who, in her younger years, had cared for extensive perennial beds (there is nothing like the glory of a perennial bed on which love has been lavished). When she was well into her eighties, she could be seen tending the plants on either side of the terraced walkway leading to her front porch steps. She had scaled back her gardening as her years increased, but she had never stopped.

Guy and I wrote five books together. All our writing grew out of a strong desire to keep our mountains wild, asking people to be aware of human impacts, asking all of us, when we go to the mountains, to protect the mountains from ourselves. In the early 1990s, when my knees were signaling that I needed to back off climbing mountains, I turned to writing short fiction. From a childhood spent scaring myself with Edgar Allan Poe, I'd been in love with short stories, a form that can deliver a remarkable emotional punch in a few well-chosen words. I had some success with publication. These stories were my own creation, separate from the work Guy and I did together. I couldn't see the future, though: that this work was preparing me for what was around the next few bends in the trail.

Before the short stories, I had written a few articles that grew out of our mountain research on a handful of women climbers and mountaineers who had struck off on their own—led their own expeditions—despite the harsh judgment and belittling remarks of society. Being a climber myself, their stories fascinated me, and it was a great adventure to read their books and do research that gave me the tools to tell their stories. (The research notes for these articles are in the archives of the American Alpine Club.)

With Guy's death in 2000, my writing life changed. I would no longer be collaborating on a subject we both embraced with equal commitment. But I already knew what I wanted to write about. During our homesteading years we had been cautious about granting interviews about our off-the-grid life. We did not want to draw a procession of visitors in the way that homesteading gurus Helen and Scott Nearing had. But our story was worth telling and Guy agreed. "I hope you will," he had answered. Not long after that conversation, Guy was gone, and I began writing what became *Losing the Garden*.

When I began this book, *Calling Wild Places Home*, in my late seventies, I saw it as a collection of essays about salient points of my life, a "backward glance," to borrow Edith Wharton's apt phrase, at influences and turning points, an accounting, a recounting, a taking into account of what had shaped a life. I was nearing the end of this writing project when I became increasingly preoccupied with the subject of aging.

It seems to have been my practice to write out what I find hard to confront, and, in that way, take in the difficult bits in small digestible pieces—always with much scratching out, revising and rethinking. It's an approach that allows the material to be absorbed incrementally, at its own pace that permits for maximum assimilation, the way a snake digests. (I have a young friend who raised a pet boa constrictor to whom he fed a meal of a mouse, or other small creature, once a week. This meal moved slowly down the boa constrictor's long digestive track. There was waste—waste is produced by snakes as well as in humans—but what remains nourishes, and so lays the groundwork for the process of further digestion, be it of a mouse or a hard-to-confront problem. I'll admit this is not an attractive image, but if you can get past your own squeamishness, you might find it, as I do, apt.)

My hiking friends asked if I was going to throw a party for eighty as I had done for my seventieth birthday. My answer was *no*.

For some complicated reason I hadn't yet sorted out back then, I'd felt the need to invite everyone I knew. I threw the party at my house. I rented a tent from the church—in Vermont a sensible precaution against rain—along with tables and chairs that I set up in my field. I posted a notice on the bulletin board at the post office and at the general store, and mailed out invitations to those farther away. I made it clear that everyone was invited. I'd supply the cake and a nonalcoholic punch; otherwise, it was a potluck birthday party.

About one hundred people showed up, some accompanied by their children and canine companions. It all took place outside, except for my friend who brought her cello—it was just cool enough that she felt the necessity to repair to the house where her fingers could manage the strings. This worked exceedingly well, since guests could warm up inside and listen to Margaret, then go outside for more socializing, food, and drink. Out there in my field we had a small fire going in a stone-lined pit, and I had distributed blankets with the idea that people would spread them on the ground to picnic upon. Instead, the blankets came in handy as shawls for those who had come in shirtsleeves.

I'm not a natural party thrower, but birthdays, I have always felt, mark an occasion that should be recognized, like graduations or marriages. The decades, especially, call for recognition. But why did I go all out for a bash of a birthday party at seventy?

That three-letter word, O-L-D, kept clamoring for attention in my head. *Old!* It didn't fit the vision I had of myself. Only old people turned seventy. I could have just let it go, ignored it. But when my thoughts went in that direction, they hit a roadblock. I would be dishonest to myself if I resisted or tried to escape the colossal plain fact that, yes, I was about to achieve this "advanced" age regarded by the world as old. At seventy, you could die from heart disease, stroke, cancer. You could develop diabetes, Parkinson's, high or low blood pressure, and, God forbid, a frightening variety of memory disorders.

What turning seventy also meant, I realized with a lightning bolt jolt, was that time was closing in. There wasn't that much time left. I was either on my way up the last climb, or heading down into a long black tunnel that closed off in a dead end. No matter how you twisted the metaphor, it meant that time was running out. Those last sandy grains were pouring through the narrow waist of the hourglass.

That hit me hard. Life had never seemed so finite before. I was reminded of Mario Cavaradossi, the political prisoner and Tosca's lover in Puccini's ever-moving, melodramatic opera. About to face the firing squad, he pours his heart into a final great outburst of song:

Oh vanished forever is that dream of love,
Fled is that hour,
And desperately I die.
And never before have I loved life so much!

Though Mario was young and I was not, he was facing his own immanent death. I was not, which seemed all the more reason for me to acknowledge the diminishing sand grains and use my time wisely. I had always been fairly well tuned to time as a commodity not to be wasted, and living with Guy highlighted this awareness. But, suddenly, at seventy, time had a "best used by" date stamped across my future. It no longer flowed onward in that poetically endless stream. Whether I liked it or not, my life *would* come to a full stop, with the words THE END imprinted on the final page.

This realization made me pay more attention to my work, my family and friends, my life itself. We all try to do this. It's the point of being alive. Death just makes the material of life—of living—more precious, as Mario's dying words point out. Yet, who would want to live to be three hundred years old, like Emilia Marty in Janáček's opera, *The Makropulos Case*? Emilia's father, an alchemist, invents a potion to prolong life and tests it on his daughter. Life, being infinite, loses its meaning. She longs to die. Who wants to end up like Emilia Marty?

The point of being alive—the beauty of it as one grows older and that end point hits you between the eyes—simply becomes keeping on with doing the things that have meaning to you. This, I came to realize, was the advantage of turning seventy. It was this not-well-understood imperative that had made throwing a blast of a birthday party seem like the right approach to inaugurate—best foot forward!—the coming decade of my seventies.

◦

I must have passed the crest a while ago
And now I am going down—
Strange to have crossed the crest and not to know,
But the brambles were always catching the hem of my gown.

—Sara Teasdale, "The Long Hill"

I continued to rock climb after the knee replacements, but only for a few more years. It is impossible to keep that edge honed if you make infrequent visits to the cliff. All the actions involved in moving upward on steep rock—placing protection or removing it, securing the safety at the belays for you and your partner—must be as natural and automatic as breathing. If you climb only every few months you will, in time, lose this. With hiking, you will become breathless going uphill if you don't hike with regularity, and if you aren't often climbing the 4,000-footers, you won't be able to ascend them with ease anymore. But with rock climbing, an inherently dangerous sport, more is at stake. I knew about losing this edge—I was, in fact, losing it—but I hadn't reached the point where I could articulate this to myself. I knew it only in the subliminal feelings of a stomach-churning, anxious-making nervousness when I thought about the climb coming up for me, even one I knew well, or a first attempt at a grade that should have been well within my ability. I'd be climbing with a dear friend. I wanted to be on the rock. I wanted that physicality, that upward movement through time and space, the tactility of edges, roughness, and all that joy under my fingertips, the close partnership fostered by the rope, and how life contracts to essentials when we go to the mountains. But these things we love can come to their own natural end, and I had enough of my climber's pride left that I wanted to be smart at recognizing when that end came for me.

I was helped in this by remembering the climbers in their seventies I had known when Guy and I were climbing regularly. There weren't many—three, at most, four. They climbed nearly every weekend at the Shawangunks, the Northeast's premier cliff.

One was Fritz Wiessner, born in Dresden, Germany, in 1900. The mountains near Dresden were a great climbing center, and Fritz was already a talented climber, schooled in the Dresden ideals of free climbing and the principle that to use aid was to cheat, when he immigrated to the United States in 1929. Two years later he was raising the standards of American rock climbing single-handed. In 1939, Fritz came within a tantalizing seven hundred feet of summiting the world's second highest mountain, K2. (Bear in mind, there are fourteen 8,000-meter Himalayan peaks; Annapurna was the first to be climbed, but not until 1950.)

Probably only a scant handful of climbers knew this about Fritz. What counted for us was that Fritz had "discovered" the Shawangunks—he had seen its potential for climbing and had begun putting up first ascents by the mid-1930s. No one, not a climber at the cliffs, when I began climbing in 1969, thought about age as it applied to Fritz, who was, by that time, moving into his seventies. What we saw was his confidence, his grace on steep rock, his enthusiasm, his animation and broad smile when we engaged him in conversations about climbing.

When he was over eighty, Fritz followed a younger climber, Jim McCarthy—well regarded for his own groundbreaking first ascents—up "High Exposure," a route Fritz had put up in 1941 with his climbing partner, Hans Kraus. The guide book calls it "THE Shawangunk climb to do." "High E," as climbers familiarly call it, is a bold route that requires a cool head when starting up that overhanging final pitch. We were at the cliffs that day, and when we saw Fritz come down, we congratulated him on climbing this celebrated route. He put off our compliments with a shake of his head. "I didn't climb it," he said. "Jim climbed it. I just followed." We smiled back. We understood that what Fritz meant was he had not led the climb. And we knew this meant that climbing was slipping away from him, because Fritz always led—he went first on the rope and took all the risks.

We continued to see Fritz at the cliffs. He climbed with Hans Kraus with whom he had pioneered dozens of climbs. They were the "Hans and

Fritz" of American rock climbing. For climbers, they were living history as we watched them walk side by side down the carriage road beneath the cliffs: short men, barrel-chested, hands behind their backs, still emanating strength, like two dwarves from a German fairy tale, off to climb a moderate route the two of them had pioneered nearly half a century before. For the harder routes that Fritz wisely felt were beyond him now—now that he was in his middle eighties—he turned to younger climbers.

Then we heard that Fritz Wiessner had suffered a debilitating stroke. He didn't hang around long after that, dying in 1988, at the age of eighty-eight. I was forty-eight then and didn't pause to think much about how Fritz had closed the chapter of his life as a climber, but now that I was at that point myself, it struck me that he had done so with dignity and great presence of mind.

Hans Kraus, born in Trieste, had been tutored as a child by James Joyce. Trained as a doctor in Vienna, Hans moved to America in 1938 to join the staff of Columbia Presbyterian Medical Center in New York City, specializing in sports medicine (he could number John F. Kennedy among his back patients). As a young climber he had gained experience on the vertical towers of the Dolomites. In 1940, desperate to climb, he was introduced to the Shawangunk cliffs by Maria and David Millar, and welcomed by the Appalachian Mountain Club's small circle of climbers. There, Hans met Fritz, and these two Europeans with skills far exceeding the current American rock climbing standards single-handedly opened the Shawangunks wide, leaving a lasting legacy of routes for all to enjoy.

The last time Guy and I saw Hans Kraus at the cliffs, he was on a climb called Layback, put up in 1941 by Fritz. Layback begins with an awkward, rather strenuous, chimney. Other than that, it's a beginners' climb, but as with a few of the easy Gunks climbs, the initial moves can make you feel like you've been sandbagged. I knew that from experience, and only engaged with that chimney because the rest of the climb was so perfect, so airy, the rock so beautiful, and so much fun. As we rounded the corner that revealed the start of Layback, we could hear scrabbling, and saw Hans—the leader was above him managing the rope—struggling to negotiate that chimney. We knew his hands were painfully arthritic, the result of catching a fall barehanded nearly a lifetime ago in the Dolomites, when the rope tore through his palms. We moved quickly past: listening to Hans's desperate scrapings against the rock was upsetting, and we did not want to watch. This was too private. Too awful. Too sad. Suddenly Hans had become an old man. It was like watching a giant topple.

At that moment, I remember thinking: *I don't want that to happen to me.*

Yet, it did, finally. And more than once. For me, it was knees. Most climbers and hikers, no matter what their age, put up with pain for various reasons and find countless ways to fight back, not wanting to give up the mountains.

One of the last times I descended from Franconia Ridge I was with Guy and some dear friends, among them Shady Hill School classmates of his. They wanted to hike the ridge, and, generously, to see the trail work we were doing up there. I was one of the youngest in this group of three couples. When we reached the bottom we were all in high spirits from a wonderful day, and one in our group lined us up and snapped a photo, our arms linked across each other's sweaty shoulders. Unexpectedly, in the midst of this happiness, the sudden realization crashed down on me that this could be the last time I'd descend from Franconia Ridge in the company of friends. (It wasn't—not quite.)

So many mountain days had made up my life, and I had taken every one of them for granted. I was only fifty-two. My knee problems had begun as a teenager, yet I had never felt handicapped. Perhaps the amount of hiking Guy and I did kept my muscles strong, but it also added to the knee joint's wear and tear. I'd been wearing knee braces for years, the type with hinged steel supports on either side. I used hiking poles at a time when poles were so rarely seen they generated the comment "Expecting snow today?" I always laughed because, why not? I swallowed increasing amounts of ibuprofen, to the point of provoking an ulcer. On that descent with the Shady Hill friends, the pain—I called it *discomfort*—had done a good job of interfering with my pleasure. I was facing the end, and knew it.

Winter climbing continued for a few more years, since snow and snowshoes provided the cushioning my knees needed. That came to an end on Lowe's Path, descending from Mount Adams in the Presidential Range. I was with Guy, descending from a visit to Gray Knob, when I found myself repeatedly falling, my balance unhinged by unstable knees. This time, I was in tears. There was no ignoring that I had become a liability, not just to myself, but to any group I might be hiking with.

Well, I wouldn't be climbing mountains, but I had plenty to keep me busy and outside and active with the work at our homestead. So my life—our lives—became somewhat circumscribed with no mountain days, but also more centered and focused with the care we now could put into our gardens and woodlot, and the pleasure of constructing a small log guest house we called Twin Firs Camp. Guy, with my knees in mind, put a few switchbacks into our steep woods paths. He continued the trail work on the Franconia Ridge and joined friends for the occasional hike, but, for both of us, Barra, our homestead, drew us closer to each other and to the land.

Those knee replacements were in 2004. Still, today, I am reminded of what it is like to be pain-free when I rise up from a sitting position, walk upstairs or down, roll over in bed, or fold my legs into the driver's seat of my car. I hike now not with the fervor Guy and I had, but with more joy, or a different kind of joy, because what I had lost has been restored: the view from a rocky high point shared with close friends over a peanut butter sandwich is not the least of it.

When Guy and I were researching and writing *Yankee Rock & Ice*, we interviewed many climbers in their seventies, eighties, and nineties, and one skier, Jackrabbit Johannsen, who was 106. What stands out in memory for me now was their vitality, yet climbing days come to an end. Robert Underhill, who learned to climb from the guides in Europe and introduced modern Alpine rope-and-belaying techniques to climbers in America in the late 1920s and early 1930s, let me see this when we visited him at his home in Randolph, New Hampshire. At ninety-one, he stood before a picture window that gave a sweeping view of the Northern Presidentials and waved his hand toward Mounts Madison, Adams, and Washington. "I don't have to go up there anymore," he said, and smiled. I was stunned.

He must have seen my jaw drop. How could anyone who had romped across that range say that—especially Robert Underhill, who had put up some of our earliest and most prized climbing routes? In his early seventies, he and his wife Miriam, famous for her groundbreaking all-women ascents in the Alps in the early 1930s, backpacked on snowshoes into the mountains in winter in pursuit of climbing all forty-eight peaks over four thousand feet. They were the first to accomplish it, at a time when the White Mountains saw almost no winter hikers. Wouldn't Robert regret, daily, that he couldn't stride up Mount Adams through steep, rough, rocky, and glorious King Ravine? Perhaps, but he had apparently made peace with it.

Now I am of an age where I not only understand Robert's words but respect him for that unabashed pronouncement.

How about Hassler Whitney? I don't know when he stopped climbing, or if he ever did, but when we climbed with him at the Sleeping Giant cliff, eight miles north of New Haven, Connecticut, when he was seventy-six, he showed no signs of having slowed down. Hassler was famous for pioneering one of the Northeast's greatest routes on New Hampshire's

Cannon Cliff in 1929. Sustained and exposed, the Whitney-Gilman was arguably the most impressive climb in the United States at that time. We had been in correspondence with Hassler about it and he offered to meet us at the Sleeping Giant parking lot to show us some original routes he'd climbed there when he'd been an undergraduate at Yale. Hassler had gone on to a brilliant career as a mathematician and educator at Harvard and the Institute for Advanced Study at Princeton, and by then had not climbed on the Sleeping Giant cliff for more than fifty years.

We arrived with our full rack of climbing gear, our specialized shoes, and our Perlon rope. (The rope Hassler would have last used on the Sleeping Giant would have been made of hemp—not strong enough to catch a falling climber.) We were accompanied by Ken Nichols, a young Connecticut climber interested in his state's rock climbing history, and whose protection devices for ascending cliffs out-classed ours by a generation.

Hassler had driven up from Princeton, and when he stepped out of his automobile, ready for climbing, he carried one thing—his lunch, in a small brown paper bag. He handed this to Guy, who put it in his pack. Without a glance at our equipment, Hassler started up the rock, explaining over his shoulder that he remembered this route and would stop if he reached a move he might want the rope for. We watched as he smoothly and rapidly progressed up the face in old sneakers, our mouths agape, gazing up, over-burdened by coils of rope and the most up-to-date equipment available. Did Hassler take this in? It all seemed so bizarre: if you passed him on the street you would see an old man, yet here he was soloing a route that, for safety, required the use of the rope. We were, naturally, concerned. But *he* seemed perfectly at home. Should we eschew the rope and start up, untie our specialized rock shoes, and climb in our sneakers? The three of us felt pretty silly staring at Hassler, now forty feet up. He finally stopped—to our relief—and called down that he'd wait for us to climb up with the rope for the next move.

The takeaway must have entered me at a subliminal level to be stored away for later, years later—something about seizing opportunities, trusting yourself, saying yes to just about everything, but not forgetting that good judgment remains an essential part of the equation too.

My favorite story concerning closing down a climbing career is about Lester Germer, who, when I began climbing at the Shawangunks, was probably the most widely known and best loved individual in the community of rock-climbing regulars. Lester—tall, spare, bespectacled, and white-haired—took me up my second-ever rock climb. I didn't know then that he had come within a whisker of winning a Nobel Prize when he and his colleague discovered something important involving the electronic microscope, or that Lester was one of Bell Labs' top physicists, or an expert on mushrooms, or enough of an authority on ants to publish a witty treatise about them, or that he had spent World War I as a fighter pilot. Lester motored down from Ithaca, where he had moved to the faculty of Cornell in his (partial) retirement, and every weekend he defied age by leading those new to climbing up his favorite routes.

That first weekend, in October 1971, we were at the cliffs and heard that Lester would turn seventy-five in one week. This meant he and I shared a birthday. When we saw him that Sunday afternoon as he prepared to take one more party up a climb conveniently near the Überfall, I said, "Lester, I was born on October 10th, too!"

"Yes," he replied with a twinkle, "but what century?"

We shared a laugh. Guy and I walked down the carriage road to fit in a last climb, while Lester started up the cliff. When we returned, we saw a knot of climbers around the base of the route called Double Chin. The first pitch presents the climber with the kind of big overhang for which the Gunks is infamous—not hard, as the holds are good, but with steep moves that take a bit of effort to surmount. Lester started up, we were told, hesitated, came back down, sat on the ledge, and then, without a word, started back up toward the overhang. He had a perfect safety record, and had never taken a leader fall in twenty-six years of climbing. It is technically fair to say that was still the case. The coroner told us the next day that Lester's heart attack was so massively sudden that he was dead before his belayer caught his fall.

Lester's name and the circumstances of his death got carried down as Gunks legend, a magnificent ending for a magnificent man. I believe we all wished—and I continue to wish—we could all be so lucky.

It's not only climbers who grow old doing things they love that require a good deal of physicality. Where I live, I see loggers driving massive and skillfully loaded trucks, farmers mowing acres of hay fields, foresters walking miles of woodlots.

I possess a six-acre clearing, about two acres of which need cutting twice a year. Not long after I moved here and spread the word that I was looking for someone with a small tractor to mow my field, I received a visit from Ernie French. We had never met, though we lived only a short distance apart. In a few words we reached an agreement, and Ernie began mowing for me. Sturdy and solid, he sat astride his tractor seat—it had no cab—like a throne, sun-browned arms rivaling Vulcan's at his forge or Schwarzenegger flexing in a pose. We became friends, and I enjoyed working in my garden while Ernie was running his tractor around my field. We were working in tandem, like a team, and I often found myself recalling Caleb Garth's words from George Eliot's *Middlemarch*:

> You must be sure of two things: you must love your work, and not be always looking over the edge of it, wanting your play to begin. And the other is, you must not be ashamed of your work, and think it would be more honourable to you to be doing something else. You must have a pride in your own work, and in learning to do it well. . . .
>
> No matter what a man is—I wouldn't give twopence for him, whether he was the prime minister or the rick-thatcher, if he didn't do well what he undertook to do.

Ernie was only two years older than me. He had used his body hard all his life and, as the years piled on, I could see how hard it was for him to get on and off that tractor seat, or to walk the uneven ground when he paced close to my stone wall where the tractor couldn't get, clipping out saplings. It was hard for him to see, now, too. He often wiped his eyes with the handkerchief he kept stuffed in his back pocket. More troublesome to both of us, Ernie got so he couldn't hear me well at all. My voice is soft, with no carrying power, hard for older ears to hear; we had talked about his struggles with hearing aids, all mostly unsuccessful.

For some time we'd been communicating by postcard: I'd send Ernie a postcard in early spring saying I hoped he'd be mowing for me again—twice a year, after July 4th and late September. Sometimes he would call me to confirm, but due to the hearing issue it was a one-sided conversation. That didn't really matter. I would just wait for Ernie to show up. He always did.

I'd be inside, working, when I'd hear the unmistakable roar and clank of his tractor beginning its initial swath through my field, the grass four feet deep. The tractor noise receded as he moved away from the house, and grew noticeably louder as he cut the side field closest to my windows. No wonder Ernie was nearly deaf! He had never worn ear protectors. He'd be at it for an hour, and then stop for lunch, if you could call it that: peanut butter crackers, four to a pack. I'd go out and we'd attempt to chat, mostly jokes about how little he ate, and how little he drank, too. But I exerted little influence. He knew it and I knew it, so we laughed about it. I was pretty sure he listened to his wife, Betty, who understood him in every way better than anyone.

Ernie was past eighty, or nearly, when he ran into a post that held my telephone wires. We examined it, its cables spilling out, and I called the phone company. He was most chagrined. After that I found myself keeping an eye on him when he mowed around my pond. Those edges were soft, and the sides dropped down a foot or more to the water. It was a deep pond, about ten feet.

The day Ernie went into the pond I had a young friend, Annie, here and we were doing garden work together. I became aware that the tractor noise—always considerable—had stopped, and didn't start up again as it should have. So we walked to where we could get a better view. It was off the edge, partly in the water, canted at what appeared to be forty-five degrees. Somehow Ernie had managed to crawl off that elevated seat and was stumbling toward us.

We shouted some, attempting to understand what he wanted us to do, but even Annie's robust voice had difficulty getting through. So I went into the house, called my friend Chris, who mows fields and knows Ernie, and left a message. It was late Sunday afternoon. I was pretty sure that tractor was going to spend the night in my pond. I called Betty, too, and let her know that Ernie was all right, but she might want to come take him home.

Annie and I were trying to urge Ernie to sit on my porch and wait for Betty, when, to my surprise and joy, we heard a tractor moving fast down my road and Chris appeared in his truck with his son Chase driving the tractor, here to the rescue of Ernie. The efficiency with which father and fifteen-year-old son handled this job appeared, to my eyes, like the final performance of the best-rehearsed play ever staged: no dropped lines, no false entrances, no botched cues, merely an impressive synchronization that had that tractor hauled onto dry land in minutes. And there was Betty, waiting in her car in my driveway.

I wasn't sure what would happen about Ernie and mowing the next year, and resolved to wait and see the course things would take. He wanted to come back and finish, and so he did, with a young friend in tow to keep an eye on him, a smart precaution I was glad to see. Meanwhile, I'd had a conversation with Chris, who agreed to pick up the job of mowing when the time came. We'd leave that to Ernie.

Before the next summer's mowing came around, Ernie telephoned me to say he thought he'd better quit while he was ahead. He didn't hem and haw about it. It was a straight declarative sentence. I could hear him, but he couldn't hear me thanking him for all he'd done and how much fun it had all been. I wrote him that later. "You're in good hands with Chris," Ernie said, and hung up. And so ended nearly two decades of Ernie's riding that mower like a NASCAR driver around my field. He didn't want to give it up—that work, that life. But he did. When the right moment came.

Now when my hiking friends asked what was I going to do about turning eighty, I knew I had already crossed that bridge too. Eighty was just another upward rung in the same ladder. Instead of a party, I suggested, we could take one of our well-loved local walks. That seemed the best way to celebrate that I could imagine.

But it was not to work out that way.

My friend Tania, an expert at assembling people around food, asked if I would save the Saturday that was nearest to my birthday because she and another dear friend, Sue, wanted to gather our hiking friends at Sue's, as she is a champion at hosting. Our hiking group is small. This generous offer appealed. A lovely idea!

Then I heard from one of the hikers that she'd received the email invite list. List? I queried. How could five or six hikers have turned into a list? This was received with a shrug and laugh. I tried to ignore what this could mean, but, of course, I couldn't and in the next days I began to get the sense that the list was long, which was supposed to be a surprise. In a small rural town with a tight-knit community, it's like rowing upstream against the river's spring breakup to keep anything a "surprise."

As it turned out, my literary agent was planning a visit right at this time. We had never met, though we'd been working together for an active five years. We knew each other very well, on the level of writing and endeavoring to get words into print, but what was going to happen when we met face to face? As much as I welcomed Craig's appearance, I was conscious of an undeniable nervous-making spread of wondering how this was going to go.

The date of the party arrived. I was told to show up at Sue's around lunchtime. A few days before that, my friend Carl had called to offer me a ride up the three miles to Sue's home. I had demurred, as there was no reason why I couldn't drive myself.

That morning I came to my senses. I could at least be gracious, I instructed myself, and accept Carl's offer of a ride. As we approached, I realized I hadn't thought about how many vehicles we'd pass parked along the roadside going up Sue's hill—how could I have known? When we turned into the driveway, I was amazed to see, standing in the yard, friends whom I knew had driven a distance to get here. There was Doug, flown in from France! (Behind-the-scenes planning had engineered a stateside trip that fit with this birthday party.) Here were folks with whom Guy and I had formed close friendships during our days of trail work on Franconia Ridge, and friends from my local connections—friends from hiking, from the library, from gardening, and from books and writing. There was even a sprinkling of children.

As we congregated in the dining room and began helping ourselves to an outpouring of potluck creations, it hit me that part of the beauty of achieving eighty was that friends from the mountains, most of whom were a generation or more younger than Guy and I were—hadn't seen each other in a long time. Some were parents, and some, I knew, had lost their own parents. Life moves on. Decade-marking birthdays powerfully underline this fact. When I'd planned to celebrate by taking a quiet walk, I couldn't imagine a better way to recognize turning eighty. But this was.

The day before, Craig had asked me what I was going to say.

"Say?" I asked.

"You'd better be thinking about your speech, Laura," he warned, with a grin.

The party moved outside for cake cutting. It was a perfect early October day, the sun shining with glorious light on all of us gathered together under a large maple whose leaves were turning orange. Short-sleeve weather, unlike my seventieth.

Carl was master of ceremonies, and when it came my turn to respond, all I could offer was an embracing thank-you to everyone—for being there. I had spent most of Year Seventy-Nine, I told them, deliberately, meditatively preparing for Year Eighty, and it left me—I had only just come to see this—with a feeling of gratitude. This was gratitude writ large: for friends, for work, and for health, because, well, at eighty you're thankful for the gift of each day. A cliché, but bear in mind, that at eighty each day *does* count. It's not something you're thinking about at forty or fifty, I said.

Two years ago, my friend, Arlene, had let all of us know that she was undergoing treatment for cancer, a huge shock. She and I had been rock climbing together since the mid-1980s. She was just tremendous fun to climb with! I couldn't imagine Arlene, with her vitality and spirit, struggling to fight off cancer. Time passed, and the next report from Arlene was that her cancer was in a sort of remission. We all felt great relief, because if a positive attitude could beat cancer, then Arlene had this beast licked.

Sadly, not so. My breath caught when I read in an email, sent out to over eighty of Arlene's friends by her daughter and granddaughter, that their mother and grandmother was in the care of hospice. Treatments could do no more. She was comfortable. She would be glad to hear from friends. I sent Arlene a list of climbs—by name and date—that we had done together, copied out from the records I kept, and added a few words about how much fun we'd had, how etched in my memory so many of those climbs were. It was the only way I could think to say goodbye.

Her life ended a week after I mailed that list. She died at seventy-five. That seems young to me. And that's because Arlene was never old.

That cliché about each day being a gift is a hard thought to hold on to. We don't much like being reminded of mortality. Yet, like most clichés, it springs from truth. And so we carry on, day by day, until Atropos, eldest of the Fates, steps in to snip the thread.

Epilogue

Letting Go

At some point, after the drafts had accumulated, and I was satisfied that the manuscript was ready to approach publishers, I contacted Chip Brown who had written a book about Guy, *Good Morning Midnight*, published in 2003, asking if he'd take a look. Chip quickly got back to me offering his thoughts on where and how I could, as he put it, in Melville's words, "Mine deeper." Whoa! This is going to take a lot more work, flashed through my head. Yet I quickly saw how lucky I was to get this reading from Chip. We had spent many hours together at my home in Vermont when he was working on his book, as well as when I was starting on *Losing the Garden*, talking about Guy: his decision to homestead, his relations with his sons, what mountains meant to him, and his choice to take his own life. Where was I in all this? How did I fit in? For the purposes of what I was calling a second memoir, this last bit—my role in what essentially looked like Guy's story—was what called for more work. How did I manage to live with Guy and preserve a sense of self? I could imagine that it took some courage on

Chip's part to urge me further into territory I believed I'd already given much thought to.

So I went back into the manuscript with tools in hand, principally that bulldozer, determined to plunge to the "murky bottom." As I saw it now, I, and many others, would never stop loving Guy, and here was my chance to attempt to understand my husband through my own reactions to him that make him (and perhaps myself) more forgivably human.

Guy had come back from Cannon Cliff and taken me into his plan. That was a game-changer in the sense that it began the process of letting go. Letting go of Guy. Letting go of Barra.

Knowing how much he wanted to abandon his life, knowing how miserable he'd be were he still around—his words, "I don't want to be here, Laura"—kept me from missing him. I understood that there can come a point in life in which mental anguish is so constant that death becomes the only option. However differently I felt about my own life, Guy, from what he was telling me, had reached that point.

When a spouse dies, the one left can miss the other unbearably for years, right up to the last day of life. My mother would speak of older friends who, after the death of husbands, remarried for "companionship." I know that after we had settled my father in a nursing home, she articulated to me how lonesome she felt walking into an empty house. In her case the person who was always there wasn't dead, he just wasn't *there*. He wasn't in his accustomed places—his study or his chair in the living room.

They had been married for more than fifty years, but for the last several decades I would not have called their marriage close or particularly happy. My father's drinking problem had a lot to do with this. My mother had built a life for herself around it that included selling real estate in Princeton for two decades. Yet it was hard to see how they could have been companions for each other, I thought, but I was only seeing the surfaces of things and was surprised by how much she simply missed his presence.

My case was different: Guy was so set on getting out of life. His attempt to jump off Cannon Cliff failed, I believe, because he knew in some unignorable portion of his finely tuned nineteenth-century moral code that he couldn't run out on me like that. He owed it to me to be a part of his death.

We had always worked on projects together.

Reaction to a suicide is "How could this have been prevented?" That was mine too when Guy told me he wanted to return to Cannon Cliff. But I saw, almost in the same instant, that his mind would not be changed, that he felt he had no choice, that suicide was his only answer to his own unceasing mental turmoil. My response—that if this was his plan, I needed to be in a better position—came from an equal determination to buy time. I hoped he would change his mind. Knowing Guy, I did not count on it.

During those eighteen months I began to learn how to let go. After his death, when I began putting his clothes aside for the local rummage sale, I found among his socks and T-shirts, as he certainly intended, a suicide note he'd written dated April 13, 1992. I learned then that he'd had suicide—his own—in mind for a long time: "I think I've been hung up too long on wondering how you could get along without me. . . . I am going on the assumption that I was just getting worse and worse, and becoming a drag on your life. I'm not trying to say I do this for you—of course not, I do it for myself. I guess I'm just trying to justify why it's probably as well for you once you work out a new life."

His note confirmed the instinct that had led me to support Guy in what he wanted to do. It was his own life, after all. Whenever, during those months together, I had attempted to do otherwise, it set us at odds. I could not see inside, where Caliban had established his camp and driven Ariel out. That island had darkened to the point where seeking his own death appeared to be Guy's only release, the only one that seemed reasonable to him. I needed to respect this even if I could not understand it.

This helped me to let him go.

The cover of *Losing the Garden* included some words by Albert Camus: "An act like suicide is prepared within the silence of the heart, as is a great work of art." In Guy's case, his suicide was prepared in his head perhaps more than in his heart. Did he see it "as a great work of art?" Did I?

Our friend Louis Cornell said, "Laura, if Guy had frozen himself behind the outhouse, do you think he'd have gotten such coverage in the press?" Doug used the word "choreographed" to describe Guy's death. My friend Rebecca warned against seeing Guy's suicide as a romantic act, and her words startled me into realizing that was how I saw it. One friend used the words a hero's journey, certainly a romantic way to look at Guy's suicide. I think it was his charisma that directed those who knew him, or only knew about him, to see his suicide in that way. And it somewhat appalls me now, years later, that I saw it that way, too. All of us, most of all me, were taking our cues from Guy.

In Amor Towles's *The Lincoln Highway*, one of the characters asks himself whether we can be sideswiped by our own best character traits and so blinded to how we, possibly, should have acted. In Towles's novel a great deal of harm came from someone who possessed a forgiving nature. My tendency is to agree with people, to be amenable. I want to make room for what they have in mind. I don't like arguing or debating, perhaps to a fault. I can see the other's point of view, and that blocks me from asking questions that, in many cases, should be asked, even if they make the other person unhappy or mad at me.

How did Guy see his own desire to take his own life? This was never clear to me since his unhappiness at the reception of our books, and his other regrets that he expressed in the final pages of his unpublished memoir didn't strike me as worth killing oneself over. Whereas I saw them as a part of the ups and downs of life, Guy wrote, "Considerations like these have left me with a sense of dissatisfaction about what I've accomplished all my life." What was at the bottom? What wouldn't he articulate? It was more a matter of *wouldn't* than *couldn't*. Could it have been the fear of his own mental condition? Accompanied by a freezing, paralyzing terror where the demons rampaged and would not be controlled? Thinking of his son Johnny diagnosed with a mental illness in a hospital in Anchorage, Alaska, Guy wrote, "And though I've grown a protective covering of smiles and talk, I too am alienated from my fellow humanity and dwell in a private world of storm and darkness." He wrote, also, in "Prospero's Options," in an attempt to come to grips with his conflictive mood swings: "Both in me. I know that the same high positive impulses of Hawee's [Guy's father] have been prominent in me at times—wonderful tendencies. But the same demons which drove Johnny to destruction have always intervened—where, after all did Johnny get them from?" As I read this, Guy is blaming himself for Johnny's mental illness; at the same time what he is saying is a convenient way to own up to the Caliban within himself.

Rebecca wrote me: "I think Guy had an inner sense of exceptionalism. . . . Instead of doing the hard work of facing the ugly, difficult sides of himself, Guy chose to wall himself off, romanticize and singularize his demons. We all went along. . . . Even going so far as to accept that this is perhaps the flip side of genius. . . . It can take a lot of work . . . and a lot of practice to change our ingrained habits of building a world based on a false sense of self."

I think Guy spent much of his life hiding his own mental condition, if not from himself, from others. It was very easy to buy into his "myth," which I did immediately and wholeheartedly, unaware that I was doing so, and in the process becoming complicit in what Guy wanted others to see, or not to see. Again, Rebecca: "For Guy I think it was easier to make up a story with bold characters and lots of intrigue, romance and beauty—than to face his truly frightening inadequacies and darkness. Leaning on Caliban and Ariel was much less scary than embracing Guy Waterman."

How do I feel about my supportive role? However I answered that, it resulted in my efforts to protect Guy and his image. Subliminally I recognized that maintaining the image of the united couple living a kind of idealized if eccentrically offbeat life as homesteaders, climbers, and mountain defenders was armor for Guy: a protective carapace, his defense against . . . what? Whatever destructive impulses his Calibanistic mental state (i.e., depression) could throw at him? How I acted toward Guy was so much a part of who I am: a supportive person who does well being mentored by a strong and trustworthy leader. I not only loved Guy, but I believed in him. I resonated with him. Our moral codes were similar: he believed in doing the right thing. One of his favorite quotations was from T. H. White's *The Once and Future King:*

> "Well, anyway," Merlin said, "suppose they did not let you stand against all the evil in the world?"
> "I could ask," said the Wart.
> "You could ask," repeated Merlin.

I've come to see these positive impulses that made up the "Ariel" in Guy's temperament embraced endeavors he could believe in—Barra, and the wilderness causes we championed. He invited me to share the journey with him. I jumped on board without a second thought or a backward glance.

So, who and what was Caliban? What was Guy's "heart of darkness." Whatever it was, though it caused me anguish, being a supportive person, a Piglet, as a kind friend pointed out, I was good at living with it. I know I gave him much strength and comfort, but I could not keep him from taking his own life. He needed to recognize that if he championed taking responsibility, taking responsibility for his own mental issues—those demons!—was crucial. There was an ironic price to the freedom of Guy's suicide. I had acted similarly toward my father, so troubled by alcohol, though again, we never talked about it. My sadness at his condition overrode my anger. Basically, I loved him. His "I am who I am" that he said to my mother was the equivalent of Guy's "Talking doesn't help." Both statements closed the door on discussion. Both—husband and father—were not asking for help. Both had walled themselves shut. And I, a Piglet, was ill-equipped to break down those walls.

Guy's suicide was seen as intentional, an act that took great force of will. Indeed, his suicide was as well planned, as deliberate, as anything he ever undertook; he would not have seen it as "a work of art," he was not *that* ego-driven, but there was a certain creative process going on. It was not something that took direct and sudden action, like pulling a trigger. It merely required the mindful determination to sit, just sit, sit down in a frigid spot on the mountain of his own choosing; to let the cold fill him. Unlike putting a bullet in your brain, it would take an indefinite period of time. There would be every opportunity to change his mind and walk down the mountain to the hearth-fires of Barra and life again. But he did not. His body was found on Mount Lafayette, on Franconia Ridge, not far north of the summit against a shelter of rocks that made a corner so that he looked both north, to where his sons had died, and west toward Vermont and our homestead. Perhaps it was not so terribly hard for him to sit still in the cold.

Discovering climbing and then meeting Guy at the cliffs were two powerful influences that abruptly changed my life. My heart was no longer in editing books—if it ever was. New York held nothing more for me, though I wouldn't have missed those years for anything. What Guy offered: the experiment of homesteading and of both climbing and the stewardship of mountains were "causes"—ways of life—I could embrace. Looking back to my experience as a student in Paris and the derailment of that with Moral Re-Armament, I can see how living by absolutes could engage me—sinking my teeth into something useful that Barra and the care of mountains meant. My ancestral roots go back to the New England Puritans, so, in a sense, I am genetically set to be comfortable with ideas and ideals. Perhaps as much to this point, my father's scholarship was firmly rooted in the colonial period. The names of Cotton Mather and Jonathan Edwards made up our dinner table conversation. I understood—at least on some level—the meaning of and limitations of a life devoted to good works: a life of purpose.

I have been asked if I regretted not having children. Motherhood, after all, being a parent, steering a child into a happy, useful life can satisfy in a fulfilling way. But I wasn't looking for that. Guy was clear that he didn't want a second family. I never thought of myself as a stepmother to his sons. I thought of them as my friends, and being their friend seemed the best way I could connect with them. What Guy and I created together was more than enough for me in terms of a fulfilling life. And as the years have gone by I see more clearly, and unabashedly, that I was not cut out to be a mother. What was important to me in our life together continues to be deeply meaningful to me: the stewardship of mountains with updates in our books, writing articles, and, on my own home ground, carrying on gardening, simple living, and the opportunity to engage in village life, particularly through our library. In our years together, Guy was the leader, the innovator. I have found it a smooth transition to the life I live now since the person I was before I met Guy is, at core, who I have always been.

Guy believed in self-reliance. It ruled his life, along with that need for control. Both worked for him in productive ways that led to a fruitful homesteading life, books written in the hope that his ideas that encouraged greater care of wild places, particularly in the Northeast's alpine zones, would be taken up by the next generation of mountain lovers. By the time he reached sixty he was already planning his own death. He was growing old. Conversations with Doug and Rebecca helped me see that Guy knew that growing old was beyond his control. The importance he put on self-reliance blocked the flexibility he needed to cede control.

Yet Guy surprised me once in a rare moment of openness by saying, "I wanted to do this trip because I wanted to be able to ask for help." This was a challenging winter walk from the summit of Katahdin through the Hundred Mile Wilderness in Maine on the Appalachian Trail. Guy was with his friend Dan Allen. Both men were cresting sixty, both born on the same date: May 1, 1932.

Ask for help? I'd never given a second thought about asking a hiking or climbing partner for help—if it were needed. "Did you have the opportunity?" I asked.

"I did!" And Guy described how they were snowshoeing through deep snow on a sidehill trail hauling heavy sleds. Guy's sled kept drifting downward, dangerously close to a steep edge—then slipped over. Guy found himself hanging on for dear life and calling out for Dan. Together the two men hauled Guy's sled up through the snow to safety.

To me this would have been part of the excitement, the fun of the mountain experience, tense at the time, but not an issue of proving something to yourself—not a test of character. But for Guy, asking for help—any kind of help—I see now, gave him a chance to give up control. He had calculated that on this trip of nearly two weeks there was a good chance that he might have that opportunity to "ask for help"—that turned out to be merely saving the sled, not a troubled mind.

Is it that Guy could not, would not, let himself see that he was loved? Shortly after his death, our close climbing friend Mike Young said, "Guy told me that everyone comes to see you, Laura." I could see, in Mike's eyes, that he recognized his own sadness that Guy should feel that way. We both knew that Guy was the magnet, the charismatic personality. That he could not see this love, would not acknowledge it, was bad news.

Love, self-love, acknowledging love, I have come to see was difficult, I'd go so far as to say impossible, for Guy. He took great pride in what he could accomplish in the mountains, especially above treeline, in the challenging conditions of winter wind and cold. Few were his equal, he told me. But pride is not the same as love. And that he seemed unable to acknowledge love—what this bad news meant for me was that it turned him silent, a wall of silence that shut me out, making me both sad and angry. When I tried to break down that wall I was never successful.

That Guy could not acknowledge love is the most injurious part of toting around a bag of nineteenth-century demons *or* twentieth-century depression that can be unpacked on the psychiatrist's couch.

Nonetheless, this episode with Dan and the sled was a rare instance of ceding control, perhaps the only instance. In a short conversation Guy and I had during those crucial last eighteen months I reminded him that early in our marriage he had said he looked forward to growing old with me. Without losing a beat, he replied, "I have."

He was, by then, sixty-seven, which, to me, was not old. Later, he said, "I don't want to put this off. I could wait for a year or two, but I don't want to risk reaching the point where I can't climb to the summit."

He was the youngest in his family of five. He'd seen how his siblings handled their aging, as well as how some of his contemporaries did. Guy didn't want to get anywhere near the compromises aging would demand of him. Self-reliance, the need for control of his life, the fear of the accommodations that are a part of growing old, as I see it, all weighted the scales.

What I have come to see most clearly now is how Guy's need for control affected me. He controlled me, though I was unaware of this since I always felt listened to, and our actions emerged from joint discussions. Piglets like to be led by a kind and trustworthy Christopher Robin who loves them. Yet the sticking point, Guy's decision to take his own life, admitted no room for discussion and split us apart as firmly as the metal wedge he drove into the hardwood log on the chopping block. As I see it the "badly scary stuff" that Guy *would* keep buried at *any* cost had to do with those mental demons. They *must* be ruled, locked up, and the key thrown into the bottomless fiery heart of the volcano. But who was controlling whom? And then, this control that was so important to Guy, and had accomplished so much good on many levels, ended up killing him. Yet Guy was no Captain Ahab. He had no wish to sink his crew with his drive to kill the White Whale. Piglets, and Poohs too, are survivors and are good at making homes for themselves in the Hundred Acre Wood. Christopher Robins grow up and move away, and somehow, those they leave behind, go on living productive lives, and happy ones, too. Or such has been my case.

My life with Guy was over. We had said all we could say—or in Guy's case, would say. The pathways between us might have appeared to others clear as a mountain stream, transparent as the initial layer of ice that formed over our waterhole on a frosty morning, but now it led nowhere. As a man who valued taking responsibility—after all, he brought me into his plan to take his own life and obligated himself to get me in a position to continue on with mine—he *could* have looked at it as his obligation to bring me into what so deeply troubled him. Not until many years later did I understand that he could have taken responsibility for himself. Responsibilities and obligations work two ways. But that would have meant dealing with those badly scary demons.

Then, February 6, 2000, the morning he walked out the door for the last time, sitting on the ash log seat lacing up his boots, he said, "I want to get out of your way."

Surprised, I had replied, "You're not in my way, Guy." How could he be thinking he was in my way? What did that mean! How long had he been thinking this? It shocked me. Such a horrible thought and I was completely unaware of it. He also said, "Perhaps I am depressed." I could read in his face, his eyes, that those words were costing him. He wanted me to know, but those bulging eyes, his aloof posture holding me off, signaled that what he had just said was not on the table for discussion.

And so I said, "You're not depressed, Guy."

I meant it, and I had missed an opportunity. Could I, at the eleventh hour, have changed his mind? What if I had taken my hands out of the dish pan where I was washing up from breakfast and wrapped my arms around him? Just inserted myself into this crack in the wall Guy had slit open? It never occurred to me.

My response was right out of the script that was consistent with how we had always functioned. As the pliable good daughter in an alcoholic family I had learned my lines well. My role was to smooth over the bumps and hurdles. The awkward and uncomfortable moments that occurred at the minefield of the family dinner table. My knee-jerk reply to Guy's earth-cracking statement/half confession had me hanging on to my role, my lines, my training that went back to childhood.

It appalls me now. His words offered an opening, but I picked up my clues from his body language. Such revelations that come twenty years later are important to acknowledge, they're another piece in the puzzle, and I greet them with the gratitude due to another link in self-understanding. But I won't lose sleep over this confirmation of where I was then: fairly clueless, in many ways an innocent, dedicated to keeping the boat upright despite the fact that I was soon to be the only surviving passenger.

He looks up from the lacing and smiles at me. He is so intensely alive. "This time," he says, "I won't even be able to send you a postcard of how it all comes out." I smile back. I know he's thinking of when he'd return from his winter trips and tell me the story.

Guy was gone. While in my daytime thoughts he continued to be a benign, helpful, steadying, and welcomed presence, when he showed up in my nighttime dreams, he was anything but.

Those nightmares took the form of me looking for him. In them, I have lost him. I lose him in confined spaces—a building, sometimes a theater, or in a house I don't recognize that includes a gathering of people, a crowd. I lose him in public places of buildings and people—never in the woods or mountains or in scenes that we both knew and had loved together. Where I lose him is foreign to me and not welcoming. I spend the dream in an unhappy but not frantic or even anxious state, looking for him with a patient, miserable, unhurried resignation. It's more as if he's reached some place where he wants to be that does not include me. I can see him from afar; he seems unaware of me. I feel it keenly. Always he is surrounded by a crowd of people I don't know, don't even want to know, yet he knows them all. They are making much of him, the center of attention, and he appears to be enjoying their company.

These dreams follow the same course and never result in a happy ending. They never can. Yet as I continued with the work of writing, I realized that these nightmares are dissolving, they have loosed their hold. It is about time.

Guy got what he wanted and, as he saw it, needed. Without question, I have carried my life forward in ways I am intensely grateful for and could never have imagined. Still, there are times I feel our separation with an immense sorrow.

During the course of all the work, the greatest comfort (which, as it continued to grow, amazed me, and which blossomed so slowly I found I was taking as a matter of course) was the peace I found by writing my way through Guy's suicide. Through this writing came revelation, and the revelation was joyous. Comfort and joy—I had discovered that this second memoir, which I've titled *Calling Wild Places Home*, was in fact a joyous book. The writing of it had to be the most serious endeavor of my life. I could not have known, at the beginning, that my joy in this headlong dive into my own experience lay in a search for what I found in that "murky bottom." And now that I've sifted through the murk, it has turned benign. As each layer sifted through my fingers, my understanding of my own life gains clarity and loses its power to unsettle, disturb, or haunt.

Perhaps it's not surprising that I feel, now, sadness as this writing project closes down, as the journey comes to an end. But wait! The chapters of all our lives, my life, march on. There is always more to learn, more to understand from our experiences.

Part of the joy for me now is that Guy feels very present because the work I do is all of a piece with what we did together. It's the same work—writing about the stewardship of backcountry and of mountains—especially our northeastern alpine zones. Guy remains so much a part of how I continue to live my own life—not so different from how we lived at Barra—gardening, heating my house with wood, right down to picking blueberries I planted, to the books I read, to the woodsy walks I take, and mountains (smaller ones) I climb. There is comfort here.

On the heels of his death, in conversations with friends, we came upon the idea of launching the memorial fund in Guy's name and focusing it on areas above treeline. We were aware that the mountain clubs and public agencies were perennially stretched thin with backcountry projects—trails, campsites, shelters—so our plan was to help finance work needed on alpine trails, the educational summit steward programs, and scientific research. The Waterman Fund has been a presence in the mountains across the Northeast for more than twenty years now. The work we do is a big part of my life that keeps Guy present not just for me but for others who loved him.

I push back from my desk and stand up, walk across the room, and open the door that leads out to my porch. I take several deep breaths in the fresh morning air. Sunlight is filling my garden, and I am close to tears with missing Guy. This heavy sadness takes me back to those early days, after he had left. I am so filled by his presence, just beyond my vision, it's as if he is about to materialize. He smells of wood smoke, softwood sap, and freshly dug garden.

It comes back to me, from when I was writing *Losing the Garden*—the intensity of Guy's presence: welcomed, yet so emotionally charged. I learned to trust those emotions, though it took some time, and let them lead me to the bedrock depths that held a truthful core, an emotional surety. I grip the porch railing under my hands and remind myself of how much he wouldn't want to be here. The tears slowly recede.

As I conclude this book, I realize I have just spent the last few weeks with Guy, without being consciously aware of it, so completely normal did it feel. Now, this is written and I'm losing him all over again. Yet I feel elated, too, by the work itself, thankful to have gone deeper, to have thought further about it all. I've landed and settled. The ground here feels firm. "Life itself is grace," Frederick Buechner wrote. "See it for the fathomless mystery it is." Buechner is writing about human well-being. He's describing happiness. I find myself staring at my asparagus bed, which needs a good weeding. I'll tackle that after lunch.